John Whitaker

Mary Queen of Scots Vindicated

Vol. 2

John Whitaker

Mary Queen of Scots Vindicated
Vol. 2

ISBN/EAN: 9783337321741

Printed in Europe, USA, Canada, Australia, Japan

Cover: Foto ©ninafisch / pixelio.de

More available books at **www.hansebooks.com**

MARY QUEEN OF SCOTS VINDICATED.

By JOHN WHITAKER, B.D.

AUTHOR OF THE HISTORY OF MANCHESTER;
AND
RECTOR OF RUAN-LANYHORNE, CORNWALL.

IN THREE VOLUMES.

VOL. II.

LONDON:

PRINTED FOR J. MURRAY, N° 32, FLEET-STREET;
AND W. CREECH, EDINBURGH.

1788.

MARY
QUEEN OF SCOTS
VINDICATED.

CHAPTER THE FIRST.

§ I.

HAVING now gone over the EXTERNAL evidence for the forgery of the Letters, Contracts, and Sonnets, I addrefs myfelf to the examination of the INTERNAL. This I hope to place equally in fome new points of view. I fhall be the better able to do fo, by having examined the other before. I fhall, therefore, prefent my reader with a copy of the Sonnets, Letters, and Contracts, in the languages in which they were originally publifhed. To each of them I fhall fubjoin a variety of remarks, in order to point out the numerous fignatures of forgery in the belly of them. By this mode of inquifition, a new train of witneffes will appear at the bar before us. Thefe will

will depose to circumstances, of a very different nature from all that we have seen before. But they will completely coincide with them. They will be equally decisive evidences of the forgery, I think. And they will superadd, I trust, a second demonstration to the first.

I shall print the Letters and Sonnets from Mr. Goodall's edition of them. It is a standard one in itself. He had consulted the original editions, in making it*. But I shall note a few variations in Mr. Anderson's copy, which I think to be of moment. And, as Mr. Goodall first formed the paragraphs in some of the Letters, and first numbered the divisions in the Sonnets; I shall so far improve upon his plan, as to form paragraphs in all the Letters; to break the divisions into stanzas in the Sonnets, for the more commodious reading of them; and to number the paragraphs in the Letters, for the facility of referring to them. The last is peculiarly requisite to be done, in the first of the Letters. This runs out into all the length of one of Richardson's conversational epistles. Only there is an infinite difference between the two, in every other respect. Richardson's are strikingly characteristick; full of spirit, and pregnant with intelligence. But this carries no light of intelligence within it. This contains no sparks of spirit in it. And it is one complete violation of character, from the beginning to the end of it.

* Goodall, i. 39.

§ II. LET-

§ II.

LETTER THE FIRST (1).

I.—" (2) Being depàrtit from the place quhair
" I left my hart (3), it is efie to be judgeit quhat
" was my countenance, féing that I was evin als
" mekle as (4) ane body without ane hart; quhilk
" was the occafioun that quhile denner-tyme (5)
" I held".

I.—" (2) Posteaquam ab eo loco difceffi, ubi
" reliqueram cor meum (3), facilis eft conjectura
" qui meus fuerit vultus, cùm planè perinde effem
" atque (4) corpus fine corde: ea fuit caufa cur
" toto prandii tempore (5) neque contulerim"

I.—" (2) Eſtant partie du lieu ou j'avoye laiſſée
" mon cœur (3), il ſe peut aiſement juger quelle
" eſtoit ma contenance, veu ce que peut (4) un
" corps fans cœur; qui a eſté cauſe que juſques
" a la difnée (5) je n'ay pas tenue"

(1) This Letter pretends to be written, with the three next, on Jan. 24—26th, 1567, and from Glafgow*.

(2) The Queen left Edinborough on Jan. 21, attended by Huntly and BOTHWELL. Theſe peers went with her to Kalendar, a feat of Lord Living-

---

* Rebel Journal in App. No. x.

fton's

ston's near Falkirk. And on Jan. 23 she went on to Glasgow, while they returned to Edinborough*.

(3) Kalendar, where she and Bothwell parted that morning.

(4) This emphatical word "evin," Scotch, is rendered in Latin by "planè," which carries a different meaning, and in the French by nothing at all. But the subsequent words "als mekle as," truly rendered in Latin "perinde atque," are turned in French into "ce que peut.' This, says Dr. Robertson very justly, "is by no means a "translation" of the Latin†. A translation, however, it undoubtedly is of the Scotch; and, as the translator himself assures us, through the medium of this or another copy in Latin. Of *this* it apparently is not. It is, therefore, of some other. And this other had rendered the words "als mekle " as" by *quantum potuit*, I suppose; interpreting the words to mean *as much as could be*, and so giving them an import much more emphatical than " perinde atque."

(5) " Jusques a la disnée," says Dr. Robertson, " is not a translation of "' toto prandii tempore;'" " the Scottish translation "' quhile denner-tyme'" " expresses the sense of the French more properly; " for anciently *quhile* signified *until* as well as " *during* ‡." Dr. Robertson has here confounded his own ideas. If *quhile* " anciently signified *until* " as well as *during*," then the expression " quhile

* Rebel Journal in App. No. x. † Diff. 32. ‡ Ibid.

" denner-

" denner-tyme" may as properly be rendered " jufques a la difnée," as " toto prandii tempore ;" and the Scotch cannot " exprefs the fenfe of the " French more properly" than the Latin. This is plain, from the Doctor's own principles. And the very reafon adduced by himfelf, turns with forciblenefs againft him.

But, though *quhile* was fometimes ufed by the Scots formerly for *until*, as well as *during*; yet ordinarily it muft have fignified the latter only. It is merely the Englifh *while*, and muft therefore have ordinarily borne the fignification of it. And *quhill* or *quhil*, which anfwer to our Englifh *till* or *until*, muft confequently import the fame as they generally. Yet the Scotch Detection of Buchanan ufes *quhill* for *while* in the firft part of it, *quhile* for *while* in the laft, and even *quhile* for *until* in one place †. Ordinarily, however, and with the natural precifion, *quhill* or *quhil* imported *until*, and *quhile* fignified *during*. So, in the Confeffions at the end of the Detection, one man fays, " I " knew nathing *quhill* I hard the blaft of powder, " and efter yis he come hame, lay down in his " bed, *quhil* M. George Haket come ‡." So alfo the Detection itfelf fpeaks of " ane *quhyle*," " all " this *quhyle*," and " the *quhyle* ∥." But the Letters, as containing Lethington's language probably, are fteadily and uniformly right. In the prefent,

† P. 4, 7, 12, 23, 35, and 45, *quhill* for *while*; 70, 73, 74, and 77, *quhile* for *while*; and 182, *quhile* for *until*. Anderfon, ii.   ‡ Ibid. ii. 162.   ∥ P. 14 and 31, 16 and 34, and 63.

the King is said to deny something, " *qubill* I schew
" him the verray wordis *." She had worked, Mary
is made to say, " *qubill* it was twa houris upon this
" bracelet †." Bothwell " will never be blyth,"
says Livingston, " *qubill* he sé zow agane." Mary
vows fidelity to Bothwell " *qubill* deith," and
speaks of something that " sall not part furth of
" my bosum, *qubill* yat mariage of our bodyis be
" maid in publict." She is likewise requested by
the King, she says, " to remane upon him *qubil*
" uther morne ‡." And here she tells us, with the
requisite distinctiveness in the orthography and in
the meaning, that " *qubile* denner-tyme" she talked to nobody.

This ascertains sufficiently the true import of
the word here. Mary is represented as leaving
Bothwell that morning with a sorrowful heart, as
journeying to dinner with a discontented countenance, and even as eating her dinner in sullen
silence. Where she dined, does not appear. Kil-
syth most probably was the place, about 27 miles
from Kalendar through Stirling, and 15 from
Glasgow. There she was so apparently chagrined
all the time of dinner, that none of the gentlemen
and ladies in the town or neighbourhood would
venture into the room, to pay their respects of duty
to her while she was dining.

This passage, therefore, overthrows the very
point for which Dr. Robertson produces it. *Qubile*
very plainly does *not* signify *until*. The word

* Sect. xi.   † Sect. xxiii.   ‡ Sect. xxii. and xxiv,
and Letter viii. Sect. iii.

for

for that, in thefe Letters, is *qubill* or *qubil*. *Quhile* fignifies here, as *while* does among ourfelves, only *during*. The Latin " toto prandii tempore" is exactly correfpondent to the Scotch " quhile den-
" ner-tyme." The French "jufques a la difnée" is greatly deviating from it. The French was led into the miftake by a corrected copy of Buchanan's Latin, which took the word *qubile*, as Dr. Robertfon has taken it, for *qubil* or *till*; and fo rendered the paffage *ufque ad prandium*. And let me clofe this train of verbal criticifms, into which the Doctor has drawn me, with a remark that turns the whole with ftill greater force againft him. *All ferve to prove the originality of the Scotch copy.* The fimilarity of *qubil* and *qubile* has occafioned this confufion. The original Latin read it *qubile*. The corrected Latin read it *qubil*. The French followed the latter. And the French, the Latin, the corrected and the original Latin, plainly derived their variation, mediately or immediately, from a SCOTCH reading in the common original of all.

" purpojs (1) to na body; nor zit (2) durft (3)
" ony prefent thamefelfis unto me, judging yat"

" fermonem (1) cum quoquam, neque (2) quif-
" quam fe offerre mihi fit aufus (3), ut qui"

" grand propos (1); auffi (2) perfonne ne s'eft
" voulu (3) avancer, jugeant bien"

(1) The French has interpolated the word " grand," and has materially altered the fenfe by

B 4 it,

it, allowing the Queen to *have* talked, and so contradicting the Latin and the Scotch.

(2) The energetick " zit" or *yet* is omitted by the Latin, but is preserved in the French " auſſi" or *moreover*. This is another proof of the French tranſlation not being made from the preſent Latin, but from a corrected copy of it.

(3) The French " voulu" is foreign to the ſenſe. The Scotch " durſt," anſwered in the Latin " auſus," required *eſė*. And the French has omitted the requiſite words *au moi*, in anſwer to the Latin " mihi" and the Scotch " unto me."

" it was not gude ſa to do (1)."

" id non eſſe ex uſu (1)."

" qu'il n'y faiſoit bon (1)."

(1) " Jugeant bien qu'il n'y faiſoit bon," ſays Dr. Robertſon*, is not a tranſlation of the Latin " ut qui judicarent id non eſſe ex uſu." In this he has been joined by the Miſcellaneous Remarker, who affirms that the Latin " is not ſenſe, and is " not even conſiſtent with the Scottiſh copy †." I was puzzled, at the firſt reading, to know what it was that occaſioned this remark in both. But neither of them, it ſeems, was acquainted with the idiomatical ſenſe of the expreſſion " ex uſu." Such criticks are they in the Latin language! And

* Diſſ. 32.   † P. 13.

hence

hence the French became different from the Latin in one of them, and the Latin proved inconsistent with the Scotch in the other.

Thus ends, however, the first of the three sentences, that Dr. Robertson pitched upon in an unfortunate moment, as the only visible relicks of his own imaginary original in French; and as having a " spirit," and an " elegance," which neither the Latin nor the Scotch have retained*. But the Doctor has forgotten to support his hypothesis, by pointing out either the " spirit" or the " elegance" of any particular clauses in it. He has only taken two of the blunders in it, " jusques " a la disnée," and " je n'ay pas tenu *grand* pro-" pos;" and turned them into graces, by producing them as proofs of a non-translation, because— they are deviations from the Latin and the Scotch. He has then added one of his own, in fancying " jugeant bien qu'il n'y faisoit bon" to be different in signification from " ut qui judicarent id " non esse ex usu." And he has cited the words " veu ce que peut," as different from the Latin, because they are more emphatical, and as superiour to the Scotch, when they are plainly derived from them through the corrected Latin. Nor has he taken any notice of two other blunders in the French, in the substitution of " voulu" for *osé*, and in the omission of *au moi* entirely. He did not observe them. If he had, he would have turned the deformities again into beauties. They would have been equally valid arguments, for a

* Diss. 32.

non-

non-translation of the French from either the Latin or the Scotch. And they would have equally served, to give a " spirit" and an " elegance" to the French, which neither the Scotch nor the Latin have been able to reach.

Of this, of the " elegance" at least, the Miscellaneous Remarker comes forward to present us with one instance, though the Doctor had furnished us with none. His instance is a singular specimen of a spirit trifling, injudicious, and prejudiced. The Latin uses the word " vultus;" the French renders it " contenance." I select the two words that he has Italicised himself. And the French is *very seriously* asserted to be " *much* superior in " *elegance* and *accuracy*" to the Latin. The Remarker then proceeds to note another instance, not indeed of " spirit," not indeed of " elegance," in the French; but merely of " accuracy." The Latin says " se offerre," the French " s'avancer." The Latin is affirmed not to " express the mean-
" ing" of the French, because " the Queen is here
" made to speak of what happened on the road
" and before dinner." But this is only a continuation of Dr. Robertson's mistake. She is speaking of her conduct " quhile denner-tyme." And, even if she had not, " s'avancer" might as well express the advance of a person into a room, as the approach of a person upon a road.

On the whole, therefore, this first sentence of Dr. Robertson's original French, gives us no exalted ideas of the original itself. The latter may rest in that Elysium into which the Doctor has transferred it, without raising one sigh in our bosoms for the loss. It carries indeed all the signatures with it, of being the very same with the French copy yet on earth, and of being as *erroneous* and as *absurd* as that. And, what is peculiarly unfortunate for the Doctor and the Remarker together, a single sentence only, which has been picked out by both as a proof of a French copy, superiour in spirit, in elegance, and in accuracy to the Latin and the Scotch, has proved upon examination to have only one single grain of spirit more than the others, to have not even one more of elegance, and, as to accuracy, to have actually one interpolation, one omission, one impropriety, and one absurdity, in it.

II.—" Four myle (1) or I came to the towne (2),
" ane gentilman of the Erle of Lennox (3) came
" and maid his commendatiounis unto me (4);

II.—" Ad quatuor passuum millia (1) antequam
" ad oppidum (2) accessissem, homo honesto loco
" natus a Comite Leviniæ (3) ad me venit, atque
" ejus nomine salutavit (4);"

II.—" Estant encor a quatre mille pas (1) de la
" ville (2), vint a moy un gentilhomme envoyé
" par le Conte de Lenos (3), qui me salva en son
" nom (4);"

(1) " Four myle," Scotch, " quatuor passuum
" millia," Latin, and " quatre mille pas," French. The French has here so servilely followed the La-

tin,

tin, as to violate the proprieties of its own language. The Romans originally used the words *mille passuum* for a mile. But, as was sure to be the case, in time they used the greater word, and dropt the lesser. Their provincials, of course, adopted the language of their masters. And *mille* without *passuum* became the familiar term for a mile, in all the languages of Western Europe. Yet the French translator so little attended to this, that he followed the Latin implicitly; and, as this had " quatuor millia passuum," he set down " qua-" tre mille pas," even though the French had for ages expressed the general idea, in the same manner that we have, by the word *mile*.

(2) Mr. Anderson says, in order to censure Mary, that " the residence of the Earl of Lennox " at that time was near Dunbarton *." Yet the very papers, then before him, shew the Earl to have resided equally at Glasgow †. And at Glasgow did he *generally* reside; as this city is expressly called by the Privy Council of Scotland, " the " ordinary place of his abode ‡."

(3) This was Thomas Crawford ‖, an active and gallant man in those times of confusion, and partilarly distinguished by his bold surprize of Dumbarton Castle for the rebels §. But the French copy here appears to have followed a corrected copy of the Latin; the affected " Leviniæ " of Buchanan, which is derived from the original orthography of

---

* Anderſ. i. lx.   † Ibid. and ii. 101.   ‡ Keith, 348.
‖ Goodall, ii. 245, 246, and 247.   § Crawford, 188.

the name, *Levenox*, having been altered into *Lenoxiæ*, and the French therefore giving us " Lenos."

(4) " Maid his commendatiounis unto me." This phrase, says Mr. Tytler*, is *still used in the Scottish language* to signify *he presented his compliments.* Yet the Miscellaneous Remarker observes †, that
" to say *faites mes recommendations a un tel*, is more
" certainly French, than *make my commendatiouns* is
" Scottish. *Commender*, no doubt, may be employed
" abusively in French for *recommender*; and so
" perhaps *commendatiouns* may be employed in the
" Scottish language for *recommendatiouns*; but
" there occurs no singularity of idiom here; the
" phrase *to do commendations* is in Ainsworth's Eng-
" lish and Latin Dictionary, and is explained to
" mean *aliquem salvere jubere*; and yet it has a
" very French air." The captiousness and the feebleness of this gentleman's criticisms, are strongly exemplified together here. He would make the idiom a French one, in opposition to Mr. Tytler. Yet he proves it an English one, in opposition to himself. And he concludes with asserting, in opposition to both, that it has " a very French air." The fact is, that it is a mode of expression purely Scotch and English; but that it is similar to, though not the same with, a mode of expression in the French language. It was a customary idiom of compliment in all letters at that period, both in England and in Scotland ‡.—But the adherence of

---

* P. 88.   † P. 22, 23.   ‡ Goodall, ii. 153, 161, 178, 375, &c. It is derived from " recommendations," used in Sadler's Letters, 156, which in 242, 394, and 440, is " commendations."

the French to the Latin is very close here. " Ejus
" nomine salutavit" is re-echoed in " salva en
" son nom."

" and (1) excusit him (2) that he came not to
" meit me, be ressoun he durst not interpryse (3)
" the same, because of the rude wordis that I had
" spokin to Cuninghame (4): and he desyrit that
" he suld come to the inquisitioun (5) of ye mat-
" ter yat I suspectit him of (6). This last speik-
" ing (7) was of his awin heid, without ony com-
" missioun (8)."

" (1) excusavit Comitem (2), quòd non ipse ob-
" viam processisset, id enim quò minùs auderet (3),
" in causâ fuisse, quòd verbis asperioribus Cuni-
" gamium [Cuningamium] (4) compellâssem.
" Petivit etiam ut inquirerem (5) de suspicione
" meâ adversus Comitem (6). Postrema hæc ser-
" monis pars (7) ab ipso, injussu Comitis, erat
" adjecta (8)."

" et (1) l' (2) excusa de ce qu'il ne m'estoit
" venu au devant, disant, qu'il ne l'avoit osé en-
" treprendre (3), a cause que j'avoye tensé Cu-
" ningham (4) avec paroles aigres. Il me de-
" manda aussi que je m'enquisse (5) de soupçon
" que j'avoye contre icelluy Conte (6). Ceste
" derniere partie de son dire (7) avoit esté adjoustée
" par luy, sans que le Conte luy eust com-
" mandé (8)."

(1) " *And* excusit," Scotch; " excusavit,"
Latin, without the connecting word; " *et* excusa,"
French,

French, with it. This is another proof, that the French was not tranflated from the prefent Latin, but (as I have already fhewn) from another verfion in Latin, one that had all the eight Letters in it.

(2) "Excufed *him*," Scotch; "excufavit *Comitem*," Latin; and "*l*'excufa," French. This is another proof of the fame point.

(3) "Durft not interpryfe," "quò minùs auderet," "ne l'avoit ofé entreprendre." This is another. And the remarkable coincidence in *one* word muft be purely cafual, as the French tranflator was totally ignorant of the Scotch language. We have an inftance of the like before, in the Scotch "cquntenance," the Latin "vultus," and the French "contenance." There are alfo feveral others afterwards, which are not worth a particular notice. This one remark will fuffice for all.

(4) This is Robert Cunningham, who appeared at the trial of Bothwell, and in the Earl of Lenox's name protefted againft the profecution of it.

(5) Here the turn of the Latin, by which it has avoided the idiomatick obfcurity of the Scotch, is clofely copied by the French.

(6) The matter here hinted at is the Queen's fufpicion of Lenox's concern in the murder of Rizzio. "The Earl," fays Randolph in a letter dated April 4, 1566, "continueth fick, fore trou-
" bled in mind; he ftaith in the Abby," Holyrood-houfe; "his fon hath been once with him,
" and he once with the Queen, fince fhe came to
" the

" the Caſtle" of Edinborough *. But this very alluſion proves the forgery. The murder had been committed in *March*. The Earl, whom ſhe ſuſpected of concern in it, had been reſiding in his apartments within the Palace ever ſince, and had even been to pay his reſpects to her ſince ſhe went from the Palace to the Caſtle. She muſt therefore have intimated her ſuſpicion to *him*, rather than to his ſervant Cunningham. And in the *January* following it is abſolutely ridiculous to ſuppoſe, that ſhe had *lately* uttered her ſuſpicion to the ſervant, and that the Earl was *now* afraid to come and ſee her becauſe of it. He had already ſeen her, even in April before. He had ſeen her at the Palace, probably. He had ſeen her in the Caſtle, certainly †.

But the conduct of the three copies here is remarkable. The Scotch, in its uſual ſtile of colloquial indiſtinctneſs, ſpeaks only of " him ;" the Latin very properly ſubſtitutes " Comitem ;" and the French accordingly ſpecifies " iceluy Conte."

(7) " This laſt ſpeiking," " poſtrema hæc ſer-" monis pars," " ceſte derniere partie de ſon dire." The French is only the Latin repeated.

(8) Here the departure of the Latin from the language of the original, and the adherence of the French to the Latin, are equally obſervable.

* Robertſon, ii. 359.
† This letter of Randolph's refutes Foſter's from *Berwick*, in Robertſon, ii. 360.

III.

III.—" I anſwerit to him, that thair was na
" receipt culd ſerve aganis feir, and that he wald
" not be affrayit, in cace he wer not culpabill (1);
" and that I anſwerit bot rudely to the doutis yat
" wer in his letteris (2). Summa, I maid him hald
" his tongue (3). The reſt wer lang to wryte (4).
" Schir James Hammiltoun met me, quha ſchawit,
" that the uther tyme quhen he [Lenox] hard of
" my"

III.—" Ego reſpondi, nullam adverſus timorem
" eſſe medicinam; neque, ſi extra culpam eſſet (1),
" tam meticuloſum futurum; neque me, niſi ad
" dubitationes quæ in ejus literis erant, aſperiús
" reſpondiſſe (2). In ſummâ, impoſui homini ſilen-
" tium (3). Longum eſſet cetera perſcribere (4).
" D. Jacobus Hamiltonius mihi obviam venit; is
" oſtendit ſuperiore tempore, cúm de"

III.—" Je reſponduy, qu'il n'y avoit point de
" remede contre la crainte; et que, s'il eſtoit hors
" de faute (1), il ne ſeroit pas tant timide; et que
" je n'avoye point reſpondu aſprement ſinon aux
" doutes, qui eſtoient en ſes lettres (2). En ſomme,
" j'impoſay ſilence au perſonnage (3). Il ſeroit
" long deſcrire tout le reſt (4). Le Seigneur Jaques
" Hambleton vint au devant de moy, lequel me
" declara, qu'auparavant"

(1) " Si extra culpam eſſet," Latin; "s'il eſtoit
" hors de faute," French.

(2) In the *preceding* paragraph, Lenox is reprefented as fufpected of the murder of Rizzio, and Mary is intimated to have *therefore* treated Cunningham fharply. The earl, fays Crawford, durft not wait upon the queen, " becaus of the rude wordis " that I [Mary] had fpokin to Cuninghame ; and " he [Crawford] defyrit that he [Lenox] fuld come " to the inquifitioun of ye matter yat I fufpectit " him of." The fufpicion and the rudenefs are plainly connected together. The one is hinted to be the caufe, and the other is infinuated to be the effect. And common-fenfe fhews this to be the relation between them. Yet in the *prefent* paragraph, with that fudden contradictorinefs of which we fhall meet with other inftances hereafter, the rudenefs is no longer referred to the fufpicion, but is attributed to fome doubts expreffed by Lenox in fome letter or letters of his to Mary.—I proceed however to confider another particular.

Mary is faid before to *fufpect* Lenox. She here fays, that " he wald not be affrayit in cace he wer " not *culpabill*." She therefore charges him with a fhare in the murder. But all refentment upon this account muft have been long over, at prefent. She had pardoned even Lethington in the Auguft before *. She had pardoned even Morton in the December following †. Yet thefe fhe not merely fufpected; fhe *knew* them to have been guilty of the murder. And would fhe be ftill perfecuting Lenox with *fufpicions*, when fhe had overlooked and forgiven *abfolute certainties* ? She undoubtedly would not.

* Keith, 345. † Ibid. 429. and Pref. xi.

Nor did she persecute him at all. This is plain from a single fact. The king forming a design, as he said, to leave the kingdom in August or September 1566; Lenox was so far from considering himself as a persecuted man, that he wrote her Majesty a letter, which she received on September the 29th, and entreated her to use her influence with the king, in diverting him from his resolution. This was the act of a man, who was apparently in some habits of friendliness with the Queen.

But was that the letter, which is here alluded to? It certainly was not. There was no epistolary correspondence, indeed, carried on *ordinarily* betwixt the queen and him. There were only two periods in this part of their lives, at which they appear to have corresponded at all; the present, in consequence of the king's intention to go abroad, and a later one, in consequence of the king's murder. Of both correspondences we have a particular account. Nor were there any " doutes" expressed in the FORMER of them. This is clear from two accounts of it, written at the time. " The earl of Lenox," says Monsieur Le Croc, the French embassadour, in a letter of October 15th, " has written a letter to
" the Queen, signifying that 'tis not in his power to
" divert his son from his intended voyage; and
" prays her Majesty to use her interest therein. This
" letter from the Earl of Lenox, the Queen re-
" ceived on Michaelmas-day in the morning.—
" Early next morning the Queen sent for me, and
" for all the Lords and other Counsellors.—The
" Bishop of Ross, by the Queen's commandment,
" declared to the council the King's intention; " —and

" —and that her Majesty's information hereof pro-
" ceeded not from the rumour of the town, but
" from a letter written to her by his own father,
" the Earl of Lenox; *which letter was likewise*
" *read in the Council.*" " From Glasgow," adds
the Privy Council in a formal memorial upon the
subject, " my Lord Lenox wrote to the Queen,
" and acquainted her Majesty, that altho' he had
" endeavoured to divert him," the King, from going abroad, " he nevertheless had not the interest
" to make him alter his mind.—The Earl of Le-
" nox's letter came to the Queen's hand on St.
" Michael's day, and *her Majesty was pleased to im-
" part the same incontinent to the Lords of her Coun-
" cil*, in order to receive advice thereupon. And
" if her Majesty was surprized by this ADVER-
" TISEMENT from the Earl of Lenox; these Lords
" were no less astonished to understand, that the
" King should entertain any thoughts of depart-
" ing *." This letter therefore had no *doubts*. It
was merely an *advertisement* of the King's intended
departure.

What doubts indeed, and *of what*, could *any*
letter from Lenox have expressed to the Queen *at
present?* None certainly. Nor had any been actually expressed. This is clear from a real letter of
hers, dated only three days before the present,
speaking equally of the Earl of Lenox, speaking
too in terms of blame against him; and yet resting
her blame, not upon any *doubts* expressed in a letter
or letters to her, not upon any *letter* whether with
or without doubts in it, that had provoked her to

* Keith, 345, and 348.

CHAP. I. MARY QUEEN OF SCOTS. 21

ufe *rude words* to the bearer; but *upon his and his son's speeches and contrivances against her.* " Al- " wayis," fays Mary on January the 20th, 1567, to her embaſſadour in France, " we perſave him " [the King] occupeit and biſſy aneuch to haif in- " quiſitioun of our doyngis, quhilkis, God willing, " ſall ay be ſic as nane ſall haif occaſioun to be " offendit with thame, or to report of us any wayis " bot honorably; howſoever he, HIS FATHER, and " thair fautoris, *ſpeik*; *quilkis*, we knaw, want na " gude will to make us haif ado, gif thair power " wer equivalent to thair myndis. But God mo- " deratis thair forces well aneuch, and takis the " moyen of executioun of thair pretenſis fra " thame," &c.* At *this* time Mary had plainly received no letter of doubts from Lenox, and had been provoked by it to utter no rude words to the bearer. All the offence which ſhe had *yet* taken at Lenox, was grounded on his *ſpeeches*, and on his *cabals*, againſt her. And the writing, which ſpeaks of her having received ſuch a letter, and of her having uttered ſuch words in conſequence of it, is proved by the genuine writing to be a FORGERY.

The forgery indeed lies in an *anachroniſm*. The fabricator has *anticipated* a fact. He alludes to ſome letter or letters of *doubts*, which were *really* written by Lenox, but which were written *ſome weeks poſteriour* to the pretended date of the preſent. *After the murder of the king*, Lenox wrote the Queen more than one letter concerning it, in which the rebels thought there were ſome *doubts* expreſſed by

* Keith, Pref. viii.

Lenox, concerning Mary's sincerity in bringing the murderers to trial; as they induced Lenox himself to carry copies of two of his, and the originals of two of hers, and present them in form to the English commissioners, with a charge of murder against Mary; and as they afterwards procured the originals and copies of all the rest, and lodged them equally in the hands of Cecil *. These are dated February 20th, 21st, and 26th, March 1st, 17th, and 24th, and April the xith. *All* these, however, cannot be alluded to here, because the allusion is to *one* only, to what was brought at one time and by one messenger, and to what the Queen answered with rude words to Cunningham. This therefore carries us to the *last* of them, that of April the xith, the famous letter from Stirling; in which he, who had first desired her to call a parliament, *in order* to bring on the trial; and who had then desired her to hasten on the trial *before* the parliament met, "yis "matter not beinge ane parliament matter;" now requested her to *defer* the trial *to an indefinite time*. This was actually brought to her by "Cuning-"hame," while the others were all brought by we know not whom †. And *this* expresses *doubts* concerning her very plainly. "For your awin ho-"nour," says Lenox in it, "I desire you wauld "causs apprehend and put in suir keiping the "suspect persons namit," Bothwell, &c. "avoyd-"ing your Majestie's company of tham; for *it was "nevir hard of*, bot in the tryall of sic ane odious "fact, all suspectit persons was *alwayis* apprehendit,

---

* Anderson, i. 40—49. Contents, lix. and lx. and Goodall, ii. 208—209.   † Ibid, i. 40, and 45. and ii. 106.

"qubat

"*quhat degre foever thai war of*;—utherwayis the "fufpect perfonis continewing ftill at libertie, *being* "*gret in court*, and *about your Majeftie's perfon*, "comforts and incouragis thame," &c. * On the receipt of this letter, Mary might poffibly utter fome harfh words to the bearer, Cunningham. This indeed was the only letter, for which fhe could. And the forger has been wildly inattentive to dates, in alluding to a letter which was pofteriour to the very death of the King; and wildly confufed in his ideas, in fpeaking of the Queen's fufpicion of Lenox for the murder of Rizzio, and in alluding to Lenox's doubts of the Queen concerning the murder of Darnley, at a period BETWIXT both.

The fact was this. When the forger fat down to his work of compofing epiftles for Mary, he had a void of time before him, which he muft neceffarily fill up with epiftolary incidents. The letters muft relate fome things, in order to be letters. They muft relate fome circumftances of her journey, her reception, and her converfation, in order to give a greater air of probability to them. And they muft relate fome particulars of her prefent conduct, and of her future defigns, in order to bear a charge of adultery and of murder upon them. Thefe incidents, therefore, muft all be either picked up by intelligence from the real events of her vifit, or be created by a happy exertion of the imagination and of the judgment together. But fo to create is no eafy tafk. The letters are apparently the work of a hafty effort, ftruck off at once without imagination and without judgment. They are *therefore* ftored with

* Anderfon, i. 52—54.

incidents,

incidents, which intelligence supplied. This is plain from the depositions of Thomas Crawford in England, who confirmed several of the facts related in this part of the present letter particularly *. Yet, in arranging the articles of this intelligence, the forger was liable to be abused by his negligence and his situation. He was to take such articles only, as were antecedent to the date of his letters. He was to reject all that were posteriour to it. He was to draw a very precise line betwixt both. And he was to adhere very rigidly to it. But the hurry of the forger did not allow him to be confined within such limits. He drew no line, or he overpast it. He united prior and posteriour incidents together. He combined the future and the past in his own point of time. He even went such lengths of confusion, as to anticipate an event that happened NEAR THREE MONTHS AFTERWARDS. The distance of time at which he was writing, came in to the aid of his carelessness, to conceal the blunder from him. And he plainly betrayed his forgery to the eye of the publick by it; though this eye is now opened for the first time to see it, after an acquiescence of two hundred years under it †.

* Goodall, ii. 245—246.
† Buchanan has also misled himself in his History, by trusting to his memory, and mistaking one event for another. In xix. 367. he makes Murray to hold a parliament in August 1567, when he actually held it in December following (Keith, 465.) But then Murray did really hold one in August, *the year succeeding* (Anderson, iv. part 1. 125—126.) And this his memory afterwards confounded with that. So he convenes the nobles at Stirling in the end of April and beginning of May 1567 (xviii. 356.) *because* they assembled there in the beginning of June afterwards.

(3.) " Im-

(3.) " Impofui homini filentium," Latin, and " j'impofay filence au perfonnage," French, are as fimilar to each other as they are different from the Scotch, " I maid him hald his toung."

(4.) " The reft wer lang to wryte." What remainder could there be to write? She has told us his fpeech. She has told us her anfwer. And fhe has told us the refult of both. What elfe could fhe have to tell us? Nor let fuch a queftion be thought more brifk than proper. Thefe letters are written with fuch continued abfurdity in the whole and in the parts, and they have been fo little examined hitherto with minute attention, that we can hardly be too much alive to the progrefs of the narrative in them, or too ready to queftion and interrogate the fentences as they arife before us.—The French has *added* the word " tout."

" cumming, he departit away, and fend Howf-
" toun (1) to fchaw him [Sir James] that he wald
" never have belevit that he [Sir James] wald have
" perfewit him [Lenox], nor zit have accompanyit
" him [Sir James] with the Hammiltounis. He
" anfwerit (2), that he was only cum bot to fee me
" (3), and yat he wald nouther accompany Stewart
" nor Hammiltoun, bot be my commandement (4).
" He [Lenox] defyrit that he [Sir James] wald
" cum and fpeik with him [Lenox]: he [Sir James]
" refufit it (5)."

" meo adventu audiffet, eum difceffiffe, ac Hufto-
" num (1) ad fe mififfe, qui diceret, fe nunquam
" fuiffe

" fuiffe crediturum, quód aut ipfum perfequeretur,
" aut Hamiltoniis fe conjungeret; fe vero refpon-
" diffe (2), fui itineris caufam unam fuiffe, ut me
" videret (3); neque cum Stuartis aut Hamiltoniis,
" injuffu meo, fe conjuncturum (4)."

" ayant entendu ma venüe, il s'eftoit retiré, et luy
" avoit envoyé Hufton (1), pour luy dire, qu'il
" n'euft jamais creu, ou qu'il l'euft voulu purfuivre,
" ou qu'il fe fut joinct avec les Hambletons; et
" qu'il refpondit (2), qu'il n'y avoit eu qu'une
" caufe de fon voyage, a fcavoir, pour me voir (3);
" et qu'il ne fe conjoindroit avec les Stuarts et
" Hambletons fans mon commandement (4)."

(1) This name fhews the fidelity of the French
to the Latin; " Howftoun," Scotch, being " Huf-
" tonum," Latin, and " Hufton," French.

(2) The Scotch begins a frefh fentence. But
the Latin continues the former. And therefore the
French continues it too.

(3) The Latin fays, " fui itineris caufam unam
" fuiffe, ut me videret;" and the French, " qu'il
" n'y avoit eu qu'une caufe de fon voyage, a fca-
" voir, pour me voir;" both very fimilar and very
diffufe: while the Scotch is at once different and
compact, " that he only cum bot to fee me."

(4.) The whole turn of the fentence here, and
particularly the plural termination of Stuart and
Hamilton, fhew the French to be merely from the
Latin. The Stuarts, or the family and dependents of the Earl of Lenox, were at this period in a

ftate

state of enmity with the Hamiltons, the family and dependents of the Duke of Chatelleraut.

(5) A whole sentence in the Scotch is here omitted by the Latin, and, in consequence of that, by the French. Such is the variation of the Latin from the Scotch; and such the closeness, with which the French comes treading in its steps! The Scotch, as we have reason to think from other instances hereafter, had not the sentence in it originally. The *first* and the *corrected* Latin, therefore, were equally deprived of the sentence. And for that reason the French *could* not have it.—But let us here attend to the new fact stated in this paragraph.

Lenox is said " the uther tyme," when he heard of the Queen's coming to Glasgow, to have " de-" partit away." This alludes to some journey of the Queen's, which was different from the present. It was the journey of " the uther tyme." It was some journey that was still well remembered, and that had consequently been taken a little before. And Lenox *then* " departit away" from Glasgow; when he *now* staid in the city, and sent to excuse his non-attendance on her upon the road. So plainly is that journey of the Queen's, discriminated by the letter from the present! Yet, if we proceed with the letter, we shall find it *confounding* what it has already discriminated, and we shall see the journey to be the very same with the present. It was one, in which Sir James Hamilton came to pay his respects to the Queen, equally as he did in this. It was one, in which the Queen was escorted by the Hamiltons, equally as she is in this [*]. It was one

[*] Sect. xxxii.

too,

too, in which Sir James Hamilton muſt have *then* related to the Queen the anecdote concerning Lenox, if the journey had been different from this. And indeed Sir James makes it one and the ſame with this, by his anſwer to Lenox, as reported in the letter. "He anſwerit, that he WAS only cum "bot to ſee me, and yat he WALD nouther accom- "pany Stewart nor Hammiltoun, bot be my com- "mandement." So plainly was this journey of the Queen's at once different from, and yet the very ſame with, her preſent! The circumſtances, the language, and the whole tenour of the ſtory, all unite to prove it the ſame; while the departure of Lenox at it, and the other time aſſigned for it, concur to prove it different. And all forms a very glaring evidence of that abſurdity in the parts of theſe letters, which I have noticed ſo little a while before.

But, whether we conſider the journey as different or the ſame, *either way* the mention of it proves the mentioning letter to be a forgery. This is extraordinary. Yet it is evident.

If we take the journey to be a *different* one from the preſent, the Queen is repreſented as going to Glaſgow ſome time before the 23d of January 1567, and Lenox is deſcribed as leaving Glaſgow upon the report of her coming. This muſt have been, as I have obſerved before, only a little time previous to her preſent journey. It muſt certainly have been, *ſince* the Queen began to ſuſpect Lenox of a ſhare in the murder of Rizzio, *ſince* Lenox left his lodgings in Holyrood-houſe, and *ſince* he retired to Glaſgow. He was in his lodgings, as I have

have previously shewn, on the 4th of April. But he was also there many days later. That letter, which shews he was then resident " in the Abby," and had been " once with the Queen since she came " to the castle," ought to be dated much later than it is. It was not till the *fifth* of April, that the Privy Council *agreed* to *advise* the Queen, if it might be compatible with her pleasure and health, to " remane in the castell of Edinburgh till her " Grace be deliverit of hir birth *." She entered it therefore *after* the 5th. But she also entered it *before* the 14th. She kept Easter-Sunday there, which was the 14th of April in that year †. Yet she had been for some time in the castle, when the letter was written; as Lenox had then been " once " with the Queen since she came to the castle." And the letter ought pretty certainly to be dated the 24th, as " it is written to me for certain," says the author, " by one that on *Monday last* spoke with " the Queen, that she is determined that the house " of Lenox shall be as poor in Scotland as ever it " was;" and as the Monday but one after Easter-Sunday was the 22d of April. Lenox then continued at Holyrood-house to the 24th, and beyond. The Queen also had removed before into the castle, and continued there to the time of her delivery, the 19th day of June, and to the completion of her month afterwards ‡. Betwixt the 24th and 28th of July, she left the castle for Alloa, a seat of Lord Mar's, near Stirling ‖. From that period to the

* Keith, 335.   † Goodall, i. 289.   ‡ Ibid. i. 289—290.   ‖ Ibid. 292—293.

present,

present, we have all her motions described exactly by the zeal and hostility of the rebel diary. And WE HAVE NO JOURNEY TO GLASGOW IN ANY PART OF THE WHOLE *. So evidently is this, if considered as *different* from the present, demonstrated to be all a forgery!

Nor is it less so, if considered as the *same*. It was taken, says the letter, " the uther tyme." The slightest distance of time, that we can ground upon these words, directly oversets them. In S. xxiv. we have words nearly similar, and meaning the day after next, " uther morne." If therefore we interpret those words in the sense of these, and consider them as signifying the day before the last, which is the lowest possible signification that we can give them; even then we shall be carried back to the 21st of January, the very day of Mary's setting out for Glasgow. And, as I shall hereafter shew Mary *not* to have *known* of her own setting out *the very day before*, the report of it could not possibly have reached Glasgow the very day of her setting out. This carries a decisive weight with it. But let us view the account in another light also. The Earl of Lenox is said to have *left* Glasgow, upon the report of the Queen's coming. Yet, as I have already observed, he did *not* leave it. This the testimony of Thomas Crawford satisfactorily shews, who was the very man that came to Mary on the road in the name of Lenox, and who deposed before the commissioners in England, That " as soon as the " Quene of Scotts had spoken with the King his " master

* Anderson, ii. 269—271.

" mafter at Glafgow from tyme to tyme, he, the
" faid Crawford, was fecretly informed by the King
" of all things which had paffed betwixt the faid
" Quene and the King, *to the intent he fhuld report*
" *the fame to the Earl of Lenox his mafter*; becaufe
" the faid Earle durft not then, for difpleafure of the
" Quene," occafioned (as appears from her letter
of January 20th before) by his factious pratings and
factious cabals, "*come abroad**." Our prefent letter alfo confirms the teftimony and the obfervation.
" This day," fays the writer of it, " HIS FATHER
" bled at the mouth and nofe;—I have not zit fene
" him, *he keipis his chalmer*; the King defyris
" that I fuld give him meit with my awin handis †."
And the grofs and palpable contradiction here, is
the fulleft proof of a forgery. Nature could not
deviate fo wildly from itfelf. Art alone could.
The Queen could not poffibly have afferted Lenox
to be departed from the town, and yet to be actually
in it. And as this concurs with the obfervation
before, concerning the " uther tyme;" fo both unite
to make the whole paffage furnifh us, with a fecond,
unnoticed, proof of the general forgery.

* Goodall, ii. 246.   † Sect. xvi.

§ III.

§ III.

LETTER THE FIRST CONTINUED.

IV.—" The laird of Luffe (1), Howftoun (2),
" and Caldwellis fone (3), with XL (4) hors or
" thairabout, came and met me (5). The laird of
" Luffe faid, he was chargeit to ane day of law (6)
" be the King's Father, quhilk fuld be this day (7),
" aganis his [Lenox's] awin hand-writ, quhilk he
" [Luffe] hes (8): and zit notwithftanding, knaw-
" ing of my cumming, it is delayit (9). He was in-
" quyrit to cum to him (10) [Lenox], quhilk he
" refufit (11), and fweiris that he will indure (12)
" nathing of him."

IV.—" Luffius (1), Huftonus (2), Caldoëlli
" filius (3), comitati quadraginta (4) circiter equis,
" obviam venerunt (5). Luffius dixit, fe a Regis
" patre in eum ipfum diem (7) ut caufam diceret
" (6) accerfitum, contra quám chirographo pro-
" mififfet; id chirographum penes fe effe (8): tamen
" cúm de meo adventu refcitum effet, diem prola-
" tum (9); fe accerfitum a Comite (10), ire nolle
" (11); ac jurat fe nihil unquam ab eo velle (12)."

IV.—" Luffe (1), Hufton (2), et le fils de Cauld-
" wellis (3), accompagnez d'environ quatre vingts
" (4) chevaux, vindrent au devant de moy (5).
" Luffe dict, que ce jour-la mefme (7) il eftoit ad-
" journé

" journé (6) par le pere du Roy, contre ce qu'il
" avoit promis par fon feing, et que ce feing eftoit
" par devers luy (8) : mais, que quand on fut ad-
" verty de ma venüe, que le jour avoit efté pro-
" longé (9). Et qu'il ne vouloit (11) aller par
" devers le Conte (10), qui l'avoit appellé; en
" jurant, qu'il ne luy demanderoit (12) jamais
" rien."

(1) The Latin tranflator rendering " the laird
" of Luffe" by " Luffius," inftead of *Dominus de
Luffa*, the Frenchman was compelled to take up
with " Luffe," here and immediately afterwards.

(2) The French again follows the Latin in the
variation of this name.

(3) The French here purfues the corrected Latin, which was lefs flourifhing in itfelf, and more
clofe to the Scotch; retaining the conjunctive particle, giving the Scotch name juft as it was, but
miftaking the termination for a part of the name,
and fo making " Caldwell" into " Caldwellis "
The Latin being " et filius de Caldwelle," the
French read it, " et filius de Caldwellë," and fo
became itfelf " et le fils de Cauldwellis." This
gentleman was afterwards feized by the rebels, as he
was haftening to affift the Queen juft then efcaped
from prifon *.

(4) " Forty" in Scotch, " quadraginta" in Latin, and by fome ftrange miftake " quatre vingts"
or eighty in French.

* Keith, 475.

(5) Here also the French follows a more correct translation into Latin, than the present is; the relative "me" being omitted in the last, and yet preserved in the first.

(6) "Chargeit to ane day of law," and "ut "causam diceret accersitum," are only answered by "adjourné" in French. The Frenchman did not understand the meaning of the Latin. The laird of Lusse was summoned to attend as a juryman at one of Lenox's courts. Ignorant of this, the Frenchman only says he was summoned, without specifying for what. And this alone should have shewn decisively, that the French was not the original, and that the Scotch was.

(7) "Quhilk suld be this day," Scotch; "in "eum ipsum diem," Latin; "ce jour-la mesme," French.

(8) "Aganis his own hand-writ, quhilk he hes," Scotch; "contra quám chirographo promisisset, id "chirographum penes se esse," Latin; and "contre "ce qu'il avoit promis par son seing, et que ce "seing estoit par devers luy," French. So thoroughly Latinized is the French!

(9) "It is delayit," Scotch; "diem prolatum," Latin; "que le jour avoit esté prolongé," French; another proof of the same point.

(10) "Him," "Comitem," "le Conte."

(11) "Refusit," "nolle," "ne vouloit."

(12) "Indure," "velle," "demanderoit." These three instances are three additional proofs of the same point.

V.—" Ne-

V.—" Never ane of that (1) towne came to
" speik to me, quhilk causis me think that thay ar
" his (2); and neverthelles (3) he (4) speikis gude,
" at the leist his (5) sone (6). I'se na uther gentil-
" man (7) bot thay of my company."

V.—" Nemo oppidanorum (1) me convenit, quæ
" res facit ut eos credam ab illo stare (2); præ-
" terea (3), bene loquuntur (4), saltem de (6)
" filio (5). Nullos præterea nobiles (7) video præ-
" ter meos comites."

V.—" Nùl des citoyens (1) n'est venu a moy,
" qui faict que je croy qu'ils sont d'avec cestuy-
" la (2); et puis (3) ils (4) parlent en bien, au
" moins (6) du fils (5). D'avantage je ne voy au-
" cuns de la noblesse (7), autre ceux de ma suite."

(1) This is one of those slight and incidental
strokes of forgery, which the common eye always
overlooks, but which betray the forgery very signi-
ficantly to a critical one. The letter pretends to be
written from Glasgow. The real Mary, writing
from *Glasgow*, could not possibly have called it *that*
town. She must have called it *the* town, as she
does before, or *this* town. But the forger of the
letter, writing at *another* place, and writing from a
forced combination of ideas, would be apt at times
to start aside from it. Art would intermit its controuling power for a moment. And Nature would

re-assert

re-assert her authority, laugh at the mimickries of her rival, and confound her fantastical operations.

(2) The Frenchman has made an amazing blunder here. His Latinity not carrying him far enough, to shew him the meaning of the idiom, "ab illo stare;" he translated it literally, "sont d'avec cestuy-la," and so gave it a signification directly the reverse of the original. And as "quæ res facit" runs so readily into "qui faict," so it concurs to shew how literally he was following the Latin.

(3) The Latin translating "nevertheles" by "præterea," the French renders both by "puis." And this is the more observable, as the French, by prefixing the "et," appears to have been translating from the corrected Latin.

(4) This is the region of mistakes to both the French and the Latin. "He speikis" is rendered "loquuntur" and "ils parlent."

(5) "His" is omitted equally in the Latin and in the French, though so necessary to the sense.

(6) The father, says the Scotch concerning Lenox, speaks " gude ;" or at least his son, the King, does. Mary is thus made to anticipate in reflection, what she relates in succession afterwards. Yet there is a great absurdity attending one half of the anticipation. She relates the " gude" speeches of the *son* hereafter. But she relates none hereafter from the *father*. She also *relates none before*. She has not yet seen him, she does not see him at all in this letter, to hear him speak either " gude" or bad. She tells us expresly, near the *end* of this long letter,

ter, that she had not even then seen him. "His
"father," she says, "keipis his chalmer; I HAVE
"NOT SENE HIM *." Nor can she be excused, as
alluding to the message which she received from
him on the road. This she did not consider as
"gude," because she says she made the messenger
"hald his toung." And this passage is therefore
one of those many contradictions, which I have already announced to my reader, some of which I
have exposed to his view before, and others of
which I shall be forced to expose hereafter. This
contradiction the Latin translator appears to have
observed, and to have taken a turn in order to
avoid it. "Nemo oppidanorum," he says, "me
"convenit, quæ res facit ut eos credam ab illo stare;
"præterea, bene loquuntur, saltem de filio." That the
townsmen speak well of him, or at least of his son;
is an *additional* reason assigned for believing, that
they are of his side. This is plainly too regular a
chain of thoughts, to be linked by the hand of accident. He studiously formed it, to escape an absurdity. He has escaped one by it, and has fallen into
another. He now gives the kind speeches to the
townsmen of Glasgow. He now fixes the father,
"or at the leist his sone," to be the object, instead
of the speaker, of them. And he now makes the
townsmen to utter them to Mary, when "never ane
"of that towne came to speik to" her at all. I
need hardly add, that the French has taken all the
absurdity of the Latin. We cannot expect the
mock-sun to be freer from spots than the true.

* Sect. xxxi.

And " ils [citoyens] parlent en bien, au moins du
" fils," is juſt the reflection of " bene loquuntur,
" ſaltem de filio."

(7) " Gentilman" was tranſlated before " homo
" honeſto loco natus," and " un gentilhomme."
But now, when the Latin abſurdly renders it " no-
" biles," the French, ſcorning to be leſs abſurd,
renders it " nobleſſe."

VI.—" The King ſend for Joachim ziſternicht
" (1), and aſkit at him, quhy I ludgeit not beſyde
" him? and that (2) he wald ryſe the ſoner gif
" that wer (3): and quhairfoir I come, gif it was
" for gude appointment (4)?"

VI.—Rex arceſſivit Joachimum heri (1), ac
" eum interrogavit, cur non propé ſe diverterem,
" id enim (2) ſi feciſſem, ſe citiús ſurrecturum (3);
" item cur veniſſem? an reconciliationis cauſâ (4)?"

VI.—" Le Roy appella hier (1) Joachim, et
" l'interroga, pourquoy je n'alloye loger pres de
" luy? et que (2), ſi je le faiſoye, il ſeroit pluſtoſt
" remis ſus (3); item pourquoy j'eſtoy venue, et
" ſi c'eſtoit pour faire une reconciliation (4)?"

(1) This is the firſt note of time that has occurred yet. I ſhall mark all very carefully, as they
appear before us. And I ſhall ſtop occaſionally to
ſhew, how fully they unite to prove the forgery.
But I ſhall only obſerve at preſent, that the Latin
tranſlating

translating " zisternicht" by " heri" and not *besternâ nocte*, the French was forced to use "hier," instead of *hier au soir*.

(2) The French " et que," so different from the Latin, and so according with the Scotch, shews it to have been taken from the corrected Latin.

(3) " Gif that wer," rendered " id si fecissem" and " si je le faisoye," shews the French to be only Latin Frenchified. The words adjoining in all the copies, " he wald ryse the soner," " se citiús surrecturum," and " il seroit plustost remis sus," mean that he should the sooner be raised up from his bed of sickness. He kept his bed at present *.

(4) " Item cur venissem," Latin, " item pourquoy j'estoye venue," French; and " an reconciliationis causâ," " si c'estoit pour faire une reconciliation." But how comes the King to ask this question? He knew for what purpose she came. Joachim, no doubt, as her fore-runner, brought a message from the Queen to the King, indicating her immediate visit to him, and the reasons of it. This must have been the case, whether the Queen came with friendly or with hostile intentions. And it must peculiarly have been so, when the Queen came (as I shall soon shew she did) in consequence of a message from the king himself, in consequence of his avowed repentance for his previous conduct to her, and in consequence of his expressed wish to see her.

* Sect. x. and xxi.

" and gif ze wer thair in particular (1)? and gif I
" had maid my eſtait (2), gif I had takin Paris *
" and Gilbert (3) to wryte to me? and yat I wald
" ſend Joſeph away. I am abaſchit quha hes ſchawin
" him ſa far (4); zea, he ſpak evin (5) of the mar-
" riage (6) of Baſtiane."

* " This berer will tèll you
" ſumwhat upon this (7)."

" ac nominatim, an tu hic eſſes (1)? an familiæ
" catalogum feciſſem (2)? an Paridem et Gilber-
" tum (3) accepiſſem qui mihi ſcriberent? an Jo-
" ſephum dimiſſura eſſem? Miror quis ei tantum
" indicarit (4); etiam uſque ad nuptias (6) Sebaſ-
" tiani ſermo pervenit (5)."

" ſi vous eſtiez icy (1)? et ſi j'avoye faiƈt quelque
" rolle de mes domeſtiques (2)? ſi j'avois prins
" Paris et Gilbert (3), afin qu'ils m'eſcriviſſent? et
" ſi je ne vouloye pas licentier Joſeph? Or je
" m'eſtonné qui luy en tant declaré (4); car meſme
" il a tenu propos (5) de Sebaſtian (6)."

(1) This is the firſt hint concerning the adultery.
But who the adulterer was, could never be known
from the hint. No one is addreſſed by name. No
one is alluded to by character. No one is pointed
out with the ſlighteſt particularity. But the abſurdity of all this is greatly heightened, by another
circumſtance. Mary went to ſee Darnly in his illneſs at Glaſgow, with a *real*, or with a *pretended*, regard. Acting under the influence of either, ſhe
would

would *not* take her adulterer with her. This is obvious. Yet, obvious as it is, the forger has not feen it. And Darnly is reprefented as enquiring of her fore-runner, whether the adulterer was with her. With fuch an evident abfurdity is the letter managed!

(2) " Maid my eftait," fays the Mifcellaneous Remarker *, is French, *faire un etat*, to make up a lift of the officers of one's houfhold. This letter fhews it to be equally Scotch. The Latin accordingly renders it " an familiæ catalogum fecif-" fem?" And the French thought fo little of *faire un etat*, that it turns the Latin into " fi j'avoye faict " quelque rolle de mes domeftiques." But, in *any* fenfe of the words, where is the *propriety* of them? Why fhould Darnly afk, whether fhe had made " *quelque* rolle de domeftiques," or " familiæ cata-" logum," or a lift of the officers of her houfhold? Was this the *commencement* of her royalty? or had fhe never formed her houfhold *before?* She formed it, no doubt, when fhe firft fettled in Scotland. She muft have formed it finally, if fhe had not done fo before, when fhe married Darnly. And the queftion is only one of thofe abfurdities, which croud the letters from end to end, and which are fome of the ftrongeft marks of forgery in them. When the imagination is let loofe into the regions of fiction, it requires a higher degree of judgment than what the forger was able to exert, in order to keep its excurfions within the lines of fobriety; to guard it againft extravagance, while it is indulging in invention; and

* P. 20.

to secure a strain of probability, amid the facilities of falshood.

(3) This was Gilbert Curle, mentioned in Paris's second confession *, and afterwards secretary to her in her English confinement.

(4) This is said in consequence of a peculiar disposition in the King. He was meanly suspicious. He was therefore at work continually, in prying into all the circumstances of Mary's conduct. And he was perpetually twisting and turning them, as far as his little ingenuity would allow him, to the hurt of her reputation. This appears sufficiently in Mary's *real* letter of January the 20th before. But I shall cite some of the clauses again. "Alwayis "we persave him," she says, "occupeit and bissy "aneuch, to haif inquisitioun of our doyngis ; "quhilkis, God willing, sall ay be sic as nane sall "haif occasioun to be offendit with thame, or to "report of us any wayis bot honorably, howsoever "he, his father, and thair fautoris, speik ; quhilkis, "we knaw, want na gude will to make us haif ado, "gif thair power wer equivalent to thair myndis †." By this folly of conduct he was probably the author or the spreader of many calumnies, which the fools of faction still believe against Mary. He certainly was of one, which some of the lowest are still circulating in conversation, though none of them are weak enough to lend their little sanction to it in print; the pretended amour of Mary with Rizzio ‡. And in this fictitious letter he is repre-

* Goodall, ii. 78.   † Keith, Pref, viii.   ‡ Keith, App. 124.

sented, perhaps not untruly, as carrying his suspicious curiosity so far, as to procure information of every man and woman that she took into her houshold, and even of every marriage that was negotiating among them.

(5) Here the French, following another translation in Latin, varies equally from the present and the Scotch; " car" being substituted for " etiam" and " zea." And it is useful to note these little variations from the present Latin, because they arise from what I have already proved, but which had never been observed before, a Latin copy different from the present, and having all the eight letters in it.

(6) The French, having followed the Latin in lengthening the name of " Bastiane" into " Sebas-" tian," by some mistake drops all notice of the marriage.

(7) " This berer will tell you sumwhat upon " this." What then was the bearer, Paris, to tell Bothwell concerning this? The King had asked, whether Mary had taken Paris and Gilbert to be her private secretaries. Mary reports this question in a letter to Bothwell. And she adds, that Paris himself, who carried the reporting letter, should tell him some more particulars concerning the question. What then was he to tell? I cannot possibly conjecture what. And I therefore consider the whole, as one of the multiplied absurdities, that glare upon us while we read the letters.

" This

"This Paris," says Buchanan, "was ane young man borne in France, and had levit certane zeiris in the housis of Bothwell and Setoun, and efterwart with the Quene*." He appears in the *letter* to be *juſt now* taken into the Queen's service. He accordingly says, in his second mock-confession, that he first entered into credit with her on the road betwixt Kalendar and Glasgow†; which was this very day, January 23d. Yet, though he was so lately come into her train, she had confidence enough in him THIS VERY DAY, to make him *privy to the adultery*, by giving him a purse of crowns for Bothwell‡; and even, IN A DAY OR TWO, to make him *privy to the murder itſelf*, by sending him with *this* letter *unſealed*. And all this while he was only "ane young man."

The force of folly, I may safely affirm, cannot possibly go beyond this. But let us attend to another circumstance here.

I have already pointed out a number of variations in the form and substance of the letters. Here we have one of a new nature. This marginal intimation was not in the letter, as it appeared at York. The commissioners there speak thus of the bearer: "Item, in the credit gifin to the berer, "quhome WE UNDERSTAND was Pareis §." But they *could* not have spoken in these terms, if the intimation had been then in the letter. They could not have said *they underſtood* Paris to be the bearer, if he was expressly stiled so by a reference to the

---

* Detection, 21. † Goodall, ii. 76. ‡ Ibid. ibid.
§ App. Nº vii.

side

fide of the page. And they could not have attributed their knowledge of the point to the information of the rebels, if the letter itself informed them of it explicitly. This note therefore, of Paris being the bearer of the letter, was not in the original shewn to the commissioners at York. Yet it was in that exhibited at Westminster. Hence it appeared in the English edition of the letters 1571, and appears in the present. But hence also it does *not* occur in the Latin, in the French, or in the Scottish edition of 1572. The Latin version, as I have shewn already, was made before the exhibition of the letters at Westminster, and in order to the exhibition of them in French there. Accordingly it omitted the present passage, as the original had not yet got it. The French equally omitted it, because the Latin had. And the Scotch edition of 1572 omitted it equally with both, because this professed itself to be merely a translation from the Latin, when in the letters it is evidently nothing more than a copy of the English. No translation from the Latin, or any other language, could possibly have made the English and the Scotch editions of the letters to coincide regularly, word for word, from the beginning to the end. Nothing but transcription could do this. And, what is still more, the Scotch edition had all the eight letters of the English, when the Latin had only three of them. The Scotch edition of the letters, then, was only a transcript of the English. Yet in the title-page the whole work, the letters as well as the Detection itself, were said to have been " translatit out of the " Latine, quhilk was written be M. G. B.", Mr.

George

George Buchanan. And for this reason the Scotch editor was obliged to throw out the note, though it was in the very edition which he was copying at the time *.

We have also seen a fact before, that is nearly similar to this. At the end of Section the 3d, is a whole sentence in the English edition, which does not appear in either the French or the Latin. It was therefore, as we may presume from the present instance, not in the York original of the letter, though it must have been in the Westminster. But it differs from the present, in appearing upon the pages of the Scotch edition. And this, the only difference between them, may be easily accounted for, from that being a note on the margin of the page, and this being a sentence in the body of it; from that necessarily engaging the notice of the pretended translator, and so being omitted in conformity to his pretensions; and from this very naturally escaping his notice, and so running readily into his copy.

All serves however to shew us very satisfactorily, the reason of these two omissions in the different editions of the present letter. But it also resolves a point of much more consequence to us. It proves a plain variation in the York and Westminster originals of the letter. As shewn at York, the letter *certainly* had *not* the side-note attached to it, and *probably* had *not* the whole sentence incorporated with it. But, as shewn at Westminster, it had certainly the one, and it probably had the other. Mary thus appeared at one time to have penned the

* See Anderson, ii. title page, and 133.

letter

letter in her own hand *without* the paſſages; and at another to have penned it *with* them. And we thus add one more demonſtration to the many that we have ſeen already, of the obvious and apparent forgery of all the letters, and of the ever-reſtleſs fluctuation of the ſpirit of knavery under it.

VII.—" I inquyrit him of his letteris, quhairintil
" he plenzeit of the crueltie of ſum (1); anſwerit
" that he was aſtoniſchit (2), and that he was ſa
" glaid to ſé me, that he belevit to die for glaid-
" nes (3). He fand greit"

VII.—" Ego eum de ſuis literis rogavi, in quibus
" queſtus erat de quorundam crudelitate (1); re-
" ſpondit, ſe nonnihil (2) eſſe attonitum, meumque
" ei conſpectum tam jucundum, ut putaret ſe
" lætitiâ moriturum (3). Offendebatur"

VII.—" Je l'ay enquis de ſes lettres, ou il s'eſtoit
" plaint de la cruauté d'aucuns (1). Il reſpondit,
" qu'il eſtoit aucunement (2) etonné, et qu'il ſe
" trouvoit ſi joyeux de me voir, qu'il penſoit mou-
" rir de joye (3)."

(1) The letters, as here called, or the letter, as more properly called in the next paragraph, was one which Darnly wrote to Mary from Stirling, a few days after his abrupt departure from her at Holyrood-houſe, on September the 30th 1566. But we have already ſeen, that it is dangerous for forgers to meddle with hiſtory. And this paſſage

furniſhes

furnishes us with another proof of the important truth.

Mary immediately answered that letter of Darnly's very fully *. Yet nearly FOUR MONTHS AFTERWARDS she is made to ask him, what he meant by one point in it. She is even made to ask him, in the *first* moments of her visit to him upon his illness. And she is even made to notice the *intimated cruelty of some* in it, when it intimated no such thing. His grounds of complaint were not general and vague. They were specifick. He complained, that he was not trusted with power or advanced in honour by her, and that he was without any attendance from the nobility †. And Mary, in her answer, reminded him of the honour and power, which she had given to him, and which he had turned against her; recalled to his memory her uniform offers, of making her servants to attend him; and suggested to him the disgust, which he had excited in the nobles, by the statelines of his conduct towards them ‡. There was no complaint therefore concerning the *cruelty* of some, in Darnly. Nor could there be any enquiries concerning it, in Mary.

But indeed all remembrance of such a letter must have been long effaced from the minds of both, by the scenes that had passed before them since. Mary had been ill of a violent fever. The illness continued eleven days. Her life was in the utmost danger for a part of the time. Her council actually issued a proclamation for securing the

* Keith, 349—350.   † Ibid. ibid.   ‡ Ibid. ibid.

peace,

peace, in full apprehenfion of the worft. Mary fully expected that worft. And on the 25th of October fhe lay to all appearance dead *. In all this danger the King, though formally apprized of it, with a grofs unfeelingnefs and a ftupid barbarity of foul, had never come near her. He came not till fhe was out of danger †. And all this muft have formed an object to the minds of both, much more important in itfelf, and much furer to engage their converfation when they met, than the letter before. She particularly was fo affected by it, that fhe was often heard to wifh for that laft fhelter of over-burdened nature, the grave ‡.

The baptifm of the young prince had taken place in the December afterwards, at Stirling. At this very period the King, with a fullen abfurdity of fpirit, thought proper to take up his refidence at Stirling, never to come near the Queen, never to appear in the entertainments, and fo to publifh his own folly and their common unhappinefs to all the world. Mary felt this infult fo fenfibly, that fhe was obliged at times to retire from the gaieties before her, and give vent to the fulnefs of her heart in fecret ‖. And this was furely a fubject, that would have much more demanded the attention of Mary, at her firft conference with the King afterwards; than a flight letter, with flight complaints in it, written about three months before.

But another event had alfo happened in this interval. On December the 27th, the King left

---

* Keith, Hift. 352—353, and App. 133—136.   † Ibid. pp. 135.   ‡ Ibid. Pref. viii.   ‖ Ibid. ibid.

Stirling, and retired to Glasgow, without taking the least notice of the Queen *. He was immediately seized with a dangerous illness. He was racked with violent pains. He was covered with pustules of a black and putrid nature. And his life was in the utmost danger †. This surely, from its recentness, its continuance, and its importance, would have given a topick to the King and Queen at their meeting, infinitely more attractive than a petty letter, written nearly four months before. And all these events together would have so totally superseded the memory of such a letter, that it could not possibly have been the FIRST point of their conversation, that it could hardly have been any at all.

(2) The Latin having, by some wild mistake, inserted " nonnihil" into the text, the French adopts the mistake, and substitutes " aucunement" for the word.

(3) Dr. Robertson acknowledges, that Mary shewed great kindness to Darnly in this visit; tho', with the true spirit of faction, he endeavours to turn all into artifice ‡. Yet *in these letters* she appears not to have shewed any kindness at all. *He* shews much to her, but *she* none to him. And this is such a plain proof of the forgery, that the Doctor should in common candour have pointed to it.

---

* Keith, Pref. vii. and Hist. 364. Anderson, ii. and 242. Jebb, i. † Detection, 16.
‡ i. 396.

" greit

" greit fault that I was penfive (1)."

" eo quód tam cogitabunda effem (1)."

" cependant il eftoit offenfé de ce que j'eftois ainfi
" penfive (1)."

(1) " Fand *greit* fault," " offendebatur," " eftoit
" offenfé;" and " that," " eo quód," " de ce que."
Both fhew the exactnefs of the French in copying
the Latin. And the addition of " cependant" in
the French, fhews the copier there to have been
more attentive to connection than fidelity. But
the whole furnifhes us with another proof of the
forgery. That the Queen fhould be " penfive,"
is abfurd. If fhe took the journey from a *real* regard, her fenfibilities would break from her in a
full tide of affectionate tendernefs. If fhe went
from a *pretended* one, fhe would endeavour to imitate the affectionatenefs that fhe did not feel, would
certainly carry on the hypocrify of tendernefs for a
while, and could not poffibly have been penfive at
the VERY FIRST encounter.

Dr. Robertfon fays thus concerning Mary's vifit
to Glafgow at this period : " Notwithftanding the
" King's danger, fhe amufed herfelf with excurfions
" to different parts of the country, and fuffered near
" a month to elapfe before fhe vifited him at Glaf-
" gow *." But furely the Doctor fhould in *honefty*

* i. 395. This is only the flanderous ribaldry of Buchanan
repeated again, fee 63—64. Anderfon, ii. and 259. Jebb, i.

have shewn that she *knew* of the illness, before he adduced this heavy charge against her. He should certainly in *policy* not have referred to a letter, as he does immediately afterwards, which proves she did *not* know of it. In the very next page he speaks of " a letter written with her own hand to " her ambassadour in France, just before she set out " for Glasgow." And *this* proves decisively, that *she knew nothing of the illness till she actually set out*. It is the letter which I have noticed before, as dated the 20th of January, only *the very day before she set out*. In it she speaks of the King particularly. She mentions " with some bitterness," says Dr. Robertson, " the King's ingratitude, the jealousy with " which he observed her actions, and the inclina-
" tion he discovered to disturb her government; " and at the same time talks of all his attempts " with the utmost scorn." YET SHE SAYS NOTHING OF HIS ILLNESS. Dr. Robertson indeed has much aggravated the manner, in which she mentions the King. These are the words: " For the King our " husband," she says, " God knawis alwayis our " part towartis him ; and his behaviour and thank-
" fulnes to us is semblablement well knawin to God " and the warld. Specialie our awin indifferent " subjectis seis it, and in thair hartis, we doubt not, " condemnis the samyne. Alwayis we persave him " occupeit and bissy aneuch to haif inquisitioun of " our doyngis, quhilkis, God willing, sall ay be sic " as nane sall haif occasioun to be offendit with " thame, or to report of us any wayis bot honora-
" bly, howsoever he, his father, and thair fautoris, " speik ; quhilkis, we knaw, want na gude will to
" mak

" mak us haif ado, gif thair power wer equivalent
" to thair myndis. But God moderatis thair forces
" well aneuch, and takis the moyen of executioun of
" thair pretenfis fra thame; for, as we believe, thay
" fall find nane, or varray few, approveris of thair
" counfalis and devyfis imaginit to our difplefor
" or miflyking *." There is nothing in all thefe
expreffions of Mary's, but a calm confcioufnefs of
her own innocence, and a firm confidence in her
own fecurity through that, againft the enquiries
and contrivances of the King concerning her. YET
SHE SAYS NOTHING OF HIS ILLNESS. Had fhe
known of it then, fhe muft have mentioned it.
Had fhe alfo intended to fet out the very next day
on a vifit to him, fhe muft have mentioned her intention. She would have done it *in order* to fhew
her reconciliation to him, if it had been all *fictitious*. And, if it had been *genuine*, fhe could not
have concealed it. It would have burft from her
in fpite of herfelf. Hence " no tokens of fudden
" reconcilement appear" in the letter. They *could
not*. She knew not of the only fact, that could
produce them in a mind like hers; the dangerous
illnefs of the King, attended with " fymptoms vio-
" lent and unufual," and " commonly imputed to
" the effects of poifon" at the time. She heard
of it *after* fhe had written the letter. She heard of
it from himfelf too, with a meffage expreffing his
grief for the paft, profeffing his reformation for the
future, and requefting her prefence immediately.
And fhe immediately hurried away to fee him.

* Keith, Pref. viii.

" The

" The Queen," say Crawford's Memoirs, " was
" *no sooner informed of his danger*, than she *hasted*
" *after him* *." " Hearing and advertised," says
the Bishop of Ross in an *un-answered* publication
at the time, " that HE WAS REPENTANT AND SOR-
" ROWFUL, and that he DESIRED HER PRESENCE;
" she *without delay*," though it was, as Buchanan
himself has told us, " in the deip of a schairp
" wynter †," " thereby to renew, quicken, and re-
" fresh his sprites, and to comfort his hart, to the
" amendment and repayring of his helth lately by
" sicknes sore impaired, *hasted with such spede as*
" *she conveniently might*," with such weather and at
such a season, " to see and visit him at Glasco ‡;"
probably setting out in the *forenoon* of January 21st,
reaching Linlithgow, sixteen miles off, *that* night,
and getting to Kalendar, about eight miles farther,
the *next* §. So clear, so honourable, and so generous, is the Queen's behaviour in this business! So
strong too is the twist of mind in her historian!
And with such a sideling pace does it carry him,
through all this period of the history!

But let me make another remark upon the present passage in the letter, for the better detection of
the whole. That Darnly was " astonished" at the
visit, and that Mary was " pensive" in the very first
moments of it; is said with the same view as Dr.

* P. 12. † Detection, 17. Anderson, ii. and 242,
Jebb, i. ‡ Defence, 12. Hence also Barnstaple in Jebb, i.
407, calls it " profectio tam longa, tam impedita."

§ Appendix, Nº x. And hence Barnstaple says, " Morbi rumor
" cúm primúm increpuit," then the Queen set out, Jebb, ibid.
A fall of snow probably prevented her from moving faster.

Robertson

Robertson says, that "the sudden transition will appear with a very suspicious air, and will be considered by them [who are acquainted with the human heart] as the effect of artifice." In this assertion, I think, the Doctor shews *himself* to be very little acquainted with the human heart indeed. Or, to speak more properly, and to do justice to the Doctor's understanding, his sagacity became a ready servant to popular prejudice, and an officious slave to the folly of the times. Mary certainly *visited* Darnly in his illness at Glasgow. But *why* did she visit him? From artifice, say the letters, and that writer who, like Buchanan, has incorporated them into history. This, the writer intimates, is plain from her not visiting him till he was "out " of all danger." The fact is not true, and the inference is totally false. This very letter shews him not to be out of all danger. "He has," it says, "almaist slane me with his braith, it is worse " than zour uncle's, and zit I cum na neirer unto " him, bot in ane chyre at the bed-fit, and he " being at the uther end thairof *." "He declairit " unto me," it tells us, " his seiknes, and that he " wald mak na testament, but only leif all thing to " me †." But, not to imitate the Doctor in erecting history upon forgery, I turn to the cotemporary memoirs of Crawford. The Queen, they affirm, " notwithstanding her resentment of the past in" jury," the murder of Rizzio, " was extremely " moved to find him *in so bad a condition*, and " waited very carefully upon him for the space of

* Sect. xx. † Sect. viii.

" ten

" ten days, till, *the strength of his nature overcoming*
" *the venom of his disease*, he was able to abandon
" that place *." And " after this discovery of Ma-
" ry's sentiments," says the Doctor, with a reference to the letter of January 20th, and to her not
visiting him at first, " it was scarce to be expected
" that she would visit the King" at all †. Yet this
very circumstance overthrows his whole argument.
If she had been acting from design, *she would have
gone at first*. The design would have been *best pro-
moted* by *that*. So unhappy is the Doctor in his
reasonings! But he is worse than unhappy. When
the Queen does *not* go to Glasgow, she is reproached
with a " neglect" of the King, with no longer feeling
" conjugal affection" for him, with " not even put-
" ting on the appearance of this passion," and with
" amusing herself notwithstanding the King's dan-
" ger ‡." When she *does* go, then she is equally
condemned, as acting purely from design. " To
" those who are acquainted with the human heart,"
we are *then* told, " this sudden transition will appear
" with a very suspicious air, and will be considered
" by them as the effect of artifice §." Thus is the
former charge even made to confirm the latter.
And a bold and false assumption is made to pervert
a true fact, in the hands of this party-writer.

Indeed every generous spirit must feel a strong
tenderness of pity for the unhappy Queen, assaulted
with all the enginery of fraudulence by her unprin-
cipled brother, and abused with all the perversions

---

* P. 12. The Queen was absent only ten days in all, by the
Journal, N° x. Appendix.   † i. 396.   ‡ i. 395.
§ i. 396.

of sophistry by a modern historian. She could not go to visit the King in his illness, *before* she knew of it. Yet she is traduced for not doing so. She is traduced, as if she *had* known of his illness. Yet all the while the traducer has full evidence that she did *not* know, lying directly before him. But party seals up his eyes. And the sun shines in vain upon wilful blindness. She goes at last, however. She is very kind in her behaviour to the King. All the world speaks of her tenderness. But the writer, who was blind before to the SUN, can now discern the MOTES that are *not* there. He can now penetrate below the semblance of tenderness, and see cruelty and murder lurking under it. Thus does the violence of party, when party is the prevailing tone of the nation, work wildly in bosoms that are otherwise the seats of honour. And thus did Murray, in the stern flagitiousness of his ambitious policy, turn that high act of generosity and love in Mary, into an infernal deed of covered malignity; and so

Pour the sweet milk of Concord into Hell!

But let it also be remembered, in display of THE PROVIDENCE OF GOD OVER MAN, that, if Mary was singularly unhappy in the variety of attacks upon her, she has been peculiarly fortunate in the instruments of her defence. No other person, in such circumstances, can appeal to such justifying documents as she can. We see this strikingly exemplified in the preservation of that very letter, which I have noticed above. Written only the day before she set out to visit the King, it shews, in the most satisfactory manner, that she had not *even then* heard of his illness, and that she did not *even then* intend to visit him. Such a letter, written in such a critical moment, is a very extraordinary monument in itself. It seems to have been peculiarly preserved for the confutation of those slanderous writers, who have been long arising among us. Yet, what shews it not to have been *humanly* preserved for that purpose, it has never been applied to the purpose before. And it is now applied, because a new æra is begun in the nation; when all the records of Mary's innocence are daily coming forward to the eye of the public; when all the petty libellers of her name are shrinking abashed before them; and when her honour will be finally laid open, with a meridian splendour of evidence.

§ IV.

§ IV.

LETTER THE FIRST CONTINUED.

VIII.—" I departit to fupper (1). This beirer
" will tell zow of my arryving (2). He prayit me
" to returne: the quhilk I did (3). He declairit
" unto me his feiknes (4), and that he wald mak
" na teftament, bot only leif all thing to me (5);
" and that I was the caus of his maladie (8), becaus
" of the regrait that he had that I was fa ftrange
" unto him (6). And thus (7)"

VIII.—" Ego difceffi ad cœnam (1). Qui has
" fert tibi de meo adventu narrabit (2). Rogavit
" me ut redirem, quod et feci (3). Suum mihi
" morbum (4) explicavit; feque nullum teftamen-
" tum facturum, nifi id unum, quód omnia mihi
" relinqueret (5); me autem fui morbi [caufam]
" fuiffe (8), quód molefté tuliffet me tam alieno
" erga fe animo fuiffe (6). Ac poftea (7)"

VIII.—" Je m'en allay foupper (1). Celuy qui
" vous porte ces lettres vous fera entendre de ma
" venüe (2). Il me pria de retourner, ce que je
" fay (3). Il me declara fon mal (4), adjouftant,
" qu'il ne vouloit point faire de teftament, fi non
" ceftuy feule, c'eft qu'il me laifferoit tout (5);
" et que j'avoye efté la caufe de fa maladie (8),
" pour l'ennuy qu'il avoit porté que j'euffe l'affec-
" tion tant efloignée de luy (6). Et puis apres (7)"

(1) This

(1) This shews the paragraph preceding to relate the interview *immediately on her arrival,* and the paragraph before that to tell the King's *antecedent enquiries from her forerunner.*

(2) This sentence has been misplaced. It should be at the head of the paragraph preceding. There it is wanted. And here it is impertinent. " This " beirer," Scotch; " qui has fert tibi," Latin; " celuy qui vous porte ces lettres," French.

(3) All the conversation that follows, therefore, is what is represented to have passed in the evening of the Queen's arrival at Glasgow, January 23d, and *after supper.*

(4) What was the King's sickness? Crawford's Memoirs assert, that it " was generally reported " the effect of POYSON *." Melvill says, that " he " went to Glasgow, where he fell sick; *it being al-* " *ledged, that he had got* POISON *from some of his ser-* " *vants* †." Buchanan and Knox assert positively, that he was POISONED. Some of Mary's friends, both antient and modern, Blackwood, Causin, and Carte, affirm his disorder to have been THE SMALL POX. These letters assert it to have been the GREAT POX. Mr. Goodall and Dr. Robertson cannot decide with certainty, concerning its nature and its cause. Only the latter intimates, that it was commonly imputed to poison at the time. And Dr. Stuart gives this strong reason for suspecting, that the King was actually poisoned. " From what is " observed by Melvill," he says, " from the cir- " cumstance of the subsequent murder of the King,

* P. 12.   † P. 77.

" and

" and from the characters of Murray and Bothwell,
" Morton and Lethington, there is a high probabi-
" lity that they had corrupted some of his domes-
" tics to take this method of destroying him *."
The practice of poisoning, indeed, seems to have
been as dreadfully common at this period in Scotland, as we know it to have once been since in
France. The King was alledged at the time, we
see, to have been poisoned. Bothwell's family is
said by Buchanan to have been "in France de-
" famit of poysoning;" and his servants are said
to have been, " for the same caus, sum tortu-
" rit, sum imprisonit, and all suspectit †." But
we know from an authority equal to Buchanan's,
though anonymous, even from a letter of April
the 3d, 1566, to Cecil; that one of Bothwell's
servants confessed himself, and four of his fel-
low-servants, to have agreed upon assassinating
or *poisoning* Bothwell, at the instigation of Lethington; and that the other servants, upon exa-

* See Goodall, i. 324. Robertson, i. 394. and Stuart, i. 187. The Doctors Stuart and Robertson refer to Keith, 364, for Bishop Lesley asserting the disorder to be the Great Pox. But why do they refer to *Keith* for this? Why do they not refer to the Bishop himself? Even for this short reason, that they did not know where the Bishop had said so, and yet supposed Keith to have known. The fact is, I believe, that Keith has made a mistake concerning the Bishop, and that the latter no where asserts what the former quotes him for.

† Detection, 51. Anderson, ii. and 255. Jebb, i. The mother of Murray is said in Jebb i. 405, to have been an adept
in poisoning, *a Countess of Soisons* in her day. And Elizabeth
is intimated in Moyse 128, to have put forth her hand in ex-
periments of poisoning upon King James.

mination,

mination, confessed the same*. Morton also was strongly suspected of poisoning the Earl of Mar first, and the Earl of Athol afterwards; and was more than suspected of poisoning Lethington †. And, to mount up to the first and leader of this profligate triumvirate MURRAY, the Queen was apprehensive herself of being poisoned by some Protestants about her; Ruthven actually gave her a ring, as a pretended security from their poison; Murray actually considered the security as intended against *himself*; and actually urged Mary to punish Ruthven, for furnishing it ‡. The King therefore was assuredly poisoned. Crawford's and Melvill's united allegations prove decisively the general opinion at the time to have been, that he was. The actual murder of the King so speedily afterwards, confirms that opinion, and corroborates those allegations, very strongly. And the practice of poisoning, so familiar to the wretches concerned in the murder, lends a great addition of weight to all, and carries all into a moral certainty.

That he was poisoned then, was the *first* opinion. This appears from Crawford and Melvill. That he had either the Small or the Great Pox, was only a subsequent surmise. Yet, what is very surprizing, both the surmise and the opinion make their appearance together in this letter. Thus Darnly is called " this pokische" or pocky " man ;" *not* having the small pox, as Dr. Robertson interprets the word §, as Blackwood intimated at the time, as

* Keith, App. 167.   † Leslæi Vita, 10, in Anderson, f. Melvill, 118. Jebb, ii. 268. Crawford, 347—348. and Moyse, 32, and 35.   ‡ Keith, App. 125.   § Hist. i. 394.

Causin

Caufin intimated afterwards, and as Buchanan's Latin intimates here, in direct contradiction to his own Detection*, by its version of the main word into " variolato;" *but* infected with *the* pox, that greater one, to which the word *pocky* has always been emphatically referred. And accordingly the Queen refuses to sleep with him, because " he be-" hovit to be purgeit" firſt †. Yet another paſſage hints, that he was poiſoned. " He is not over " mekle deformit," it ſays, " zit he hes RESSAVIT " verray mekle: he has almaiſt ſlane me with his " braith; it is worſe than zour uncle's; and zit I " cum na neirer unto him, bot in ane chyre at the " bed-feit, and he being at the uther end thairof ‡." That theſe words were meant to intimate he was poiſoned, we know from Buchanan himſelf §. So contradictory is Buchanan, to poiſon the King in one part of this letter, and to give him the ſmall pox in another. So contradictory too is this very letter, as, in the compaſs of a few lines only, to pronounce the King a pocky man, and yet to inſinuate that he was poiſoned! All this ariſes from the contrary opinions entertained generally at the time. It was firſt believed, that he was poiſoned. It was afterwards ſurmiſed, that he was poxed. The former, no doubt, was the report of the phyſicians, the ſervants, and the Queen. The latter was the counter-report circulated by the poiſoners, I ſuppoſe, to ſhield themſelves from detection; and afterwards varied by a miſtake in Buchanan, Blackwood, and Cauſin, into a report of the ſmall pox. And two of

* P. 16.   † Sect. xii.   ‡ Sect. xx.   § Detection, 50—51. Anderſon. ii. and Jebb. ii. 254—255.

theſe

these reports very astonishingly meet together in the Scotch of this letter, and even all three in the Latin of it. This therefore proves the forgery very evidently. Different people at different times might think differently, concerning the disorder. But one person could not at one time. The Queen, particularly, could not intimate that the King was poxed, and yet in the same breath insinuate that he was poisoned. And she could still less declare his disorder to be poison, to be the great pox, and to be the small pox, all in one instant.

(5) " Mak na testament, but only leif all thing " to me," Scotch; " nullum testamentum facturum, " nisi ad unum, quód omnia mihi relinqueret," Latin; " ne vouloit point faire de testament, sinon " cestuy seule, c'est qu'il me laisseroit tout," French. The exact conformity of the French to the Latin is remarkable.

(6) This is another proof of the forgery. The King's disorder is ascribed to the pox, to poison, and to regret. The last, to be sure, is a most dangerous cause of sickness, especially in minds so finely and elegantly organized, as Darnly's was. It worked very violently in him. Regret racked him with dreadful pains in his body. Regret threw out the black and putrid pustules all over him. And regret gave a baleful taint to his breath. It was both the poison and the pox to him.——" That " I was sa strange unto him," Scotch; " me tam " alieno erga se animo fuisse," Latin; " que j'eusse " l'affection tant esloignée de luy," French.

(7) " Thus,"

(7) Thus," Scotch; "postea," Latin; "puis
" apres," French.

(8) *Causam* is by some neglect of the press omitted in Goodall's edition. It is in Jebb's*. And it is also in the French.

" he said, Ze ask me (1) quhat I mene be the cruel-
" tie contenit (2) in my letter? It is of zow alone,
" that will not accept my offeris and repentance (3)."

" inquit, me rogas (1) quid sibi velit illa crudelitas
" cujus mentio est (2) in meis literis? Ad te unam
" id spectat, quæ meas pollicitationes ac poeniten-
" tiam recipere non vis (3)."

" vous de demandez (1), dit-il, que veut dire ceste
" cruauté dont je fay mention (2) en mes lettres?
" Cela s'addresse seulement a vous, qui ne voulez
" recevoir mes promesses ny ma repentance (3)."

(1) How strangely does this come in here! The question was asked before supper. He then "an-
" swerit," that—he was astonished and glad to see her. But after supper, without any fresh question, he answers to the point at once. Just so it is with " words froze in northern air." The question is put in autumn, and the answer is spoken in the spring following.

(2) " Quhat I mene be the crueltie contenit,"
Scotch; "quid sibi velit illa crudelitas cujus mentio

* i. 271.

" eſt," Latin; "que veut dire ceſte cruauté dont
" je ſay mention," French.

(3) The King is made to account for the cruelty falſely averred to be intimated in his letter to the Queen, and to ſay that he meant the Queen's cruelty to him, in not accepting his offers and repentance. Here the forger becomes more entangled in his own perverſions of the hiſtory. There were no offers made, there was no repentance averred, in the letter. Let his own hiſtorian tell us the contents of it. " He wrote to Mary," ſays Dr. Robertſon *, " and mentioned two things as grounds of diſguſt. " She herſelf, he ſaid, no longer admitted him into " any confidence, and had deprived him of all " power; and the nobles, after her example, treated " him with open neglect, ſo that he appeared in " every place without the dignity and ſplendor of " a king." Where is the repentance, and where are the offers, in all this? But let us go to that which is Dr. Robertſon's authority for his account of the letter, an addreſs of the Privy Council of Scotland to the Queen Dowager of France. " In the letter " he wrote the Queen," they ſay, " he grounds a " complaint on two points; one is, that her Ma- " jeſty truſts him not with ſo much authority, nor " is at ſuch pains to advance him, and make him " to be honoured in the nation, as ſhe at firſt did. " And the other point is, that nobody attends him, " and that the nobility deſert his company. To " theſe two points the Queen has made anſwer †." Where then, let me repeat, is the repentance of

---

* i. 376.   † Keith, 350.

Darnly in this letter, and where are his offers? No where. Yet the forger has the impudence to insert both. And Dr. Robertson has the modesty, even when he gives an account directly contrary to the forger's, not to hint at the slightest fraud in him.

" I confes that I have failit, bot not into that quhilk
" I ever denyit (1); and sicklyke hes failit tò (2)
" sindrie of zour subjectis, quhilk ze have forge-
" vin (3).

IX.—" I am zoung.

X.—" Ze will say, that ze have forgevin me
" oft tymes, and zit yat I."

" Fateor a me peccatum esse, sed non in eo quod
" semper negavi (1); peccavi etiam adversus (2)
" quosdam civium tuorum, quod mihi abs te con-
" donatum-est (3).

IX.—" Ego sum adolescens.

X.—" Ac tu dicis, quód post veniam sæpe abs
" te datam, adhuc"

" Je confesse, que j'ay grandement offensé, mais
" non en ce que j'ay tousjours desnié (1); j'aussi
" peché a l'encontre (2) d'aucuns de vos citoyens,
" ce que vous m'avez pardonné (3).

IX.—" Je suis jeune.

F 2   X.—" Vous

X.—" Vous dites cependant, qu'apres m'avoir
" souvent pardonné (3),"

(1) This alludes to the King's share in the assassination of Rizzio. That share he publickly and
formally denied. And to make him deny it now
to Mary, is only giving him a proper consistency of
character. But Mary never believed him. This
appears from the abstract of her answer to his letter,
as given us by the Privy Council. " To these two
" points," they say, " the Quene has made answer,
" that if the case be so, he ought to blame himself,
" not her; for that,—altho' they who did per-
" petrate the murder of her faithful servant, had en-
" tered her chamber with his knowledge, having
" followed him close at the back, and had named
" him the chief of their enterprize; yet would she
" never accuse him thereof, but did always excuse
" him, and was willing to appear as if she believed
" it not *." And, after such an answer as this to
his letter, even Darnly himself could not have had
the folly to deny it to the Queen again.—" Grande-
" ment" is *added* in the French.

(2) The Latin has here made a strange mistake,
and drawn in the French after it. " Sicklyke," in
such a manner, " hes failit tò," have also failed in
their duty, " sindrie of zour subjectis," meaning
Murray, Lethington, &c. But the Latin, with a
wildness that I hardly know how, upon any principles of construction, to account for, has rendered the
clause thus, " peccavi etiam adversus quosdam civium

* Keith, 350.

" tuorum;"

" tuorum;" and the French comes fhambling behind it in the fame aukward pace, " j'auffi peché " a l'encontre d'aucuns de vos citoyens." And yet, grofs as this corruption of the meaning is, it was firft obferved by Mr. Goodall, and produced as one of his proofs againft the originality of the French*.

(3) " Zour fubjectis," by the republican pen of Buchanan, is abfurdly rendered " cives" in Latin, and is therefore changed into "citoyens" in French. " Quhilk ze have forgevin," meaning which fubjects, in confequence of the blunder above is thus tranflated, " quod mihi abs te condonatum eft," and " ce que vous m'avez pardonné."

" returne to my faultis (1). May not ane man of
" my age, for lacke of counfell (2), fall twyfe or
" thryfe, or inlacke of his promeis, and at laft (3)
" repent himfelf, and be chaftifit be experience (4)?
" Gif I may obtene pardoun, I proteft I fall never
" mak fault agane (5). And I craif na uther thing,
" bot yat we may be at bed and buird togidder, as
" hufband and wyfe (6); and gif ze will not con-
" fent heirunto, I fall never ryfe out of zis bed. I
" pray zow, tell me zour refolutioun. God knawis
" how I am punifchit for making my"

" ad peccata redeo (1). Nonne homo, quâ ego
" fum ætate, confilio deftitutus (2), bis aut ter labi
" poteft, aut pollicitis non ftare, ac deinde (3) fui

* See i. 91—93.

" errati

" errati pœnitere, et rerum ufu (4) corrigi? Quód
" fi veniam impetrare potero, polliceor me nun-
" quam pofthac peccaturum (5). Nihil autem
" aliud peto, nifi ut communi mensâ et lecto, tan-
" quam conjuges, utamur (6): ad hæc nifi tu confen-
" tias, nunquam ex hôc lecto refurgam. Te rogo,
" ut mihi indices quid decreveris. Novit autem
" Deus quid pœnarum feram, quód Deum"

" je returne en femblables fautes (1). Une homme
" de mefme age que je fuis, et deftitué de confeil
" (2), ne peut il pas faillir deux ou trois fois, ou ne
" tenir pas quelque-fois promeffe, et apres (3) fe
" repentir de fa faute, en fe corrigeant par l'ufage
" des occurrences (4)? Que fi je puis obtenir par-
" don, je promets cy apres de ne plus offenfer (5).
" Je ne vous demande rien d'avantage, finon que
" nous ne faifions qu'une table et un lict, comme
" ceux qui font mariez (6): a cela fi vouz ne con-
" fentez, je ne releveray jamais de ce lict. Je vous
" prie, de me faire entendre ce que vous avez deli-
" beré: car Dieu fcayt quelle peine je porte, de
" ce que j'ay"

(1) " Ze have forgevin me oft tymes, and zit
" yat I returne to my faultis," Scotch; " poft ve-
" niam abs te datam, adhuc ad peccata redeo,"
Latin; and " apres m'avoir fouvent pardonné, je
" returne en femblables fautes." The Latin departing from the Scotch in the turn of the expreffion, the French departs too.

(2) " Ane man of my age, for lacke of counfell,"
Scotch; " homo quâ ego fum ætate, confilio defti-
" tutus,"

" tutus," Latin ; and " une homme de mefme age " que je fuis, et deftitué de confeil," French.

(3) " At laft," Scotch ; " deinde," Latin ; " apres," French.

(4) " Experience," Scotch ; " rerum ufu," Latin ; " l'ufage des occurrences," French.

(5) " Gif," Scotch ; " quòdfi," Latin ; " que fi," French.

(6) All this fpeech of Darnly's is in direct violation of hiftorical truth. He was *not* the man which he is here reprefented to be. He was *very different.* His great aim was not the happinefs of conjugal affection. " So far as things could come to our " knowledge," fay the Privy Council of Scotland, " he has had no ground of complaint ; but, on the " contrary, that he has the very beft of reafon to " look upon himfelf as one of the moft fortunate " princes in Chriftendom, could he but know his " own happinefs, and make ufe of the good for- " tune which God has put into his hands *." But without one atom of ability for bufinefs, and without one particle of difcretion in dignity, he was childifhly eager for authority. He was a mere eunuch in ambition. " Multum cupiit, nihil potuit:" And, to obtain this authority, he entered into the bufinefs of murdering Rizzio in the very prefence of the Queen, then feveral months gone with child. This was fuch an act of brutal favagenefs, as fhews him to have been a monfter in feeling and in folly.

* Keith, 350.

And a speech like this put into his mouth, therefore, is a violent breach of the unity of character, and a full evidence of the general forgery.—" At " bed and buird togidder as husband and wyfe," Scotch; " communi mensâ et lecto, tanquam con- " juges, utamur," Latin; and " nous ne faisions " qu'une table et un lict, comme ceux qui sont " mariez," French.

" God of zow, and for having na uther thocht but " on zow (1); and gif (2) at any time I offend " zow, ze ar the caus, becaus, quhen ony offendis " me, gif, for my refuge (3), I micht playne unto " zow, I wald speik it unto na uther body (4): bot " quhen I heir ony thing, not being familiar with " zow, necessitie constrains me to keip it in my " breist (5); and yat causes me to tyne my wit for " verray anger (6)."

" mihi te fecerim, ac nihil aliud nisi te cogitem " (1): quòd si (2), quando te offendam, tu ipsa " in causâ es, nam, cúm aliquis me offendit, si id " perfugium haberem (3), ut apud te queri possem, " ad neminem alium querelam deferrem (4); sed " si quid audio, nec te familiariter utor, cogor " id in pectore clausum tenere (5); quæ res ita me " angit, ut mentem et consilium mihi prorsus ex- " cutiat (6)."

" fait de vous un Dieu, et que je ne pense a autre " chose qu'a vous (1); que si (2) je vous offense
" quelque-

" quelquefois, vous en eftes caufe, veu que, quand
" on m'offenfe, fi j'avoye ce refuge (3), que je me
" peuffe plaindre vers vous, je ne feroie ma com-
" plaint a autre (4) ; mais fi j'entend quelque
" chofe, et que je n'aye familiarité avec vous, je
" fuis contraint de la retenir clofe en mon cœur
" (5); ce qui tourmente tellement, qu'il m'ofte du
" tout l'entendement et le confeil (6)."

(1) This idolatry of Darnly's is fomething like what the Heathens practifed at times. They whipt and fcourged their idols occafionally, if they did not indulge them in their wifhes. And, to fpeak ferioufly, we may here fee the impudent forgery of the letter in its proper view, if we only turn to two or three circumftances in Darnly's conduct. He entered into a *formal* and *exprefs* agreement with the ruffians who committed the murder upon Rizzio, of doing it even " in prefence of the " Queen's Majefty," and of fupporting them after- wards for it. He even *folicited* them to do it. He even intended to have done it *with his own hand*, if they had not undertaken it for him *. At laft he not only united with them to do it, but actually *infifted* upon their doing it *in her very pre- fence*, and *at her very table*; the devoted victim flying behind her for refuge, laying hold even of her garments for protection, and even throwing his arms round her waift for fecurity; even there being ftabbed by one of the villains *over her fhoulders*, with fo much fury too, that he was obliged to leave

* Goodall, i. 268 and 264.

the dagger in his body; being then forced from his hold, while *cocked pistols were presented to herself;* being dragged away bleeding and screaming into an adjoining chamber, and being instantly dispatched there with a variety of wounds*. And, when

---

* The person who presented the pistol to her, is said by Barnstaple in his Maria Stuarta (Jebb, i. 396) to have been "Andreas Carreus." But Bedford and Randolph, in a letter at the time, mention "Andrewe Car of Fawdenside," as the person "whom the Queen sayth *would have stroken her with a dagger.*" And they say it was "one Patrick Balentine,—who, also her "Grace sayth, *offered a dag against her belly with the cock down*" (Robertson, ii. 357). These two peculiar monsters of enormity ought to be dragged forth into particular view, and their names branded with a particular mark of infamy, for their conduct upon this occasion. The honour of humanity demands it at our hands.

Let me also remark, that Mr. Goodall, i. 247—272, has thrown a new light upon the motives and plan of this horrid transaction, but has confounded history and himself concerning one circumstance leading to it. "David," says Buchanan, Hist. xvii. 345. "interea singulos circumibat, animosque per- "tentabat, quid de absentibus decreturus quisque esset, si a re- "liquo conventu Πρoξυλoς legeretur." This he understands to mean, That David asked each what each would vote for concerning the exiled lords, if each was chosen a lord of the articles. But it clearly means, as it had always been interpreted to mean (Spotswood, 194). That he asked the lords singly how they would vote, if he, David Rizzio, should be chosen speaker by the parliament. Πρoξυλoς can never signify a lord of the articles. Buchanan's appellation for those lords in general, the only time (I believe) that he mentions them, is "Apolecti" (Hist. ix. 167). Nor can Πρoξυλoς signify any officer of state, except the speaker or president of an assembly. The same interpretation is also given, as Mr. Goodall himself acknowledges, in Knox's history of the times; who equally with Buchanan

when the provost and citizens of Edinborough came down to the rescue of their Queen, so outrageously insulted by this body of banditti under the conduct of her husband; these brutal wretches, with an addition of savageness, declared to her face, that, if she offered to speak to the people, "they "should cut her in collops, and cast her over the "walls ;" and their brutal captain, concurring in all their utmost savageness with them, called to the crowds, and commanded them to retire *. This is perhaps, when contemplated in all its varieties of horror, the time, the place, the woman, and the Queen; such a woman, and such a Queen; the pregnancy, the far-advanced pregnancy; the persons who were the actors, the man who was the leader, the deed, the mode, and the language; beyond any thing that occurs, among all the wildest eruptions of brutality and barbarism, in the human history. Yet the forger of this letter had the stupid effrontery, to make Mary the god

Buchanan hints at the design of giving the Chancellorship to David (i. 272). And it occurs also in Crawford's Memoirs. "David," says the author, "—was likely to be chosen Chan- "cellor (Speaker or President) in Morton's stead," p. 7. The fact indeed is obviously false, for the two grand reasons assigned by Mr. Goodall (i. 271), that David was not naturalized, and therefore could not be Chancellor to the kingdom; and that David did not understand Scotch, and therefore could not be Speaker to the parliament. But the faction circulated the lie. And all the factious, the Buchanans, the Knoxes, and the rabble-rout of sedition, with even some of the honest and the judicious, particularly the worthy and respectable author of the Memoirs, swallowed the lie without consideration.

* Keith, 331—332. App. 123. Melvill, 64. and Crawford, 10.

of Darnly's idolatry, and to affert he had no other thought but on her; at a time too, when this execrable fact, with all its train of horrible particulars, was yet fresh and lively in the minds of the whole nation. He wanted to raise the character of the King, and to sink that of the Queen. He was therefore compelled to change the whole tenour of history, to cast the two characters anew, and to give each the other's part in this play of his. And he thus betrayed the forgery directly to every mind.

But what says Dr. Robertson to this act of the King's? He says, as all mankind have ever said, and as common sense and common decency must for ever say. " Every circumstance here," he tells us, " fills us with horror.—The place, chosen for " committing such a deed, was the Queen's bed-" chamber," a closet within it. " Though Mary " was now in the sixth month of her pregnancy," near the end of her seventh *, " and though Riz-" zio might have been seized elsewhere without " any difficulty, THE KING PITCHED UPON THIS " PLACE, that he might enjoy the malicious plea-" sure of reproaching Rizzio with his crimes be-" fore the Queen's face †." And he afterwards says in general of the King, that " by his folly and " ingratitude he lost the heart of a woman, who " doated on him to distraction ‡." If however Dr. Robertson says true, the letters are the most impudent of liars. Or, if the letters are true, the Doctor must exchange situations with them. Two

* Keith, 331.   † i. 358.   ‡ i. 400.

such

such intelligences cannot preside in one orb of history. Either the one or the other must be dislodged from it. The Doctor is undoubtedly true; and yet, strange to tell! *according to the Doctor himself*, the letters are *not* false. The Doctor himself still considers them as true. He formally vindicates their authenticity. He gravely interweaves them with the thread of his history. And he founds his accumulated slanders of Mary, in a peculiar manner, upon them. But how is this? *Can light and darkness blend in the same sphere? Can the letters be at once convicted of gross and deliberate falshoods in facts, and still be authentic in themselves?* They certainly cannot. The Doctor himself is compelled to go against them. And still the Doctor asserts them to be genuine.

YET BRUTUS IS AN HONOURABLE MAN!

(2) In the clause preceding, "autem" is added n Latin, and "car" in French. In the present, " and gif," Scotch, is answered by "quòd si," Latin; and "que si," French.

(3) "For my refuge," Scotch; "si id perfu-
' gium *haberem*," Latin; and "si j'*avoye* ce re-
' fuge," French.

(4) "I wald speik it to na uther body," Scotch;
ad neminem alium *querelam deferrem*," Latin;
nd " je ne *feroie* ma *complaint* a autre," French.

(5) "Keip it in my breist," Scotch; "in pectore *clausum* tenere," Latin; and " la retenir *close* en mon cœur," French.

(6) " Causes

(6) "Caufes me to tyne my wit," Scotch, to lofe my underftanding *; "*mentem et confilium mihi prorfus excutiat*," Latin; "il m'ôte du *tout l'entendement et le confeil*," French. And "yat caufes me," Scotch; "*quæ res ita me angit, ut*," Latin; and "ce qui *tourmente* tellement, qu'il," French. All thefe paffages concur to prove beyond a poffibility of doubt, that the French was not the original, that the Latin was the original to it, and that the Scotch was no tranflation from either. Indeed the fact is fo ftrikingly apparent in thefe and a thoufand other paffages, that a reflecting mind is amazed at firft, to think the difcovery was left to Mr. Goodall.

XI.—" I anfwerit ay unto him, bot that wald be
" ovir lang to wryte at lenth (1). I afkit quhy he
" wald pas away in ye Inglis fchip (2). He de-
" nyis it, and fweris thairunto (3); bot he grantis
" that he fpake with the men (4)."

XI.—" Ego femper ei refpondebam, fed nimis
" longum effet omnia perfcribere (1). Rogavi eum
" cur difceffum adornaret in iftâ nave Anglicâ (2).
" Ille id pernegat, adjecto etiam juramento (3);
" fed confeffus eft fe cum Anglis (4) colloquu-
" tum."

XI.—" Je lui refpondoye toujours, mais il fe-
" roit long de tout efcrire (1). Je luy ay demandé

* Sonnet 1xth.

" pourquoy

" pourquoy ils deliberoit s'en aller en ce navoire
" Anglois (2). Ce qu'il nia, voire avec jure-
" ment (3); mais il a confeffé avoir parlé avec
" les Anglois (4)."

(1) This is another proof of forgery. That the Queen fhould repeat all the King's defences of himfelf, and fhould not repeat her replies to them; is contrary to every principle of the human heart. Our natural fondnefs for ourfelves, puts us conftantly upon a conduct the very reverfe of all this. We fhorten the defences, we lengthen the replies. Or, if we are fair enough to give the full fubftance of the former, we are always partial enough to do fo by the latter. And we fee this very Queen acting accordingly in this very letter; relating the meffage of apology fent her by Darnly's father, reciting the addition made to it by the bearer, but rehearfing all the fubftantial part of her reply to the former, and finally declaring that fhe filenced the latter. Yet the forger was obliged to take this unnatural courfe, as no other would carry him to his aim. To make the Queen reply to thefe pretended allegations of Darnly's, muft have been to refute them at once. And he might as well have refuted them, in the opinion of every man of judgment; as he has betrayed the forgery which he wanted to profecute, by not doing it. But he thought, no doubt, as Partridge the almanackmaker is faid to have fpoken, and as knaves of all times naturally think, that the men of judgment are to the fools of the world only as one to a hundred,

dred, and that, if he could gain thefe, he cared little about thofe. The event indeed feems to have juftified his choice awhile. The almanack-predictions of Partridge retained their credit for years. The letters of Murray have not yet loft theirs. But the men of judgment will turn the tide of opinions, at laft. Partridge has been long confidered as an impoftor. And Murray is daily haftening to join him in that ftate of obfcurity, where the letters and the almanacks will repofe upon one fhelf, once the favourites of many, and now the contempt of all.

(2) Here a frefh evidence of the forgery prefents itfelf before us. At this time, January 23d, 1567, all defign of paffing away in an Englifh or any other fhip, had been long laid afide. It was taken up at leaft four or five months before, about September 26th *. Darnly mentioned it to Le Croc, the French embaffadour. " He told me,"— fays the embaffadour in a letter of October 15th, " that he had a mind to go beyond fea, in a fort of " defperation. I faid to him what I thought proper " at the time, but ftill I could not believe that he " was in earneft." But as Lenox informed the Queen in a letter which fhe received on Michael-

---

* It was after the Queen's departure from Stirling (Keith, 345); and fhe departed about September the 25th. " She " departed ten or twelve days ago," fays a letter of October the 8th (Keith, 348). Lenox alfo came to Stirling " while the " Queen was abfent," ftaid there " two or three days," went back to Glafgow, wrote a letter to the Queen, and fhe received it " on St. Michael's day" (Keith, 348). She departed and he came, therefore, on the 25th.

mas

mas-day, it had been taken up even long before this time. " FORMERLY," he says, " both by *let-ters* and *messages*, and *now* also by communication with his son, he had endeavoured to divert him" from it *. Le Croc afterwards says, in a postscript to his own letter, " now I believe he will not go out of the kingdom, though I perceive that he still entertains some displeasure †." Accordingly, Sir Robert Melvill says in a letter of Oct. 22d from London, " sens my depairture I heir *he is stayit*, bot hes not sens come neir the Quene ‡." And that Le Croc was right in his belief, and Melvill in his intelligence, time shewed. The ship, which Darnly had in readiness, was dismissed; and he still continued in Scotland. But this perversion of the history was made, for the purpose of new-decorating the character of Darnly. And that infamous pimp to the lust of power in Murray, Buchanan, was not afraid to venture upon the same perversion, even in history itself. "Ibi," at Holyrood-house, " cúm rescitum esset," he says in full opposition to his own Detection §, " Regem *convalescere*, ac vim veneni ætatis vigore et corporis firmitate naturali superatam," a fact that happened, as appears from the rebel journal itself ‖, in the end of January 1567; " novum de eo tollendo consilium initur: aliquot etiam e nobilitate in conscientiam sceleris asciti: *cúm interea ad reginam delatum esset*, Regem de fugâ in Galliam aut Hispaniam cogitare, eâque de re

---

* Keith, 348. † Ibid. 345—347. ‡ Ibid. 351.
§ P. 17. ‖ App. Nº x.

" cum

" cum Anglis, qui navem in æstuario Glottæ stan-
" tem habebant, collocutum *." Here the remarkable coincidence of the letter and the history, in an impudent distortion of the facts, shews the history to have been modelled upon the letter. Buchanan condescended to adopt the falshoods of another, though he was himself an Original Genius in lying. He felt his mind impregnated with a peculiar portion of that spirit of falshood, which is so largely possessed by the great " Father of Lies," and which he so liberally communicates to some of his chosen children. And he exerted this spirit in his history, as in all probability his equal and rival in falshoods had previously exerted it in the letters, not merely for the petty purpose of accommodating either to the other, but with the grand view which he uniformly pursued in both †; that of abusing Mary, his patroness and benefactress, of branding her forehead with the hottest iron of infamy which his understanding could provide, and of breaking down all the fences and guards of truth, in the eagerness of his knavery against her.

But Mary herself has told us a circumstance concerning him, that serves sufficiently to account for his flagitious conduct. " Buchanan," she said, " is
" KNOWN TO BE A LEWD MAN and ATHEIST ‡." He was one of those wretched men therefore, who suffer their passions to beguile their understandings, who plunge into scepticism to escape from sensibility, who destroy the tone of their minds while they are blunting the force of their feelings, and at last

---

* Hist. xviii. 350.   † App. N° xii.   ‡ Goodall, i. 311

become

become devoid equally of principle and of shame, ready for any fabrication of falshood, and capable of any operation in villainy *.

(3) This is perhaps a more impudent stroke of forgery, than any which we have hitherto met with. That the King's design of going abroad, which was first taken up in July or August at least, and even owned in September, should be referred by the history and the letter to the January succeeding, is certainly a very bold measure in impudence. But it is a greater, surely, to make Darnly *deny* that he had ever such a design, to make him *swear* to the denial, and to make Mary *not* reply either to the affirmation or to the oath. The King, as I have already shewn, imparted his design to his father in August or July before. " Formerly, both by let-

* Buchanan does not appear to have used much art, in working up the falshoods, even of his Detection. He particularly seems to have often taken the very ready method of a fool's falsifications, by giving the acts of his patrons to Mary, and Mary's to his patrons. This is strikingly apparent in the story of the proposed divorce at Cragmillar (Anderson, ii. 13—14. and Jebb, i. 241); where the overture, which was actually made by Murray and Lethington (Goodall, ii. 316—321), is attributed to Mary; and the very objection, which Mary herself made to it, is ascribed by this inverter of history to one of them. See also Anderson, i. 14. Defence of Mary. But in 1720, it seems, another Buchanan appeared at London, with another set of Mary's letters. These were eleven in number, all written to Bothwell, and found in his secretary's closet since his death (Keith, 367). Yet, as there was no Elizabeth to lend her bold sanction to these forgeries, they sunk at once under their own weight of imposition, " and dropp'd dead-born from " the press."

" ters

"ters and meſſages, and now alſo by commu-
"nication with his ſon, he had endeavoured to
"divert him" from it. The King alſo mentioned it to the French embaſſadour, as I have
equally ſhewn, about the 26th of September,
at Stirling. "He told me there, that he had
"a mind to go beyond ſea, in a ſort of deſ-
"peration." YET HE IS HERE MADE TO DENY
IT. "Since that time," adds Le Croc, "the
"Earl of Lenox, his father, came to viſit him;
"and he has written a letter to the Queen, ſigni-
"fying, that it is not in his power to *divert his ſon*
"*from his intended voyage*, and prays her Majeſty
"to uſe her intereſt therein." YET DARNLY IS
STILL MADE TO DENY THE DESIGN. "This let-
"ter from the Earl of Lenox," ſays Le Croc, "the
"Queen received on *Michaelmas-day* in the morn-
"ing; and that ſame evening the King arrived
"here about ten of the clock. When he and the
"Queen were a-bed together, her Majeſty took
"occaſion to talk to him about the contents of his
"father's letter, and beſought him to declare to
"her the ground of *his deſigned voyage*; but in
"this he would by no means ſatisfy her." YET
DARNLY IS STILL MADE TO DENY THE DESIGN.
"Early next morning," Le Croc goes on, "the
"Queen ſent for me, and for all the Lords and
"other counſellors: as we were all met in their
"Majeſties preſence, the Biſhop of Roſs, by the
"Queen's commandment, declared to the council
"the King's intention to go beyond ſea, *for which
"purpoſe he had a ſhip lying ready to ſail*; and that
"her

" her Majesty's information hereof proceeded not
" from the rumour of the town, but from a letter
" written to her by his own father, the Earl of
" Lenox: *which letter was likewise read in council.*"
YET THE DARNLY OF THE LETTERS SWEARS HE
HAD NO SUCH PURPOSE. " And thereafter the
" Queen prayed the King to declare, in presence
" of the lords, and before me, the reason of *his pro-*
" *jected departure*; since he would not be pleased
" to notify the same to her in private betwixt
" themselves. She likewise took him by the hand,
" and besought him for God's sake to declare if
" she had given him any occasion for *this resolution*;
" and entreated he might deal plainly, and not
" spare her. Moreover all the lords likewise said
" to him, that if there was any fault on their part,
" upon his declaring it, they were ready to reform
" it. And I likewise took the freedom to tell him,
" that *his departure* must certainly affect either his
" own or the Queen's honour; that if the Queen
" had afforded any ground for it, his declaring the
" same would affect her Majesty; as on the other
" hand, if he should *go away* without giving any
" cause for it, this thing could not at all redound
" to his praise."—Yet forgery, with all " the rash
" dexterity of wit," represents the King as SWEAR-
ING he NEVER MEANT TO GO AWAY. " After
" several things of this kind had passed amongst
" us, the King at last declared, that he had no
" *ground* at all given him for *such a deliberation*;
" and thereupon he went out of the chamber of
" presence, saying to the Queen, Adieu, Madam,
" *you*

"*you shall not see my face for a long space*; after which he likewise bad me farewell; and next, turning himself to the lords in general, said, Gentlemen, Adieu. *He is not yet embarked*; but we *receive advertisement from day to day*, that *he still holds on this resolution, and keeps a ship in readiness.*" Yet Mary is described by this ANNIUS of Scotland, as ADMITTING his DENIAL of any such resolution, WITHOUT OBJECTION and WITHOUT REPLY. And, as Le Croc subjoins in a postscript to this letter, " during the five or six days I continued " at Lisleburgh," Edinborough, " after the Queen " left it," who left it on the 7th or 8th, and reached Jedborough on the 8th or 9th, of October *; " the King, who had gone to Glasgow, sent " me word to come and meet him half way be- " tween Lisleburgh and Glasgow. I obeyed him, " and found his father, the Earl of Lenox, with " him. We had *much* communing together, and " I remonstrated to him *every* thing that I could " think of: and *now I believe he will not go out of* " *the kingdom*; though I can perceive that he still " entertains some displeasure. I came hither to " Jedburgh, *on purpose to signify to the Queen*, what " *the King had spoken unto me*, and *what I had said* " *to him* †." Yet the Queen is pictured by this caricatura-painter, as swallowing the OATHS of the King that he had NEVER formed such a resolution, WITHOUT HESITATION and WITHOUT ANSWER. But, what aggravates the impudence of all this, the false account of the whole was drawn up,

* Goodall, i. 237, 303, and 308.   † Keith, 346—347.

inserted

inferted in the letters, and publifhed to the Scotch parliament, to the Englifh commiffioners, and to the world, at a time when the true was known to fo many; when the whole had been ftated in a letter from Lenox to Mary, had been canvaffed in converfation betwixt Lenox, Darnly, and Le Croc, and had even been formally brought before the privy council. And this gives a ruffian air of effrontery to the *letters*, fuperior to any which the *hiftory* can bear; the latter not being publifhed till fome years afterwards, and the former within a few months only from the real incidents.

(4.) The coincidence of the letter and the hiftory here is remarkable. He grants, fays the former, " that he fpake with the men." He, fays the latter, " eâ—de re cum Anglis, qui navem in æftu-
" ario Glottæ ftantem habebant, collocutum." And what fhews the Latin tranflation to have been made by the hand of Buchanan himfelf, " the
" men" of the Scotch are rendered " cum Anglis" by the Latin, and confequently " avec les Ang-
" lois" by the French. Only the hiftorical forger is not fo impudent, as the epiftolary is. He fet his name to the hiftory, he did not to the letters. This would pull back the forward fteps, even of immodefty itfelf. Accordingly Buchanan in his narrative plainly allows, that the King *had* formed a defign of going abroad; while Lethington in the letters makes him deny it, and even to fanction his denial by oaths.

" Efter this I inquyrit him of the inquifitioun (1)
" of Hiegait (2). He denyit the fame, quhill I
" fhew him the verray wordis was fpokin. At
" quhilk tyme (3) he faid, that Mynto had adver-
" tifit him, that it was faid that fum (4) of the
" counfell had broucht an letter to me to be fub-
" fcrivit, to put him in prefoun, and to flay him
" gif he maid refiftence (5). And he (6) afkit the
" fame at Mynto himfelf; quha anfwerit, that he
" belevit ye fame to be trew. The morne (7) I
" will fpeik to him upon this point (8). As to
" the reft of Willie Hiegait's, he confeffit it (9),"

" Poftea rogavi de quæftione (1) Gulielmi (2)
" Hiegait. Id quoque negavit, donec ipfa verba,
" quæ prolata erant, ei detuliffem. Tum (3) dixit
" fe certiorem a Minto factum, dici quendam e
" concilio literas de fe mittendo in carcerem, ac,
" nifi pareret (5), occidendo, ad me detuliffe ut
" fubfcriberem: ac fe (6) idem ex ipfo Mynto quæ-
" fiffe; eumque refpondiffe, fibi verum videri. De
" hôc capite (8) eum cras (7) conveniam. Quod
" ad reliqua de Gulielmo Hiegait, ea confeffus
" eft (9),"

" Apres je l'ay enquis touchant la difpute (1) de
" Gillaume (2) Hiegait. Ce qu'il a auffi defnié,
" jufques a ce que je luy ay rapporté les mefmes
" paroles qu'il avoit proferées. Alors (3) il dit,
" qu'il eftoit adverty par Minto, qu'on difoit,
" qu'un (4) du confeil m'avoit apporté des lettres,

" afin

" afin de les figner, pour le faire mettre en prifon,
" voire, s'il n'obeiffoit (5), pour le tuer ; et qu'il
" (6) enquift le femblable de Minto ; qui refpondit,
" que cela luy fembloit vray. De ce chef (8) je
" luy en parleray demain (7). Quant au refte
" touchant Gillaume Hiegait, il l'a confeffé (9),".

(1) The Frenchman, deceived by the ambiguity of the word "quæftione," rendered it "difpute," and fo altered the whole meaning.

(2) "Hiegait," Scotch ; "Gulielmi Hiegait," Latin; "Gillaume Hiegait," French. "Quoque," Latin, and "auffi," French, are added.

(3) "At quhilk tyme," Scotch; "tum," Latin; "alors," French.

(4) "Sum," Scotch ; "quendam," Latin; "un," French.

(5) "Maid refiftence," Scotch ; "nifi pareret," Latin ; "s'il n'obeiffoit," French.

(6) "And he afkit," Scotch ; "ac fe quæfiffe," Latin ; "et qu'il enquift," French.

(7) Mary appears before to have pretendedly written this part of the letter, the evening after her arrival at Glafgow, the evening of January 24th, 1567. And "the morne" or next day muft mean Jan. 25th.

(8) "This point," Scotch ; "hôc capite," Latin; "ce chef," French. This Mynto was "Johne
" Stewart, of Mynto, Knycht, proveft of Glaf-
                                        " gow,"

"gow," and deeply embarked in the rebellion afterwards *.

(9) All this tale concerning William Hiegait is very confusedly told here, and affords us another evidence of the forgery. On the 20th of January 1567, the day before the Queen set out for Glasgow, she wrote a letter to her embassadour at Paris. I have already made good use of it in her favour. But I have still more to make. In this letter she explains the business, which is here alluded to. " A servand of zouris," she says, " namit William " Walcar, came to our presens, being for the tyme " at Sterveling, and declarit to us how it was not " only oppinly bruted, bot alsua he had hard be " report of personis quhome he esteimit lufferis of " us, that the King, be the assistence of sum of our " nobility, suld tak the prince our sone, and crown " him; and being crownit, as his fader suld tak " upon him the government," *the very plan of usurpation* that was afterwards pursued by *Murray*, instead of Darnly; " he [Walcar], being pressit, " nominat *William Hiegait* in Glasguo, alsua zour " servand, for his cheif author.—Quhairupon we " tuke occasion, with diligence, to send for Hie- " gait, quha being *inquirit* in our counsell, of his " communicatioun had with Walcar, he denyit, " als weill apairt as being confronted togidder, that " evir he talkit with the said Walcar upon ony sic " purpossis. Onlie this far he confessit, that he " hard of a bruit how the King suld be putt in

* Keith, 437.

" ward;

"ward; and for his author in that poynt, namit a
"fervand of the Erle of Eglintonis callit Cauld-
"well; qua being alfua fent for and examinat,
"expreffitlie denyit that evir he fpak or entrit in
"fic termis with William Hiegait. This purpois of
"the bruit of the Kinges warding, wes fchewen be
"Hiegait to the Laird of Mynto, quha agane de-
"clarit it to the Erle of Lenox, and be him the King
"was maid participant thairof: by quhais defyre
"and commandement Hiegait agane (as he alle-
"geit) fpak Cauldwell*." This incident appears to be very different from all the foregoing. It is recent enough, to have employed the converfation of the King and Queen, at their interview on Jan. 23d—24th, &c. The date of the letter reciting it, is only Jan. 20th before. But then it is fo told, as Mary could not have told it. She tells it on Jan. 20th. She is again made to allude to it three days afterward. Let us compare the allufion and the recital together.

The *adulterous* Mary fays, that fhe enquired of the King concerning the inquifition of Hiegait before her council, and that he denied it before he fpecified the very words that had been fpoken. But why fhould Mary interrogate Darnly concerning this inquifition? He knew nothing of the *fact* of the inquifition. Nor could Mary want to know any thing concerning *that*. And, as to the *object* of the inquifition, all that part of it which alone he could have denied, viz. that he himfelf was to take the Prince, crown him, and ufurp all the

* Keith, Pref, viii.

royalty

royalty as regent to him; this did not appear in Hiegait's inquifition at all. It was only in Walcar's declaration to the Queen herfelf. And the very words fpoken muft have been Walcar's, not Hiegait's. On the mention of thefe, the King excufed himfelf for having entertained fuch a fcheme, by the intelligence which he received from Mynto, of a defign to fend him to prifon, and to put him to death if he refufed to go. But, by the King's account, *Mynto* had apprized *him* of this reported defign; *he* afked Mynto concerning it, and *Mynto* told *him* he thought the report true; when in fact Mynto told it, not to *him*, but to his *father Lenox*, when *Lenox* was the perfon that communicated it to the *King*, and when the *King* afterwards fpoke, not to Mynto, but to *Hiegait*, about it. Nor was this reported defign fuch, as the King is here made to reprefent it, that " fum of the counfell had " broucht ane letter to Mary to be fubfcrivit, to " put him in prefoun, and to flay him gif he maid " refiftence." It was merely, that the King " fuld " be put in ward." Nor did Mynto declare *more* to Lenox, nor did Lenox communicate *more* to the King, nor did the King fpeak of *more* to Hiegait. And then as to " the reft of Willie Hiegait's," which " he confeffit," it is this very point again, about fending him to prifon. With fuch wild confufion is this incident alluded to by the *adultercus* Mary on the 23d of January, though it is very clearly related by the *innocent* Mary on the 20th before! What *Walcar* faid, is attributed to *Hiegait*. What *Lenox* faid, is given to *Mynto*. What the King faid to *Hiegait*, is addreffed to *Mynto*. The

great

CHAP. I. MARY QUEEN OF SCOTS. 93

great object of all is made very different. And, as the whole drift of the paragraph is calculated to exculpate the King, for having embarked in a measure, so violent, absurd, and unnatural, which was remotely suggested in all probability by the very man, who executed it afterwards in all its parts, and who would soon have wrested the scepter out of the weak hands of such an usurper, when once it had been wrenched by him out of the Queen's; so it proves the fact by endeavouring to excuse it, and, what is infinitely more important, proves to a demonstration the forgery of the letters, by its confused and erroneous statement of the history.

" bot it was the morne after my cumming (1) or
" he did it."

" nec id nisi postridie quám veneram (1)."

" mais non jusques au jour d'apres mon arrivée
" (1)."

(1) This is also a dash from the pen of forgery. This part of the letter pretends to be written the day after Mary's arrival at Glasgow, or on Jan. 24, 1567. Hence the letter speaks before of what the King did " zister-nicht," and of the conversation that passed with him before and after supper. And, as we shall soon see, it was written in the evening or night of this day. The " morne" or day " efter" her " cuming," therefore, must be the very day on which she was writing. She relates the

discourse,

discourse, that took place betwixt her and the King the evening before, concerning William Hiegait. About one point in it, she says, she will ask him again the next day, Jan. 25th. But concerning another, she says, he did not own this till the day afterwards. Yet how comes the letter-writer to call this day " the day after her coming," when it was that very day on which she was pretendedly writing? From the same principle, on which we have seen the very town in which she was pretendedly writing at the moment, denominated *that* town. The mind cannot be kept continually under the restraint of fraud. It will assert its native freedom at times. It will break away from the prescribed line of ideas. And, imperceptibly to itself, it will throw out some circumstances, that betray the bondage in which it is acting. Mary, writing of what had been confessed the day of her writing, would have called it *this* day. Nature could not have acted otherwise. But Lethington and art, putting themselves in Mary's and Nature's place, could not so far divest themselves of their own propriety, as to refrain from calling it *the day after her coming*. And they discovered themselves by the act.

§ V.

§ V.

LETTER THE FIRST CONTINUED.

XII.—" He wald verray fane that I suld ludge in his ludgeing (1). I refusit it, and said to him, that he behovit to be purgeit, and that culd not be done heir. He said to me, I heir say ze have brocht ane lytter with zow; bot I had raither have passit with zow (2). I trow he belevit that I wuld have send him away prisoner (3). I answerit that I wuld tak him with me to Craigmillar, quhair the mediciner (4) and I micht help him, and not be far from my sone."

XII.—" Magnopere cupiebat ut ego in ejus hospitio apud eum diverterem (1). Ego recusavi, ac dixi ei opus esse purgatione, nec id hic fieri posse. Dixit se accepisse, quód lecticam mecum attulissem; se veró maluisse mecum uná proficisci (2). Credebat, opinor, quód in carcerem eum aliquó (3) amandatura essem. Ego respondi, quód ductura mecum essem ád Cragmillarium, ubi et medici (4) et ego possemus ei adesse, neque longé a meo filio abesse."

XII.—" Il desiroit fort que j'allasse loger en son hostel (1); ce que j'ay refusé, luy disant, qu'il avoit besoin de purgation, et que cela ne se
" pouvoit

" pouvoit faire [icy]. Il adjouſta, qu'il avoit en-
" tendu que j'avoye amené une litiere, et qu'il euſt
" mieux aymé aller enſemble avec moy (2). J'eſ-
" time qu'il penſoit que je le vouluſſe envoyer
" priſonnier quelque part (3). Je reſpondy, que
" je le meneroye avec moy à Cragmillar, afin que
" là les medicins (4) et moy le peuſſions ſecourir,
" et que je m'eſloignaſſe de mon fils."

(1) " Ludge in his ludgeing," Scotch; " in ejus
" hoſpitio *apud eum* diverterem," Latin; " loger
" en ſon hoſtel," French, from the corrected Latin.

(2) " *T*heir ſay *ze* have brocht ane litter with
" *zow*, bot *I* had rather have paſſit with *zow*,"
Scotch; " Dixit *ſe* accepiſſe quod lecticam *mecum*
" attuliſſem, *ſe* veró maluiſſe *mecum* uná proficiſci,"
Latin; " il adjouſta, qu'*il* avoit entendu que *j'*avoye
" amené une litiere, et qu'*il* euſt mieux aymé aller
" enſemble avec *moy*," French.

(3) " Send him away priſoner," Scotch; " in
" carcerem eum *aliquó* amandatura eſſem," Latin;
" envoyer priſonnier *quelque part*," French.

(4) " Mediciner," Scotch; " medici," Latin;
" medicins," French.

" He anſwerit, that he was reddy when I pleiſit (1),
" ſa I wald aſſure him of his requeſt,"

" Ille reſpondit, ſe, ubi vellem, paratum eſſe (1)
" modó de eo quod peteret ſecurum ſe facerem."

" Il refpondit, qu'il eftoit preft d'aller, où je vou-
" droye (1), pourveu que je le rendiffe certain de
" ce qu'il m'avoit requis."

(1) Here is a fair print from the cloven foot of forgery. This letter makes the Queen to propofe Craigmillar the very evening of her arrival, and the King to exprefs his readinefs to go to Craigmillar whenever fhe pleafed. But the fecond depofitions of Paris affert, that fhe fent Paris from Glafgow to Edinborough in order to confult Bothwell and Lethington, " lequell eft meilleur pour ' loger le Roy, a Craigmillar, ou a Kirk-a-field ;" hat fhe charged him to make hafte, becaufe fhe :ould not ftir till he returned with his anfwer, ' haftez vous de revenir, car je ne bougeray d'ici, : jufques au temps que m'aures raporte la reponfe ;" and that Lethington and Bothwell reurned for anfwer, Kirk-a-field would be a proper lace, " le Kirk-de-field feroit bon *." Thefe two :counts ftand in direct oppofition to each other. 'hey therefore ferve, like two contrary poifons, iutually to counteract themfelves. And they are oth counteracted by the fulleft force of truth. homas Nelfon, one of Darnly's attendants, was :orn in England to fome circumftances concernig the murder of the King. His is therefore a ial depofition. And he afferts what proves Paris's id the letter to be both forgeries. " He wes ' actual fervand to the King," he fays, "the tyme ' of his murder, and lang of befoir, and came

* Goodall, ii. 77—78.

" with

"with him from Glafgow the time the Quene con-
" voyed him to Edinburgh. Item, the deponar
" *remembris* it wes dewyfed *in Glafgow*, that the
" King *fuld haif lyne firft at Craigmillar*; bot be-
" caus he had na will thairof, the purpois
" wes altered, and conclufioun taken that he fuld
" ly befyde the Kirk-of-field *."

XIII.—" He defyris na body to fé him (1). He
" is angrie quhen I fpeik of Walcar (2), and
" fayis, that he fall pluk the eiris out of his head,
" and that he leis (3). For I inquyrit him upon
" that (4), and yat he was angrie with fum of the
" Lordis (5), and wald threittin thame. He de-
" nyis that, and fayis he luifis thame all (6), and
" prayis me to give traift to nathing againft him
" (7)."

XIII.—" Cupiebat ne a quoquam confpiceretur
" (1). Irafcitur quoties ei mentionem Walcarii
" facio (2), ac fe dicit, aures ei e capite avulfurum,
" ac mentiri eum ait (3). Nam de hâc re eum
" interrogâram (4), ac de eo quód iratus effet qui-
" bufdam procerum (5), atque eis minaretur. Id
" negat, et ait omnes fibi charos effe (6), ac me
" rogat ne quid fecus de fe crederem (7)."

XIII.—" Il defiroit de n'eftre veu de perfonne
" (1). Il fe fafce toutes les fois que je luy parle de
" Walcar (2), et dit, qu'il luy arrachera les oreilles

* Goodall, ii. 241 and 244.

" de

"de la teſte, et qu'il a menty (3). Car je l'avoyé
"interrogé de cela (4), et de ce qu'il s'eſtoit cour-
"roucé contre aucuns des ſeigneurs (5), et les
"avoit menaſſez. Ce qu'il nie, et dit qu'il les
"ayme tous (6), et me prie que je ne croye point
"autrement de luy (7)."

(1) "Deſyris," Scotch; "cupiebat," Latin; "deſiroit," French; "na body to ſé him," Scotch; "ne a quoquam conſpiceretur," Latin; "de n'eſtre veu de perſonne," French.

(2) This intimation makes the alluſion to the ſtory of Walcar and Hiegait before, more confuſed than ever. Walcar had ſaid as from Hiegait, that by report the King was to crown his ſon, and uſurp the government in his name. What Walcar thus ſaid has been already given to Hiegait, but is now taken from him again, and reſtored to its right owner. And we ſhall ſoon ſee a ſimilar ſtroke of contradictorineſs, in another alluſion to this very ſtory.

(3) That Walcar *lied*, is plainly not true. Such a plan had been ſuggeſted, no doubt, by the arti- cles of the doubling Murray, to the poor head and poorer heart of this unhappy King. Mary thought ſo much of it, as to mention it in her letter to her embaſſadour at Paris. And we have a ſtrong confirmation of the truth of it, which Mary had not then; in the adoption of the very ſame ſcheme only a few months afterwards by Murray, and in the full execution of it by him, to the ruin of Mary and her fortunes for ever.

H 2 (4) That

(4) That Mary ſhould have now aſked him concerning this, is utterly incredible upon every ſuppoſition. The King was in a very weak and languiſhing condition. She had flown to him on the news. She was juſt arrived. She had only ſupped ſince her arrival. She was now ſitting at the foot of his bed. And that ſhe ſhould, in theſe circumſtances and at this time, hint a ſyllable concerning a reported deſign of his in his health, for ſeizing the crown from her; is ſo wildly incredible, as to convict the letter of forgery at once.

(5) This alludes more immediately to what the Queen notices in her letter of January 20th. "Hie-
" gait ſaid further, as Walcar reportit to us, that
" the King culd not content nor beir with ſum of
" the noblemen that war attending in our court, bot
" othir he or thay behovit to leif the ſamyn *."
But then both refer to what happened on the 30th of September before. "The ſame evening," ſays the privy council of Scotland in a formal letter of October 8th, to the Queen Dowager of France,
" the King came to Edinburgh, but made ſome
" difficulty to enter into the palace, by reaſon that
" three or four lords were at that time preſent with
" the Queen, and *peremptorily inſiſted* that they
" might be gone *before* he would condeſcend to
" come in: which deportment appeared to be abun-
" dantly unreaſonable, ſince they were three of the
" greateſt lords of the kingdom," ſuppoſed to be Argyle, Murray, and Rothes †, "and that thoſe
" Kings, who by their own birth were ſovereigns

---

* Keith, Pref. viii.   † Goodall, i. 284.

" O

"of the realm, have never acted in that manner towards the nobility. The Queen however received this behaviour as decently as was possible, and condescended so far as to go meet the King without the palace, and so conducted him into her own apartment *." But surely this was not an incident, that could have engaged a moment's attention from both, at such an interview as the present, and in the first evening of it. If the Queen had come with a real regard for him, she *could* not have led most distantly to the subject. If she had come from a pretended one, she *would* not.

(6) That Darnly should be made to assert this, in direct opposition to the speaking fact above; was the design in introducing the subject. But then it serves, with almost every other circumstance here, to prove the plain spuriousness of the letter, and the old fraudulence of the writer.

(7) "Give traist to nathing aganis him," Scotch; "ne quid *secus* de se crederem," Latin; which, connected as it stands with " ait omnes sibi charos esse," desires Mary not to believe but that they are all, as he says, dear to him. Though this is not the sense of the Scotch, yet, the Latin being so, the French was forced to accommodate itself to it; autrement de luy."

' As to me, he wald rather give his lyfe or he did
' ony displesure to me (1).

* Keith, 348—349.

XIV.—

XIV.—" And efter this he schew me of sa mony,
" lytil flattereis, sa cauldly and sa wysely (2), that
" ze will abasce thairat (3). I had almost forzet,
" that he said, he culd not dout (4) of me in yis
" purpois of Hiegaite's; for he wald never belief yat
" I, quha was his proper flesche, wold do him ony
" evill; alsweill it was schawin that I refusit to sub-
" scrive the same (5):"

" Quod ad me attinet, se malle de vitâ discedere,
" quám quicquam committere quod me offende-
" ret (1).

XIV.—" Ac postea tantum minutarum adula-
" tionum tam moderaté ac tam prudenter effudit
" (2), ut tibi res admirationi sit futura (3). Pene
" oblita eram, quód dixit, in hôc negotio Hiegait
" non posse de me quicquam suspicari (4); se enim
" nunquam crediturum, quód ego, quæ propria
" ejus caro essem, quicquam mali ei facerem: etiam
" se rescisse, quód ego ei rei subscribere recusas-
" sem (5):"

" Et quant a ce qui me touche, qu'il aymeroit
" mieux mourir, que de faire chose qui me peut
" offenser (1).

XIV.—" Or apres il m'a usé de tant de petites
" flateries, avec tel poids et discretion (2), que vous
" en seriez estonné (3). J'avoye, peu s'en faut,
" oublié ce qu'il dit sur le fait de Hiegait, qu'il ne
" peut soupconner de moy (4); et qu'il ne croira
" jamais que moy, qui suis sa propre chair, luy
" fasse aucun desplaisir; et qu'il scavoit bien, que
" j'avoye refusé de souscrire a cela (5):"

(1) These

(1) These wild and absurd attempts to colour over the wretched character of Darnly, I have already noticed with the proper severity. But, lest perseverance should attract credit, let me only subjoin Le Croc's account of his conduct so late as the 23d of December before. His bad "deport-" ment," says this honest embassador, who was also a kind of confidante to him, " is *incurable*; " nor *can there be ever any good expected from him*, " for several reasons *."

(2) " Cauldly," Scotch, which then meant *coolly and calmly*, as Mary's commissioners say to Elizabeth, " we replyed *cauldely* and myldlye, without " ony railing †;" and translated accordingly in Latin, " moderaté;" has, by a misunderstanding of the Latin, been rendered in French " avec poids," *with weight*; as if the French author took his idea of the Latin word from that passage in Sallust, "' nihil pensi neque moderati habere."—" Schew " me *of* sa mony lytil flattereis." This, says the Miscellaneous Remarker, is a French expression, because it is similar in its structure to the French here, " m'a usé de tant *de* petites flateries ‡." He might as well have said that it was a Latin one, because it is equally similar to the Latin here, "' tantum minutarum adulationum effudit." And indeed we know the French to be merely derived from the Latin.

(3) I have already shewn the absurdity of Mary's relating all the exculpatory topicks of Darnly, with-

* Keith, Pref. viii.   † Goodall, ii. 218—219.   ‡ P. 20—21.

out any specified reply to them. But I now wish to urge *another* point concerning it, as a proof of forgery. Why should Mary relate all these to her *adulterer?* Why should she thus labour to soften and extenuate the King's conduct in a letter to *Bothwell?* Is this nature, or is this art? Nature it certainly is not. No adulteress was ever so far abandoned, as to wish or allow herself to exculpate her husband. She would much rather seek for all occasions to censure *him*, in order to excuse *herself*. She would be so far from repeating all his long defences of himself, without recording her answers to them; that she would hardly permit herself to repeat them at all, that she would certainly repeat her answer to each defence, and that she would give her answer every advantage of force. She would do this to *any* correspondent. But she would peculiarly do it to *Bothwell*. And, even to *him*, she had one special reason for doing it. She is described even in these very letters, as jealous of Bothwell's wife. She is made to mention her jealousy over and over again. Then why, in the name of common sense, should she rehearse to Bothwell the King's long vindications of himself, which must have such a tendency to plant a jealousy of Darnly in him? She did not do it, in order to counteract one jealousy by another. Had she, her behaviour must have been more kind to Darnly, and more distant to Bothwell. But she avows, even in this very letter, her fullest regard for Bothwell, and her highest contempt for Darnly. And she therefore employs herself so laboriously, in reciting all that

Darnly

Darnly spoke in his own justification, not because it was natural for her to do so; but because it was necessary to the policy of forgery that she should, because nature was to be sacrificed to art, and because the forgers trusted the sacrifice would be, as it has now been for two hundred years, totally unobserved by the world.

(4) "Dout," Scotch; "suspicari," Latin; "soupçonner," French.

(5) This is the contradiction, to which I referred a few notes before. The point alluded to is called the purpose of *Hiegait*; and yet it is evidently the information of *Mynto*. The latter had said, that some of the council were reported to have brought an order for the Queen's signature, which was to send Darnly to prison, &c. And it is now added, that Mary had refused to sign the order. What Hiegait had alledged was merely this, that it was reported Darnly was to be sent to prison. This is much short of the other. This says nothing of an order actually presented to Mary for sending him. This has no connection, therefore, with Mary's refusal to sign the order. Yet the two informations are confounded. And Mynto's is given to Hiegait.

But let us now, at this present reference to the inquisition before the council, examine all the parts of it again; lest, while we are active in exposing the forgery, we should press some points into the cause, that have no concern in it. The real fact is, as we have shewn before, that Walcar acquainted the Queen with a reported design in Darnly to dethrone

throne her, to crown her son, and to reign in his name; and that Hiegait informed the council of an equally reported design in Mary, to send Darnly to prison. By these two informations we are to try the notices in the letter. To which of these, then, does it refer, when it says, that Mary asked Darnly concerning " the inquisitioun of Hiegait," and that " he denyit the same" till she shewed " the " verray wordis was spokin?" By the name of Hiegait, it should refer to the real information given by Hiegait, that it was reported Darnly was to be sent to prison. Yet this it cannot mean, because Darnly *denies* the allegation, till she shewed him the very words of it. Had it meant the real information of Hiegait, Mary would *not* have enquired about it, and Darnly would *not* have denied it. She is even made to say afterwards, that she thinks he believed, even on her present visit to him, she would send him to prison. It means therefore the information of Walcar, that the King designed to seize the reins of government, under the appearance of acting as regent to his son. And yet the letter speaks afterwards of " the rest of Willie " Hiegait's," which Darnly " confessed" the day afterward. What did he " confess" then? The same that he denied before, concerning the plan of dethroning the Queen? Or the fact, of Hiegait's communication to Mynto, of Mynto's to Lenox, of Lenox's to the King, and of the King's to Hiegait? Yet the *latter* he has equally denied with the *former*. *Mynto*, he says, was the person who informed him of the design. And with *Mynto* it was that he talked about it. So thoroughly confounded was

was the letter-writer, by his half-recollection of this inquisition, of which we have so full an account in Mary's letter! He little thought of such a letter being preserved, to expose his ignorance, and to detect his imposture.—But let us go on.

The letter-writer makes Mynto inform the King of a report, that some of the council had brought an order to Mary, for confining the King, and for putting him to death, if he resisted the execution of the order. The King is described as asking Mynto his opinion, concerning the truth of the report. And Mynto is represented as declaring his belief in the truth of it. But, says the *acted Queen*, "the morne I will speik to him upon this point." Yet before "the morne" comes, Mary speaks to her readers upon the point; and only, by a blunder rather extraordinary in so short a compass, miscalls it Hiegait's for Mynto's. For she knows immediately, and without speaking any farther to the *King* about it, that he knew she had *refused* to sign the order. And though the next day (as I shall soon shew) she writes the remaining half of this long letter, yet she never speaks to the point any more.—But I proceed to another circumstance.

Walcar's information, and Mynto's intelligence, are both attributed in different places to Hiegait. Yet Mynto in one place, and Walcar in another, have each their several allotments. And then "the rest of Hiegait's" is noticed, either as different *or* the same; if as the same, then being most impertinently noticed; if as different, then being nothing at all.

So

So confusedly, and so contradictorily, are these allusions to the *subject* of Mary's letter managed by the forgers! Confusedness upon such a recent point, and from such a pretended writer, is sufficient of itself to betray the hand of imposture in the whole. But contradictoriness does it still more strongly. And, which is what I wish to remark at the close, these intimations concerning an order produced by some of the council to Mary, for seizing the person of the King, and for slaying him if he made resistance; and concerning the King's belief, even at the very instant of her really or pretendedly kind visit to him, that she meant even then to commit him to ward, so directly contrary to his own avowal, that he knew the Queen had already refused to sign an order for his committal; are wholly false in themselves. The Queen's letter of January 20th is a full proof that they are. She who wrote an account of Walcar's information and of Hiegait's intelligence to her embassadour, must certainly have written an account of such an order and such a refusal, had they been true. And this concurs with all to shew, not merely the artificial, but the awkward and the blundering, fabrication of these celebrated letters.

―――

" but as to ony utheris (1) that wald persew him,
" at leist he suld sell his lyfe deir aneuch (2); bot
" he suspectit na body, nor zit wald not; but wald
" luse all yat I lufit (3).

XV.—

XV.—" He wald not let me depart from him,
" bot defyrit yat I fuld walk with him (4). I mak
" (5) it feme that I believe that all is trew, and
" takis heid thairto, 'and excufit myfelf for this
" nicht that I culd not walk (6). He fayis, that
" he fleipis not weil (7)."

" quód fi quis (1) fuam vitam peteret, facturum
" ut fatis magno ei conftaret (2) : fed fibi neminem
" nec fufpectum effe, nec futurum ; fed fe omnes
" dilecturum quos ego diligerem (3)."

XV.—" Nolebat permittere ut a fe difcederem,
" fed cupiebat ut uná fecum vigilarem (4). Ego
" fimulabam (5) omnia videri vera, ac mihi curæ
" effe, atque excufavi quód illâ nocte vigilare non
" poffem (6). Ait fe non bene dormire (7)."

" que fi quelqu'un (1) cherchoit a luy ofter la vie,
" qu'il feroit en forte qu'elle luy feroit cherement
" venduë (2) ; mais que nul ne luy eftoit, ou feroit,
" fufpect ; ains qu'il aymeroit tous ceux que j'ay-
" moye (3)."

XV.—" Il ne vouloit point permettre que je
" m'en allaffe, mais defiroit que je veillaffe (4)
" avec luy ; et je faingnoye (5) que tout cela me
" fembloit vray, et que je m'en foucioye beaucoup,
" et en m'excufant que je ne pouvoye veiller pour
" cefte nuict-la (7), il dit, qu'il ne pouvoit bien
" dormir (7)."

(1) " Ony utheris," Scotch ; " quis," Latin ;
" quelqu'un," French.

(2) It

(2) It is very observable, in what contradictions this negligent letter-writer involves himself. The King now *threatens* to fell his life dear enough, at least, to such of the lords as were seeking it. Yet, a very little before, he denies that he threatens them, and avers that he loves them all. So contradictory, in the compass of a few minutes, is the Darnly of the forgers! The denial is put into his mouth, to raise his character for good-nature. The threat is put in, to enhance his reputation for bravery. And both are to be exalted, at the expence of consistence.—" At leist," Scotch, is omitted by the Latin and the French.

(3) As a *proof* of this, that comes nearest to the date of the present letter; let me produce once more the Queen's own letter of January 20th. Her authority is *at least* as good as his. But in reality it is much better. She puts her name to what she says. And even Lethington did not dare to put it to what Darnly says. " For the King our husband,
" God knawis alwayis our part towartis him; and
" his behaviour and thankfulness to us is semblable-
" ment well knawin to God and the warld; specia-
" lie our awin indifferent subjectis seis it, and in
" thair hartis, we doubt not, condemnis the samyn.
" Alwayis we persave him occupeit and bissy aneuch
" to haif inquisitioun of our doyngis, quhilkis, God
" willing, sall ay be sic as nane sall haif occasioun
" to be offendit with thame, or to report of us ony
" wayis bot honorably; howsoever he, his father,
" and thair fautoris, speik, quhilkis we knaw want
" na gude will to mak us haif ado, gif thair power
" were

" were equivalent to thair myndis. But God mo-
" deratis thair forces well aneuch, and takis the
" moyen of executioun of thair pretensis fra thame;
" for, as we believe, they sall find nane, or verray
" few, approveris of thair counsalis and devysis
" imaginit to our displesor or mislyking *." Let
me also repeat what I have said before in other
words, that this letter, however Dr. Robertson
has misrepresented it, gives us the picture of a soul,
feeling but firm, touched but not provoked, looking down from its dignity with concern upon the
injuries that it had received, and looking up from
its innocence to God against the injuries that it
knew to be meditated. And this picture being
drawn undesignedly by the hand of Mary herself,
and at a very critical minute of her life; it thence
becomes the more valuable.

(4) " Walk," Scotch, meaning to *wake*. " It
" chance oft to the infirmities of man," Ninian
Wingate says in 1562, " that he sall on slepe
" quhen he suld erast [chiefly] *walk*;—ze *walkin*
" nocht furthe of zour dreme;—*awalke, awalke* †."

(5) " I mak," Scotch; " simulabam," Latin;
and " je faingnoye," French.

(6) This is the night of her arrival, January 23;
in which she very naturally excused herself from sitting up late with him, because she was tired with her
journey.

* Keith, Pref. viii. † Ibid. App. 2c6.

(7) The

(7.) The turn of the French must have arisen, I suppose, from some mistake in or concerning the corrected Latin.

" Ze (1) saw him never better, nor speik mair
" humbler. And gif I had not ane prufe of his
" hart of waxe, and yat myne wer [not] of ane
" dyamont (2), quhairintill na schot can mak brek,
" bot that quhilk cummis furth of zour hand, I wald
" have almaist had pietie of him. Bot feir not, the
" place fall hald unto the deith. Remember, in
" recompence thairof (3), that ze suffer not zouris
" to be wyn be that fals race that will travell no
" les with zow for the fame (4).

XVI.—" I beleve thay have bene at schoullis
" togidder. He hes ever the teir in his eye; he
" salutis every body, zea, unto the leist, and makis
" pieteous caressing unto thame, to mak theme
" have pietie on him (5). This day his father
" bled"

" Nunquam vidi (1) eum meliús habere, aut loqui
" humiliús. Ac nisi experimento didicissem, quám
" esset ejus cor cereum, meum adamantinum (2),
" et quale nullum telum penetrare posset, nisi quod
" e tuâ manu veniat, propé erat ut ejus miserta
" fuissem: sed ne time, præsidium ad mortem
" usque custodietur. Tu vide (3), ne tuum capi
" sinas

' finas a gente illâ perfidâ, quæ non minore con
' tentione tecum de hôc ipfo aget (4).

XVI.—" Arbitror in eadem fcholâ doctos fuiffe. Ifte femper in oculis habet lachrymam;
falutat omnes, etiam ufque ad infimos, et miferis
modis eos ambit, ut ad fui mifericordiam eos per-
ducat (5). Hodie patri ejus fanguis e naribus"

Je (1) ne l'ay jamais veu mieux porter, ne parler
' fi doucement; et fi je n'euffe appris par l'expe-
' rience, combien il avoit le cœur mol comme cir,
' et le mien eftre dur comme diamant (2), et lequel
' nul trait ne pouvoit percer, finon defchoché de
' voftre main, peu s'en euft fallu que je n'euffe eu
' pitié de luy : toutesfois ne craignez point, cefte
' forterefse fera confervée jufques a la mort ; mais
' vous regardez (3) que ne laiffiez furprendre la
' voftre, par cefte nation infidele, qui avec non
' moindre opiniatreté debatra le mefme avec vous
' (4).

XVI.—" J'eftime qu'ils ont efté enfeignez en
mefme efcole. Ceftui-cy a tousjours la larme a
l'œil; il falüe toute le monde, voire jufques au
plus petits, et les flate d'une facon pitoyable,
à fin qu'il les ameine jufques d'avoir compaffion
de luy (5)."

1) " Ze faw," Scotch; " vidi," Latin; " je
' eu," French.

2) " Not," Scotch, omitted in Latin and
French, and, as the fenfe fhews, inferted in the
Scotch by fome miftake of the prefs.

(3) " In

(3) "In recompence thairof," Scotch, omitted in the Latin and French.

(4) Meaning Bothwell's wife.

(5) This affords us a very extraordinary evidence of the forgery, in a plain and palpable contradiction. An author, who writes from a set of imaginary ideas, and has therefore no real archetypes in nature to direct him, is almost sure to fall into contradictions. The present is a very great one. Darnly at this very time kept his bed. He had done so for some time past. He was particularly in bed during all this conversation. "I cum," says Mary herself soon afterwards, "na neirer unto "him, bot in ane chyre at the bed-feit, and he be- "ing at the other end thairof." And, as she says only a little before, "he desyris na body to sē him." Yet here we are told, that "he salutis every body, "zea, unto the leist, and makis pieteous caressing "unto thame, to mak thame have pietie on him." He, who sees nobody, is saluting every body; "tout le monde," says the Frenchman. He salutes even the very lowest of the people. He makes piteous caressings to all orders of life at Glasgow—*from the upper end of his bed*. And he, who desires to see no one, who has seen none since the Queen came, even now has had a grand COUCHE'E, and has been practising all the humilities of politeness to the crowds about him.

" at the mouth and nose; ges quhat presage that
" is (1). I have not zit sene him, he keipis his
" chalmer (2). The King desyris that I sald give
" him meit with my awin handis (3); bot gif na
" mair traist quhair ze ar (4), than I sall do heir
" (5).

XVII.—" This is my first jornay (6): I sall end
" the same ye morne (7)."

" et ore fluxit; tu conjice quale id sit præsagium
" (1). Nondum eum vidi, continet enim se in
" cubiculo (2). Rex poscit ut meis manibus sibi
" tradam cibum (3); sed tu nihilo magis isthic
" sis crediturus (4), quàm ego híc ero (5).

XVII.—"Hæc est mea primi diei expeditio (6);
" eandem cras finiam (7)."

" Aujourdhuy le sang est forty du nez et de la
" bouche a son pere; vous donc devinez mainte-
" nant quel est ce presage (1). Je ne l'ay point
" encor veu, car il se tient en sa chambre (2). Le
" Roy me requiert que je luy donne a manger de
" mes mains (3); or vous n'en croyez pas par dela
" rien d'avantage (4), pendant que je suis icy (5).

XVII.—" Voyla j'ay despeché pour mon pre-
" mier jour (6), esperant achever demain le reste
" (7)."

(1) This

(1) This is the first hint about the murder. And a most dark one it is. Yet it is singled out in a short abstract of the letter, by the busy apprehensiveness of the commissioners of England, as a very particular one *.

(2) This is a false fact, and so proves the forgery. All the intimations here concerning Lenox, imply him to have been ill, and to have *therefore* kept his chamber. Yet the *present* Mary has already informed us, that this very day Lenox sent a gentleman to her four miles before she reached Glasgow, to pay his respects of duty to her, and to excuse his non-attendance upon her in person, *not* because he was sick, but " be ressoun he *durst* " *not interpryse the same*, because of the rude wordis " that I had spokin to Cuninghame." He was therefore not sick that afternoon. Yet *the very evening* of that afternoon he is here represented as sick. And, what pins down the point decisively, the very gentleman, who came from Lenox to the Queen, afterwards deposed in England, that " the " said Erle *durst* not then, *for displeasure of the* " *Quene*, come abroad †." So thoroughly does this agree with the former part of the letter! And so compleatly are both in opposition to the present!

But let me make another observation upon this part of the letter. I have already shewn the forger of the letter to have confounded his understanding by the indistinctness of his memory, to have taken incidents that happened in the April of 1566, and

* Appendix, N° vi. † Goodall, ii. 246.

to have fixed them in or about January 1567. And the prefent paffage in the letter corroborates what I have faid. In April 1566 this very contradiction was realized. Then Lenox actually excufed himfelf from attendance at Edinborough, firft becaufe he was fick, and then becaufe "he durft "not enterprize the fame *."

(3) This was a very pretty office for the Queen. It fhews the regard of Darnly for her extremely. Her Majefty was to become nurfe to his father. Yet " he wald rather give his lyfe or he did ony " difplefure to her." And he had been feverely " punifhit for making his God of her, and for " having na uther thocht bot on her." So much at odds are the parts of this letter! Yet the Queen's refufal to do this menial office to one of her Earls, of attending him in his chamber of ficknefs, and " giving him meit with her awin handis," was moft injudicioufly intended to injure her character with the reader. " Thefe cocknies," faid Condé, " make " me to think and fpeak, juft as they would think " and fpeak in the fame fituations." And, in the fottifhnefs of forgery, a Lethington became a mere cockney!

(4) Meaning ftill Bothwell's wife.

(5) The French has made a great blunder here, miftaking the fenfe of the Latin, " quám ego hic " ero," confidering it to mean *as long as I fhall be bere,* and therefore rendering the claufe " pendant " que je fuis icy."

* Anderfon, i. 52—53, and ii. 106—107.

(6) This passage is a memorable one. It was one of those, which first detected the vain pretensions of the French to originality *. And it is very astonishing, how Buchanan could miss the meaning of so easy a word, familiar as it still is in all the distant extremities of the island, and hedged and fenced in as it is by the context. It shews him to have been very careless in making the version.

(7) The passage before shews this part of the letter to have been written Jan. 24th, the day after the Queen's arrival. And the present passage intimates, that the letter was to be finished on Jan. 25th,

---

" I wryte all things, howbeit thay be of lytill wecht,
" to the end that ze may tak the best of all to
" judge upon (1). I am in doing of ane work
" heir (2) that I hait (3) greitly (4). Have ze
" not desyre to lauch (5) to sē me lie sa weill, at
" ye leist to dissembill sa weill, and to tell him (6)
" treuth betwix handis (7) ?"

" Omnia scribo, etsi non sunt magni ponderis, ut tu
" optima seligendo judicium facias (1). Ego in
" negotio (2) mihi maximé (4) ingrato (3) versor.
" Nunquid subit cupiditas ridendi (5), videndo me
" tam bene mentiri, saltem dissimulare tam bene,
" ac (6) interim vera dicere (7) ?"

* Goodall, i. 93.

" Jo

" Je vous efcry toutes chofes, encor qu'elles foient
" de peu d'importance, afin qu'en eflifant les meil-
" leures, vous en faffies jugement (1). Je fuis
" occupée en une affaire (2) qui m'eft infiniement
" (4) defagreable (3). Ne vous prent-il pas envie de
" rire (5), de me voir ainfi bien mentir, au moins
" de fi bien diffimuler (6), en difant verité (7) ?"

(1) This is the apology made by the writer, for inferting fo long an account of what the King faid to the Queen. Bothwell was to felect what he thought the principal ftrokes in the King's fpeech, and to judge from them with regard to his future proceedings. But, not to dwell on the abfurdity of her not felecting them herfelf, what were the ftrokes, principal or fubordinate, that could lead him to form any judgment concerning the murder? For the future proceedings muft relate to the murder only. Could the difcourfe concerning the *letter* lead him? Could the hint of her *penfivenefs?* Could the King's declaring, that he would leave her all he had, that fhe was cruel to him, that fhe refufed to accept his repentance, and that his regret for this had given him his diforder? None of thefe circumftances, furely, could either have retarded or haftened the murder? Let us go on then, and fee if we can find any other that could. Could the King's confeffion afterwards, his petition for pardon, his promife of amendment, and his avowal of his former idolatry for Mary? Or could his anfwer concerning the Englifh fhip, concerning Hiegait, Mynto, and Walcar, concerning his defire

to sleep with the Queen, her refusal to let him, and his readiness to attend her to Craigmillar? Could his desire to see no one, his declaration of love for all the lords, his expressions of peculiar regard for Mary, his flatteries to her, her so fully expressed attachment to Bothwell in spite of all, and his general courtesy and humility to all the world? Certainly they could not. They could not separately. They could not collectively. They could not even serve as lights, to regulate the proceedings of Bothwell in *preparing* for the murder. The murder indeed was already determined. "Ibi," at Holyrood-house, " cum rescitum esset," says Buchanan, " Regem convalescere, ac vim veneni æta-
" tis vigore et corporis firmitate naturali superatam,
" novum de eo tollendo consilium initur—; con-
" sulunt omnes festinandum, antequam plané con-
" valesceret *." And accordingly the commissioners at York, from the suggestions of Murray and his *fellows*, and as a proof of the Queen's " procure-
" ment and consent to the murder of her said hus-
" band," say she appears in this letter to have
" toke her journey from Edenburghe to Glasco,
" to visit him being theare sick, and purposely of
" intent to bringe him with her to Edenburghe †."
It was therefore determined, according to the rebels themselves, and according to their own comments upon this very letter, to murder the King at Edinborough. What influence then could any of the many particulars in the King's conversation have, towards regulating the mode of the murder?

* Hist. xviii. 350.   † Appendix, N° vi.

None

None at all, certainly. And the apology for this long rehearſal is as abſurd, as the rehearſal itſelf is unnatural.

(2) " Heir," Scotch, omitted in the Latin and French.

(3) Here the author has thrown a ſlight touch of remorſe into the character of Mary. This is more judicious, than any other part which I have yet obſerved of his management. And Milton, even in deſcribing the great author of wickedneſs in the univerſe, ſays ;

> Cruel his eye, but caſt
> Signs of remorſe and paſſion, to behold

the nature of his crime in its conſequences.

(4) Behold the gradation, in which the two tranſlations ſucceſſively " out-ſtep the modeſty" of the original. " Greitly," Scotch, is " maximé," Latin, and " infiniement," French. It ſhews the tendency, which all mankind have to exaggerate.

(5) This is very unnatural. Mary was the moment before under lively compunctions of remorſe. She is now laughing at her own cleverneſs of deceit. The tranſition is much too quick and ſudden for nature. She could not have paſſed from the one to the other at a ſtep. There muſt have been ſome intermediate ſteps between them. And the want of theſe ſhews the workmanſhip of a man, writing concerning a remorſe which he never felt, and therefore capable of paſſing from remorſe to triumph in an inſtant.

(6) " Him,"

(6) "Him," Scotch, omitted in Latin and French.

(7) That Mary was a professed dissembler, is what the rebels have repeatedly endeavoured to suggest. But nothing could be more opposite to her real character. A frank and open heart, like her's, can never practise dissimulation habitually. It is indeed the very game and quarry, at which dissimulation is ever shooting. And Mary was, throughout her whole life, a dupe to her own honesty, and a sufferer from the dissimulation of others. Accordingly Darnly himself, in one of his most excentric sallies of extravagance, in his conspiracy with Morton &c. for murdering Rizzio and usurping the crown, when " they said they " feared all was but craft and policy," on some proposals from the Queen after the murder, " the " King would not credit the same, and said, That " SHE WAS A TRUE PRINCESS, and HE WOULD SET " HIS LIFE FOR WHAT SHE PROMISED *."

" Betwix handis," Scotch; " interim," Latin; omitted in French. " It is not easy," says Mr. Goodall †, " to express in Latin the meaning of " the words *betwixt bands*. Buchanan's word *in-* " *terim* not only falls short, but makes his Latin " sentence stand, as it were, at variance with itself: " which the Frenchman observing, he omitted it " altogether." Buchanan should have translated

---

* Ruthven's own account of the murder, Keith, App. 128.
† i. 85.

the words by *fubinde*. This would have met the meaning compleatly. But it is of more confequence to remark, that the occurrence of fuch an idiom as this in the Scotch, which is indubitably Scotch in itfelf, and has even nothing parallel to it either in Latin or in French, is a ftrong proof for the originality of the Scotch. Proverbial modes of expreffion like this, are fome of the fureft figns of an original. They enter not into tranflations. They are only the effufions of a mind, not converfing with foreign idioms at the moment, but expatiating in its native language, and throwing out its ideas in the freedom of popular and colloquial diction. And we have another idiom of the fame nature hereafter *, which even Buchanan, though a Scotchman, underftood ftill lefs than this; both of them being merely forms of fpeech, appropriated to the familiarities of common life.

" He fchawit me almaift all (1) yat is in the name
" of the Bifchop and Sudderland (2), and zit I
" have never twichit ane word (3) of that ze
" fchawit me; but allanerly be force, flattering,
" and to pray him (4) to affure himfelf of me (5).
" And be pleinzeing on the Bifhop, I have drawin
" it all out of him: ze have hard the reft (6).

XVIII.—" We ar couplit with twa fals races;
" the devil finder us, and God knit us togidder for

* Sect. xxij.

" ever,

"ever, for the maift faithfull coupill that ever he
"unitit. This is my faith, I will die in it."

"Omnia (1) mihi aperuit fub nominibus Epifcopi
"et Sutherlandi (2), nec tamen adhuc collocuta
"fum, aut verbo attigi (3), quicquam eorum quæ tu
"mihi declarâfti; fed tantúm vi adulationum et
"precum (4) ago, ut a me fit fecurus (5): et con-
"querendo de Epifcopo, omnia de eo expifcata
"fum: cætera audifti (6).

XVIII.—"Nos fumus conjuncti cum duobus
"infidis hominum generibus: diabolus nos fejun-
"gat, ac nos conjungat Deus in perpetuum, ut
"fimus fidiffimum par quod unquam junctum eft.
"Hæc mea fides eft, in eâ volo mori."

"Il m'a tout (1) defcouvert foubs le nom de
"l'Evefque et de Sutherland (2); et toutesfois je
"ne luy ay encor parlé, ny dit un feul mot (3), de
"ce que vous m'avez declaré; ains feulement je le
"pourfuy par force de flateries et prieres (4), afin
"qu'il s'affeure de moy (5). Et me plaignant de
"l'Evefque, j'ay fceu toutes chofes de luy, et en-
"tendu le refte (6).

XVIII.—"Nous fommes conjoints avec deux
"efpeces d'hommes infideles; le diable nous
"vueille feparer, et que Dieu nous conjoingne a ja-
"mais, a ce que foyons deux perfonnes tres-fidele;
"fi jamais autres ont efté conjointes enfemble.
"Voila ma foy, et veux mourir en icelle."

(1) "Almaif

(1) "Almaift all," Scotch; "omnia," Latin; "tout," French.

(2) This alludes, I fuppofe, to fome quarrel between Robert Stewart, bifhop of Caithnefs, and uncle to the King, and the Earl of Sutherland, who married his fifter *. But we know nothing of the quarrel. Had any record conveyed us an account of it, I doubt not but we fhould have found fome falfe hint concerning it here, to have expofed the forgery.

(3) "Never twichit ane word," Scotch; "nec adhuc collocuta fum, aut verbo attigi," Latin; "ne ay encor parlé, ny dit un feul mot," French. The wordinefs and languor of the Latin and French is generally very obfervable, in comparifon with the Scotch.

(4) "Allanerly be force, flattering, and to pray him," Scotch, words that mean merely this, *only of neceffity, to flatter him, and to pray him*, have been ftrangely mifunderftood by the Latin, and have therefore been thus rendered by it, and its fhadow, the French, " vi adulationum et precum," and " par force de flateries et prieres." And the Mifcellaneous Remarker very gravely informs us thus: ' *Beforce, flattering*, this is very remarkable; the ' French were wont to ufe the word *force* as an ad-
' jective; hence, *par force flaterie* means by *much*
' flattering †." Even in this very inftance, the vord *force* is ufed, not as an adjective, but as a fub-ftantive.

* Keith, 205.   † P. 21.

ſtantive. So unfortunate is the author in his remarks! The French formerly ſaid " par force *de* " flaterie." This the French tranſlation of the preſent paſſage ſhews. They now ſay, " par force " flaterie," without the *de*. But the word *force* is equally a ſubſtantive in both, whatever the French dictionaries, and the Miſcellaneous Remarker may unite to ſay to the contrary. And, even if it was not, how can the words " beforce, flattering," run into " par force flaterie?" *Authors, before they write, ſhould*—think.

(5) How ſoon is the ſcene ſhifted here! This is not nature, but a play. This very evening " he " was ſa glaid to ſé her that he belevit to die for " glaidneſs." This very evening alſo, he has declared he has been " making his God of her, and " having na uther thocht bot of her." Yet he ſoon ſeems to believe, that " ſhe wald have ſend " him away preſonner." But he inſtantly recovers himſelf, and " wald rather give his lyfe or he did " ony diſpleſure to her." And yet, after all, ſhe is obliged to flatter him, and to pray him to be aſſured of her. " One of nature's journeymen" might give this repreſentation. Nature herſelf could not.

(6) " Ze have hard," Scotch; " audiſti," Latin; " et entendu," French, blunderingly.

XIX.—

XIX.—" Excuſe I wryte evill, ze may ges ye
" half of it (1) : bot I cannot mend it, becaus I
" am not weil at eis (2); and zit verray glaid to
" wryte unto zow quhen the reſt are ſleipand (3),
" ſen I cannot ſleip as they do, and as I wald
" deſyre, that is, in zour armes, my deir luſe,
" quhom I pray God to preſerve from all evill,
" and ſend zow repois (4) : I am gangand to ſeik
" myne till the morne, quhen I ſall end my Bybill
" (5);"

XIX.—" Excuſa quód malé pingam, dimidium
" te oportet divinare (1); ſed ego ei rei mederi
" non poſſum, non enim optimé valeo (2); et tamen
" magnâ fruor lætitiâ ſcribendo ad te cúm alii
" dormiant (3); quando ego dormire non poſſum,
" ut illi faciunt, nec ut ego vellem, hoc eſt, in tuo
" amplexu, mi care amice, a quo precor Deum ut
" omnia mala avertat, et quietem mittat (4). Ego
" eo ut meam quietem inveniam in craſtinum, ut
" tum mea Biblia (5) finiam;"

XIX.—" Excuſez moy que j'eſcry mal, il faudra
" que vous en deviniez la moytié (1) : mais je ne
" puis remedier a cela, car je ne ſuis pas a mon
" aiſe (2) ; et neantmoins j'ay une grand joye
" en vous eſcrivant pendant que les autres dor-
" ment (3), puis que de ma part je ne puis dormir
" comme eux, ny ainſi que je voudroye, c'eſt a dire,
" entre le bras de mon tres cher amy, du quel, je
" prie Dieu, qu'il vueille deſtourner tout mal, et
" luy donner bon ſucces (4) : je m'en vay pour
" trouver

" trouver mon repos jufques au lendemain, afin
" que je finiffe ici ma Bible (5);"

(1) This is artfully thrown in, to account for the badnefs of the writing, fo different from Mary's ufual penmanfhip. "Her hand-writing," fays Mr. Goodall, " was formed after what is commonly " called *italic print*, which it much refembled both " in beauty and regularity, and not to be eafily imi- " tated but by a fine writer *." It had not been well imitated, as is plain from this infinuation. And, that it had not, is confirmed by the fteady refufal of Elizabeth and her coadjutors in villainy, to let the originals be feen by Mary, or by Mary's commif- fioners.

(2) Why was fhe not well at eafe? From the adultery? But this had been long carried on, ac- cording to the rebels. From the projected mur- der? But this alfo, according to the rebels, had been projected before. This very diforder of the King's, fays Buchanan, proceeded from poifon com- municated to him by the Queen. Why then was fhe ill at eafe?

(3) This fhews the prefent part of the letter to be pretendedly written in the night, and late in the night, of January 24th.

(4) This wild mixture of religion with adultery and murder, carries a very ftrange and unnatural appearance with it. The human mind has been fometimes fo overborne by the fanaticifm of reli- gion or of liberty, as to reconcile itfelf to great

* i. 79.

enormities,

enormities, and to suppose assassination, regicide, and massacre, acceptable sacrifices at the shrine of God. But adultery is one of those crimes, which, in Christendom at least, have never been supposed to be even tolerated by religion. And yet Mary is most extravagantly represented, as plunged in adultery, even full of a projected murder, and still praying to God " to preserve" her partner in murder and adultery " from all evill, and send him " repois."—The Frenchman, mistaking the meaning of the Latin " quietem," translates it " bon " succes."

(5) This strange mistake, which began first from a false print or false writing in the Scotch, and has been copied without reflection by the Latin and French, was one, and the most famous one, of Mr. Goodall's decisive arguments against the originality of the French *. And it is hardly worth observing, that the Miscellaneous Remarker supposes the original word to have been *French*, in direct opposition to his own confession the very page before; which says, " Mr. Goodall has proved, beyond " possibility of cavil, that the first letter, as we " now have it, was translated into French from the " Latin copy †." Yet he supposes the word to have been *mon babil*, in colloquial English, *my chat* ; an expression, that would be as absurd in itself, as impertinent to the purpose. It is her husband's chat, not her's. *Babil* also then signified, as it still does, something worse than *chat*, imprudent or excessive

* i. 85—88. † P. 34—35.

talk;

talk; Mary herself saying in 5th letter, "il en a babillé," for *he has blabbed the secret*. And, as we now know the word for certain to have been originally a SCOTCH one, so we know the letter to be expresly denominated a BYLLE by the very manufacturers of it*.

"bot I am faschit that it stoppis me to write newis
"of myself unto zow, becaufe it is sa lang (1).
"Advertise me quhat ze have deliberat to do in the
"mater ze knaw upon this point (2), to ye end
"that we may understandis utheris weill, that na-
"thing thairthrow be spilt (3).

XX.—"I am irkit (4), and ganging to sleip
"(5); and zit I ceis not to scrible all this paper in
"sa mekle as restis thairof (6). Waryit mot this
"pokische man be (7), that causes me haif sa
"mekle pane, for without him I suld have an far
"plesander (8) subject to discourse upon."

"sed angor quód ea me a scribendo de me ipsâ ad
"te impediat, quia tam diu est (1). Fac me cer-
"tiorem, quid de re quam nosti decreveris (2), ut
"alter alterum intelligamus, ne quid ob id secus
"fiat (3).

XX.—" Ego nudata (4) sum, ac dormitum eo
"(5); nec tamen me continere possum, quó minús

* So in Buchanani Epistolæ, p. 10. Ruddiman, "sa lang
"ane lettre" is called immediately afterwards "this bill."

"(6) quod

" (6) quod reſtat chartæ deformiter conſcriberem.
" Malé ſit iſti variolato (7), qui me tot laboribus
" exercet; nam abſque eo eſſet ut materiam multo
" elegantiorem (8) ad diſſerendum haberem."

" mais je ſuis fachée que ce repos m'empeſche de
" vous eſcrire de mon fait, par ce qu'il dure tant (1).
" Faites moy ſçavoir ce que vous avez deliberé de
" faire touchant ce que ſcavez (2), afin que nous
" nous entendions l'un l'autre, et que rien ne ſe
" faſſe autrement (3).

XX.—" Je ſuis tout nuë (4), et m'en vay
" coucher (5); et neantmoins je ne me puis tenir
" que je ne barbouille encor bien mal, ce qui me
" reſte de papier (6). Maudit ſoit ſe [ce] tavolé
" (7), qui me donne tant travaux; car ſans lui
" j'avoye matiere plus belle (8) pour diſcourir."

(1) Mr. Goodall refers the words "it is ſa lang"
to the letter, and founds a criticiſm upon it againſt
the originality of the French *. But he is plainly
wrong in his reference. Mary is made to ſay, that
ſhe is going to ſeek her *repoſe*, but is vexed that *it*
keeps her from writing to Bothwell, becauſe *it* is
ſo long. This is in the true ſpirit of that *frantick
regard*, as it has been juſtly called, which the letter-
writer has attributed to her. The letter, not being
more than half-finiſhed, *could* not yet be pronounced long. And, if it could, it could not keep her
from writing news of herſelf. She was actually
writing news of herſelf, while ſhe was writing *it*.

* i. 87—88.

Accordingly,

Accordingly, the two tranflations are explicit in giving the words this meaning. Only, the Latin fays improperly " tam diu" for *tam diutina*.

(2) This we muft fuppofe to hint at the murder. But, as I have already afked, what was to be fettled by Bothwell? It had been determined to bring the King to Edinborough. The only queftion could be therefore, where he was to be lodged when he came thither. And this furely, upon every principle of common-fenfe, muft have been fettled before Mary fet out for Glafgow, or at leaft before Bothwell left her at Kalendar *the very morning of the preceding day*. Accordingly, Buchanan fays in his Detection, when he has fent the Queen to Glafgow, that " Bothwell, *as it was betwene thame befoir ac-*
" *cordit, provydis* ALL *thingis reddy that wer needful*
" *to accomplifche ye baynous act:* firft of all *ane*
" *bous,**" &c.—" Upon this point," Scotch, omitted in the Latin and French.

(3) " That we may underftandis utheris weill," Scotch, means the fame as in modern Englifh, *that we may underftand each other well.* " That nathing " thairthrow be fpilt," Scotch; " ne quid ob id fe-
" cus fiat," Latin; " que rien ne fe faffe autre-
" ment," French. Mr. Goodall has juftly remarked, that the French tranflator, not underftanding the peculiar import of the word " fecus" here, has rendered it by a word which does not convey its prefent meaning †.

* P. 18. Anderfon, ii. and Jebb, i. 242.   † i. 94.

(4) " Irkit,"

(4) " Irkit," Scotch, by some strange mis-writing or mis-print, was transformed into " nakit," and rendered "nudata" in Latin; then improved by an added stroke from the hand of the French translator, and heightened into that last extreme of blundering absurdity, " toute nuë." This therefore might well form one of those ever-memorable proofs, which Mr. Goodall brought against the pretended originality of the French, and with which he began the course that I am now compleating, I trust, of triumphant attacks upon it *.

(5) This goes on to shew, that the first part of the letter was written late in the night of January 24th.

(6) This also shews, that she is now to come soon to the end of the present day's writing. She has only a little paper remaining. And she only means to write over this little remainder. " Zit I " ceis not to scrible all this paper in sa mekle as " restis thairof," Scotch ; " nec tamen *me continere* " *possum, quò minùs quod restat chartæ* deformiter " conscriberem," Latin ; " neantmoins je ne *me* " *puis tenir que je ne* barbouille encor bien mal, " *ce qui me reste de papier*," French.

(7) " Waryit," Scotch, is a petty curse, not so strong as " maudit," French. " The day, the day," says Walter Kennedy, abbot of Corfraguel in 1558, " the terrible day sall cum," the day of judgment, " quhen the unhappy avaricious man sall *warry* the " tyme that evir he had," &c.; " the—prince sall

* i. 88—89.

" *warry* the tyme that evir he wes," &c.; "the mi-
" ſerable ignorant—fall *curs* the tyme that evir he
" tuke on hym*," &c.—" Pokiſche," Scotch;
" variolato," Latin; and, from the Frenchman's not
underſtanding a word which is only of the baſe or
colloquial Latinity, though ſo exactly the ſame with
one in his own language, rendered by him " ta-
" volé" or pock-marked, inſtead of *variolé*.

(8) Pleſander," Scotch; " elegantiorem," Latin;
" plus belle," French.

" He is not over mekle deformit, zit he has reſſa-
" vit verray mekle (1). He has almaiſt ſlane me
" with his braith; it is worſe than zour uncle's (2);
" and zit I cum na neirer unto him, bot in ane
" chyre at the bed-feit (3), and he being at the
" uther end thairof (4).

XXI.—" The meſſage (5) of the father in the
" gait.
" The purpoiſe of Schir James Hamiltoun.
" Of that the laird of Luſſe (6) ſchawit me of
" the delay."

" Non magnoperé deformatus eſt, multum (1)
" tamen accepit. Pené me ſuo enecavit anhelitu;
" eſt enim gravior quám tui propinqui (2); et
" tamen non accedo propiús ad eum, ſed in ca-
" thedrâ ſedeo ad pedes ejus (3), cúm ipſe in re-
" motiſſimâ lecti parte ſit (4).

* Keith, App. 203.

XXI.—

" XXI.—" Nuncius (5) patris in itinere.
" Sermo D. Jacobi Hamiltonii.
" De eo quod Luffæ comarchus (6) mihi re-
" tulit de dilatione."

" Il n'a pas efté beaucoup rendu diforme, toutesfois
" il en a pris beaucoup (1). Il m'a quafi tuée de
" fon halene, car elle eft plus fort que celle de
" voftre parent (2), et neantmoins je n'approche
" pas pres de luy; mais je m'affieds en une chaire
" a fes pieds (3), luy eftant en la partie du lict plus
" efloignée (4).

XXI.—" Du meffager (5) du pere fur le chemin.
" Du dire du fieur Jacques Hambleton.
" De ce que le prevoft de Luffe (6) m'a rap-
" porté touchant le retardement."

(1) " Verray mekle," Scotch; " multum," Latin; " beaucoup," French.

(2) " Uncle's," Scotch; " propinqui," Latin;
" parent," French. Bothwell's uncle here meant,
I fuppofe, was his great uncle, the bifhop of
Murray.

(3) " At the bed-feit," Scotch; " ad pedes ejus,"
Latin; " a fes pieds," French.

(4) I have already noticed this paffage, as a proof
that the letter-writer meant to intimate the King
was *poifoned* by Mary, though juft before it intimates that he was only *poxed*. And Dr. Robertfon, though his faith revolted at the former infinuation, though he did not believe the latter, though

no one could believe both, and though the infinuation of both fhewed evidently the forgery of the letter; yet continued, like a true confeffor to the caufe of party, to believe fteadily in its authenticity, and even to engraft it upon that very hiftory of his own, which was compelled to give it " the " lie direct."

(5) The French not underftanding " nuncius" to mean a " meffage," as well as a " meffenger," rendered it " meffager."

(6) " The laird of Luffe" before was " Luf-
" fius" and " Lufs." It is now " Luffæ comar-
" chus" and " le prevoft de Luffe." The French, without reflection, takes up the variation of the Latin at the moment.

" Of the demandis that he afkit at Joachim.
" Of my eftait (1).
" Of my company.
" Of the occafioun of my cumming.
" And (2) of Jofeph.
" Item, the purpois that he and I had togidder.
" Of the defyre that he has to ples me, and of
" his repentance.
" Of the interpretatioun of his letter."

" De quibus interrogavit Joachimum.
" De ordinatione familiæ (1).
" De meo comitatu.
" De caufâ mei adventûs.

" (2) De

" (2) De Josepho.

" Item, de sermone inter me et illum.

" De ejus voluntate placendi mihi, et de ejus " pœnitentiâ.

" De interpretatione suarum literarum."

" De ce qu'il s'est enquis a Joachim.

" De reglement de la famille (1).

" De ma suite.

" De la cause de mon arrivée.

" (2) De Joseph.

" Item, du devis d'entre moy et luy.

" De la volonté qu'il a de me complaire, et de " sa repentance.

" De l'interpretation des ses lettres."

(1) This gives us another proof of what I have observed just before, the ready obsequiousness of the French to the Latin at every turn. " Gif I had " maid my estait," Scotch, is in the place alluded to rendered, " an familiæ catalogum fecissem," and " si j'avoye faict quelque rolle de mes domes- " tiques." But now, when the Latin fantastically varies what is not varied in his original, the one becomes " de ordinatione familiæ," and the other " du reglement de la famille."

(2) " And," Scotch, omitted in the Latin and French.

" Of Willie Hiegait's matter (1), of his depart-
" ing.
" Of Monfiure de Levingftoun (2)."

" De negotio Gulielmi Hiegait (1), et de fuo dif-
" ceffu.
" De domino de Levifton (2)."

" Du fait de Guillaume Hiegait (1), et de fon
" depart.
" Du fieur de Levingftoun (2)."

(1) Here we have " confufion worfe confound-
" ed." We have feen before Walcar's intelligence attributed to Hiegait, but ftrengthened and improved by Mynto's; then re-attributed to Walcar; and Mynto's finally given to Hiegait. And now we fee Mynto's, Walcar's, and Hiegait's own, all ultimately and collectively affigned to Hiegait.— " Et" is added in the Latin and the French.

(2) Here, as I fhall afterwards fhew, ends the former half of the letter, that which pretends to have been written in the night of January 24.

But what do thefe fhort notices mean, that come fo ftrangely in the middle of the letter? Dr. Robertfon fuppofes them to be the *contents* of the *preceding* part of the letter, fet down originally as loofe *memorandums*, and then coming into the letter, becaufe Mary, for want of other paper, took that
of

of the *memorandums* to write upon *. This is too ridiculous in itself, to have been ever supposed by a candid and reflecting examiner of the point. The notices are *not* the contents of the preceding part of the letter. The *last* refers only to the *second* part. And the appearance of the letter here is too regular and compleat, to admit of such a casual and fortuitous advance of the notices. We might as well believe a dance of atoms to have settled into the creation of the world. Yet Mr. Hume improved the absurdity. He said, that these notices were " a memorandum of what Mary *intended to* " *add the next morning*, and *it is added* accordingly:" when all the notices referred to in the writing of the next morning, are only *one*, and the other *fourteen* relate wholly to the *prior* part of the letter. And Mr. Tytler attacked him so vigorously upon his hardy and false assertion, that he became ashamed of it, and silently withdrew it in a new edition †. Mr. Tytler indeed shewed decisively, against him and Dr. Robertson, that these were points on which Mary is made to refer Bothwell to the *bearer* for further or new information, for further in the first fourteen, and for new in the last of all; that others occur of the very same nature, at the end of the other half of the letter; and that these are expressly understood from the makers of the letters themselves, when they produced them at York, to be " the credit gifin to the berar ‡." This mode of referring to the credit of a bearer, was no uncommon one in those times. And we find Mary ac-

---

* Diss. 28. † Hist. v. 147. ‡ Tytler, 111—116.

tually

tually doing so in a letter to Lord Huntly; when " referring the rest to the beirar, quhom ze will " credit," she commits him to God*.

But, as the King's reported conversation ends here, let us examine one point of moment concerning it. Thomas Crawford, the gentleman from the Earl of Lenox who met Mary four miles from Glasgow, was produced by the rebels in England, to authenticate upon oath what the Queen said to him at the meeting, and also *what the King said to her afterwards.* " One Thomas Crawford said," as the commissioners at Westminster tell us, " that " as soon as the *Quene of Scotts had spoken with the* " *King, his master, at Glasgow*, from tyme to tyme " he the said Crawford was secretly informed by " the King of *all things which had passed betwixt the* " *said Quene and the King*, to the intent he shuld " report the same to the Erle of Lenox his master," both the King and the King's father, it seems, being his master; " and that he did immediately, at the " same tyme, *write the same word by word*, as near " as he possibly could carry the same away." This is surely as poor an expedient for communicating the King's and Queen's discourse to Crawford, as ever a distressed novel-writer was reduced to for conveying intelligence to his reader. " And sure " he was, that the words now reported in his writ-" ing, concerning the communion betwixt the " Quene of Scots and him upon the way near Glas-" gow, are the very same words, in his conscience,

* Goodall, ii. 316. See also Keith, 219, &c. and Sir Ralph Sadler's Letters, 118, &c.

" that

" that were spoken; and that others being reported
" to him by the King, are the same in effect and
" substance as they were delivered by the King to
" him, tho' not percase in all parts the very words
" themselves *." Here it is very observable, what
a mockery is played off upon the reader. Crawford's
deposition was intended to substantiate this conversation, and so derive a credit upon this and all the
letters. Yet the conversation might be true, and
the letters be false. This very man might have
received an account of the conversation in the
manner insinuated, and have communicated it again
to the rebels. But the intention of the rebels was
frustrated by the modesty of the swearer.

He does not swear, as they originally meant he
should, as they still hoped all would believe he had
sworn, and as all have actually to this day believed
he did swear, that the words stated in the letter, for
the Queen's address to him and the King's address
to her, were respectively such in expression or in
substance, as the Queen spoke and the King reported to him. No! he *seems* to do this, but he
does *not*. He swears concerning the Queen's address, that " the words NOW REPORTED IN HIS
WRYTING—are the very same words—that were
spoken." He swears also concerning the King's
address, that " others being *reported to him by the
King*, are the same in effect and substance, as
they were *delivered by the King to him* ;" not,
that the words reported to him by the King are the
same in effect with—the words reported to him by

* Goodall, ii. 246.

the

the King, as the meaning seems at first to be; but that the words SET DOWN IN HIS WRITING as "re-"ported to him by the King," are the same in effect with what were really reported. His oath concerning the Queen's address explains that concerning the King's. In both, " less is meant than " meets the ear." He swears not of either, that the words STATED IN THE LETTER are the same that were spoken and reported; but that the words STATED IN HIS WRITING are. Accordingly " the " same Thomas Crawford coming before the com- " missioners, he did present a WRITING, *which* he " said he had caused to be made according to the " truth of his knowledge; *which*, being read, he " affirmed upon his corporal oath there taken *to be* " *true*, the tenor wherof hereafter followeth, *The* " *words betwixt the Queen*," &c. That this writing contained equally the words betwixt the Queen and him, and betwixt the Queen and the King, is plain from the succeeding account given by the commissioners: " And after this [writing] was " read, the said Crawford said, that as soon as the " Quene of Scotts had spoken with the King his " master at Glasgow," &c. as before. It is then subjoined again by the commissioners, that " the " confession of the said Thomas Crawford in wryt- " ing hereafter followeth thus, *The words betwixt* " *the Queen and me*," &c. The reported conversation of the King and Queen, therefore, was equally in the writing with the very address of the Queen to Crawford. It is *this writing*, and the conversation in *it*, which he swears to be true. He swears to the truth of nothing positively in the letter; as he has hitherto been presumed to do, both by the friends and by the enemies of Mary. And as the original of this writing has been lost, and no copy of it has been preserved, we know not what it was that he swore to be true.

That he did not swear *all* to be so, is obvious from the singular management of his oath. Had he done this, he would barely have sworn, as he has for that reason been falsely supposed to have sworn, that the words *stated in the letter* were the same as spoken and reported. But he did not chuse this. He selected some parts of the address, and some parts of the conversation. To the truth of *these* he swore, with the evident disparagement of the rest. This partial and exceptive kind of testimony, indeed, threw a brand of censure upon all the rejected passages. It indirectly convicted them of forgery. Several such, carrying plain marks of forgery on their forehead, I have pointed out before. And the oath of Crawford shews clearly, that there were such in the letter. So different does the testimony of Crawford turn out to be, from what it has been uniformly considered to be; and even from what I considered it myself, before the present occasion induced me to examine it! It shews some incidents to be true in the letters, but IT PROVES OTHERS TO BE FALSE. And it thus DESTROYS THE AUTHENTICITY OF THE WHOLE AT ONCE, even in the very act of supporting it.

CHAPTER

CHAPTER THE SECOND.

§ I.

LETTER THE FIRST CONTINUED.

XXII.—" I had almaist forzet, that Monſiure
" de Levingſtoun (1) ſaid to me in the Lady Reres
" eir at ſupper, that he (2) wald drink to ye folk yat
" I (2) wiſt of, gif I wald pledge thame (3). And
" efter ſupper he ſaid to me, quhen I was lenand
" upon him warming me at the fyre, Ze have fair
" [ſair] going to ſé ſeik folk (4), zit ze cannot be
" ſa welcom to thame as ze left ſum body this day
" (5) in regrait, that will never be blyth quhill
" he ſé zow agane (6). I aſkit at him quha that
" was. With that he thriſtit my body (7), and ſaid,
" that ſum of his folkis had ſene zow in faſcherie
" (8); ze may ges at the reſt (9)."

XXII.—" Pené oblita eram, quód Dominus
" Leviſtonius (1) D. Rereſiæ dixit in aurem, dum
" cœnaret, quód præ-biberet (2) eis quos nôſſem
" (2), eâ lege ut ego re-biberem eorum nomine (3).
" Ac poſt cœnam dixit mihi, dum ad ignem calc-
" fiebam cúm ei inniterer, Bella, inquit, hujus-
" modi

" modi hominum visitatio (4); non tamen tanta
" e tuo accessu potest eis esse lætitia, quanta in
" molestiâ quidam hodie (5) relictus est, qui nun-
" quam lætus erit, donec te iterum videbit (6).
" Ego de eo quæsivi quisnam is esset. Ille arc-
" tiùs corpus meum comprimens (7), respondit,
" Unus eorum qui te reliquerunt (8); tu quis sit
" divinare potes (9)."

XXII.—" Peu s'en faut que je n'aye oublié,
" comme le Sieur de Levinstoun (1) a dit a l'o-
" reille en soupant a Madamoiselle Reres, qu'elle
" (2) beut a ceux qu'elle (2) cognoissoit, soubs con-
" dition que le pleigeroye en leur nom (3). Et
" apres souper il me dit, comme je me chauffoye
" aupres du feu, estant appuyée sur son espaule,
" Voyla une belle visitation de telles gens (4);
" mais toutesfois la joye de nostre venue ne leur
" peut estre si grande, combien est la facherie a
" celuy qui a esté delaissé seul aujourdhuy (5), et
" qui ne sera jamais joyeux, jusques a ce qu'il vous
" ayt veüe. Derechef (6) je luy demanday, qui
" estoit cestuy-la: lui m'embrassant plus estroite-
" ment (7), me respondit, C'est l'un de ceux qui
" vous ont laissée (8); vous pouvez deviner qui
" est cestuy-la (9)."

(1) "Levingstoun," Scotch; "de Leviston" before, and "Levistonius" now, Latin; "de Le-
" vingstoun" before, and "de Levinstoun" now, French. From this and other instances before and after, I suspect the French translator to have had a

Scotch,

Scotch, as well as a French, copy before him; to have kept his eye almost entirely upon the Latin; but to have turned his eye to the Scotch at times, as to proper names particularly, and to have caught some of his words from it.—But why is Lord Levingston called " Monsiure" here? He is called " my Lord Levistoun" in the rebel journal. And he was at times denominated *Monsieur*, I suppose, from some affectation of French manners in him.

(2) " He" and " I," Scotch; " præ-biberet" and " nôssem," Latin; " elle" and " elle," by some negligence, French. Lady Reres was " ane of " the cheif of the Quenis privie chalmer," says Buchanan *. She appears to have always attended the Queen.

(3) This *seems* to *prove* my suspicion above. The French has united a part of the Latin and a part of the Scotch together. " Pledge thame," Scotch, is in Latin " re-biberem eorum nomine," and in French " pleigeroye," a word (I suppose) purely English and Scotch in this sense of it, " en " leur nom," an expression purely Latin. And I shall endeavour to account for this hereafter.

(4) This also is one of the memorable passages, that led Mr. Goodall, amidst the darkness of the times in which he lived, to the discovery of the true original. The Latin, as he observes, " did " read two words wrong in this short sentence, " namely

---

* Detection, 8.

" namely, "' fair'" for "'*fair*'" or *fore*, and for
"' feik,'" fick, as it is in the edition of St. Andrew's
" in Scotland,—"' *fik*,'" *fuch*, with the firſt edition
" publiſhed in England [and in Engliſh]. "' Ye
"' have fair going to fee fick folk,'" is a mean kind
" of phrafe, uſed among people of the loweſt rank.
" It ought to have been tranſlated in this or the
" like manner, *Iter facis ægrè, ægros viſendi gratiâ*.
" —But Mr. Buchanan's miſtakes ſpoil the ſen-
" tence very confiderably, "' Bella hujuſmodi ho-
"' minum vifitatio;'" and the Frenchman could
" not mend the matter, it behoved him to follow
" his leader, "' Voyla une belle vifitation de telles
"' gens.'" I know not what others may think of
" this affair, but for my own part I would reckon,
" that this ſmall ſentence, maturely weighed, may
" be ſufficient to prove, againſt ten thouſand oaths,
" and as many acts of parliament, that theſe letters
" were originally written in the Scottiſh language*."
Such was the honeſt confidence of acuteneſs, in this
new track of diſcovery. And every generous reader
will be happy to reflect, that ſuch acuteneſs and
ſuch confidence were rightly employed; and that
fact has now come in to the aid of reaſoning, to
prove the originality of the Scotch.

But let me obſerve, in addition to this, that the appearance of ſuch a form of expreſſion in the letters betrays their ſpurioufneſs. It " is a *mean* kind of phrafe,
" uſed among people of the *loweſt* rank.". It was
equally ſo, no doubt, in the days of Mary. The
lapſe of two hundred years could not have degraded

* i. 82—83.

the language of kings and queens, into the diction of meanness, and the idioms of the lowest ranks in life. Accordingly, we see Buchanan not understanding it. It was confined to the familiarities of vulgar conversation. It was therefore not recollected by him. And it ought therefore not to have appeared in a letter attributed to Mary.

This remark, of itself, shews that Buchanan was not, as he has always been hitherto considered to be, the *actual fabricator* of the letters. Had he been, he could not have mistaken their meaning. He must have known *his own* intent in writing every part of them. He must have known particularly the drift of this proverbial form of speech, if it had come in the stream of composition to his pen, and mingled naturally with his language. And I have previously shewn Lethington, and not Buchanan, to have forged the letters.

(5) This shews Lord Levingston's speech to be made on the evening of Mary's arrival at Glasgow, on the evening of January the 23d.

(6) The printer of the French has absurdly thrown "derechef" into a new sentence.

(7) This passage was wrongly expressed by the Latin, and, in consequence of that, more wrongly paraphrased by the French. "He thriftit my body," means he gave her a secret hint with a touch of his elbow, that he had a peculiar and mysterious drift in what he said. This kind of corporal intimation is called *nudging*, in some of our northern counties. It should therefore have

been

been rendered in Latin, *ille cubitum corpori meo leniter admovit* et, &c. Yet the Latin renders it, " ille *arctiùs* corpus meum *comprimens*." And the French rises upon it with an addition of absurdity, " m'embraſſant plus eſtroitement." In this manner, and by a ſcale of miſtakes, is a mere touch of the elbow magnified into a ſtrict compreſſion, and then heightened into a more ſtrict embrace!

(8) " Sum of his folkis had ſene zow in faſche-" rie," Scotch, moſt *freely* tranſlated into " unus " eorum qui te reliquerunt," Latin, and implicitly followed in French, " c'eſt l'un de ceux qui vous " ont laiſſée." Indeed I ſuſpect, from the turn of the clauſe, and from a couple of inſtances which we have ſeen before, that originally the Scotch was as the Latin now repreſents it, that it was ſo at the York conference, and that it was altered into its preſent form for the conference at Weſtminſter. The ſenſe of the Latin is too devious from the Scotch, and yet too adheſive to the context, to be the caſual daſh of a blundering hand. And as we have already ſeen a clauſe certainly, and a ſentence probably, not in this very letter at York, and yet in it at Weſtminſter; ſo we ſhall hereafter ſee a variation, in the very words of the Weſtminſter and York originals of it.

(9) " Ze may ges at the reſt," Scotch; " tu quis " ſit divinare potes," Latin; " vous pouvez de-" viner qui eſt ceſtuy-la," French. This alſo ſerves to ſtrengthen my ſuſpicion. The ſenſe is ſtill carried on as regularly in the Latin, as it is in the Scotch; though in a very different manner.

But in this anecdote concerning Lord Levingston, as in almost every other fact alluded to in the letters, we find a proof of the forgery. Here we particularly trace the feet of the forger, in the dirt of his own steps. That Lord Levingston should know of the adultery, if there had been any; that he should know it so well, as to speak of it; that he should speak of it to one of Mary's attendants, to her confidante and intimate; that he should speak of it to her at supper, when numbers must have been present; and that he should at last speak of it to Mary herself, to Mary *leaning on his shoulder*, to Mary in a circle of guests standing around the fire; carries such a monstrous incredibility with it, that none but one of Condé's cocknies, and he a sworn foe to Mary, can believe it.

Nor is there any reason for believing Lord Levingston to have attended her from Kalendar to Glasgow. There are some strong reasons for believing the very contrary. That the Queen was escorted by a party of the Hamiltons, is insinuated in a passage before; in which Lenox sends word to Sir James Hamilton, "that he [Lenox] wald never " have beleyit that he [Sir James] wald have ac- " companyit him [Sir James] with the Hammil- " tounis," and in which Sir James answers, " yat " he wald nouther accompany Stewart nor Hammil- " toun, bot be Mary's commandement." But it is positively asserted hereafter; Mary saying, " all " the Hammiltounis ar heir, that accompanyis me " verray honorabilly." Buchanan also confirms this in his Detection, when he says of the Queen, that " to Glasgow scho gais, accompanyit with the
" Hammiltounis,

"Hammiltounis, and uther the Kingis naturall ene-
"meis," Bothwell and Huntly, who attended her
to Kalendar *. She was therefore escorted by the
Hamiltons, and not by the Levingstons, to Glasgow. And as in the other expedition to Stirling,
when Lord Levingston is equally represented to
have attended the Queen, she says, " we had zister-
" day mair then III. c. hors of his" Huntly's, " and
" Levingstoun's †;" so in this she says, what appears
the more striking from the contrast, " all the Ha-
" miltounis ar heir, that accompanyis me verray
" honorabilly;" and then adds, what *doubly* excludes the idea of any others being with her at the
time, " all the freindis of the uther," the Stewarts,
" convoyis me quhen I gang to sé him," the King.
Lord Levingston therefore *could* not have said what
he is here represented to have said, after supper on
the evening of the arrival at Glasgow.

XXIII.—" I wrocht this day (1), quhill it was
" twa houris (2), upon this bracelet (3), for to put
" the key of it within the lock thairof, quhilk is
" couplit underneth with twa cordounis (4). I
" have had sa lytill time that it is evill maid; bot I
" sall mak ane fairer (5). In the meane tyme (6)
" tak heid that nane that is heir sé it, for all the

* Anderson, ii. 17. Jebb, i. 242. and Appendix, N° x.
† Letter vii. 2.

" warld

" warld will knaw it, becaus for haift it was maid
" in yair prefence (7)."

XXIII.—" Ego hodie (1) elaboravi ufque ad
" horam fecundam (2) in hâc armillâ (3), ut
" clavem includerem, quæ fubtus eft annexa duo-
" bus funiculis (4); malé autem facta eft ob tem-
" poris anguftiam, fed faciam pulchriorem (5).
" Interim (6) profpice, ne quifquam eorum qui hîc
" funt videat, quia omnes mortales eum agnofcent,
" tantâ feftinatione in omnium oculis facta eft (7)."

XXIII.—" J'ay aujourdhuy (1) travaillé a deux
" heures (2) en ce braffelet (3), pour y enfermer la
" clef, qui eft jointe au bas avec deux petites
" cordes (4). Il eft mal fait, a caufe du peu de
" temps qu'on a eu; mais j'en feray un plus beau
" (5). Cependant (6) advifez que perfonne de
" ceux qui font icy ne le voye, car tout le monde
" le cognoift, tant il a efté fait a la hafte devant
" les yeux de chacun (7)."

(1) This is the fecond day of writing, as will appear from a note hereafter; the day but one after the arrival at Glafgow; January 25th.

(2) " Quhill it was twa houris," Scotch, till two o'clock; as Mary is faid in the rebel journal to have gone with Bothwell " to Baftian's banquet " and mafque about eleven houris, and thairefter " thay baith returnit to the abbay, and talkit quhill " twelve houris and eftir *." Accordingly the Latin fays, " ad horam fecundam." And the

* Appendix, N° x.

French,

French, coinciding exactly in idiom with the Scotch, says, " a deux heures." But let us observe the conduct of Mary here. She had come to Glasgow, on a visit to the King in a great illness. The King is still very ill. He keeps his bed. Yet what does Mary do on this visit? She sees him immediately on her arrival. She goes away to supper. She returns to him. She sits with him for some time. She excuses herself for sitting longer, because of her weariness. She sees him the next morning. But, for the rest of the day, we know not what she does. We only know, that she has very little conversation with him; that, in the evening or night of this day, she writes a long account of what the King said the night before; and that only a hint occurs, of what the King had said on this day. So greatly does she neglect him for the second day, the day after her arrival! But on the third this neglect is consummated, by what is said here, her working till two o'clock in the afternoon upon a bracelet; and by what is said hereafter, " I saw him not this evening for to end " zour bracelet." And this forms one more of the wild incredibilities, that mark the letters. Had Mary come from a *pretended* regard, as I have remarked before, she *would* not have done so; and, as she came from a *real*, she *could* not.

(3) " *This* bracelet" implies it to have been sent with the letter to Bothwell. Accordingly she bids him immediately afterward " tak heid, that " nane that is heir se it." Yet she soon afterwards says thus to him, " advertise me gif ze will
" have

" have it." Such are the contradictions, in which the letter-writer involves himself! And the second pretended confession of Paris confirms the contradiction, by declaring that he did not carry the bracelets till some time afterwards *.

(4) That *men* wore bracelets so late as this period, was unknown to me, but is plain from the letter. These were not fastened together, as they now are, by a snap-lock. They had a formal key to the lock.

(5) " I sall mak ane fairer," Scotch, implying that she would make *another*; " j'en feray un plus " beau," French, implying that she would make *it* fairer; because the Latin is ambiguous, " fa- " ciam pulchriorem."

(6) " In the meane tyme," Scotch, by a wrong punctuation was thrown into the preceding sentence; when it plainly belongs, and is given by the Latin and the French, to this. I have therefore placed it right.

(7) This is another of those contradictions, in which the unsettled ideas of a forger are continually involving him, and by which he betrays himself continually. Lord Levingston is just before represented as knowing of the adultery, as hinting it to one of Mary's confidantes at supper, and as even insinuating it plainly to Mary herself in the midst of company. Nor is Mary alarmed at his knowledge, at his hint, or at his insinuation. Yet

* Goodall, ii. 79.

now she is afraid, lest any of her present attendants should see a pair of bracelets, which she was sending to Bothwell. She seems to *enjoy* a real detection of the adultery by Levingston, and even an intimation given of it in the presence of many attendants, and even a whispered annunciation of it to herself before many persons who were close to her. And yet *now* she is apprehensive of any suspicions of it in any of her train, from the sight of one of her presents. Thus the sturdy oak, that feared no blasts of winter, in an instant is turned into a sensitive plant, and shrinks up at the approach of a finger!

XXIV.—" I am now passand to my fascheous
" purpois. Ze gar me dissemble sa far, that I (1)
" haif horring thairat; and ye caus me do almaist
" (2) the office of a traitores. Remember how,
" gif it wer not to obey zow (3), I had rather be
' deid or I did it (3); my hart (4) bleides at it
' (3). Summa, he will not cum with me, except
' upon conditioun that I will promeis to him, that
' I sall be at bed and buird with him as of befoir,
' and that I sall leave him (5) na ofter (6); and
' doing this upon my word (7), he will do all
' thingis that I pleis, and cum with me. Bot he
' hes prayit me to remane upon him quhil uther
' morne (8)."

XXIV.—"Nunc proficiscor ad institutum meum
"odiosum. Tu me adeó dissimulare cogis, ut
"etiam ipsa (1) horream; ac tantúm non (2) pro-
"ditricis partes me agere cogis. Illud reminiscere,
"quód nisi tibi obsequendi desiderium me cogeret
"(3), mallem mori quám hæc (3) committere;
"cor enim mihi ad hæc (3) sanguinem fundit (4).
"Breviter, negat se mecum venturum, nisi eâ lege,
"ut ei pollicear me communi cum eo mensâ et
"thoro usuram velut antea, ac ne sæpiús eum de-
"relinquam (5). Hoc si faciam (7), quicquid
"velim faciet, ac me comitabitur; sed me rogavit,
"ut se exspectarem in diem perendinum (8)."

XXIV.—"Maintenant je vien a ma deliberation
"odieuse. Vous me contraignez de tellement dis-
"simuler, que j' (1) en ay horreur, veu que vous
"me forcez de ne joüer pas seulement (2) le per-
"sonnage d'une trahistresse. Qu'il vous souvienne,
"que si l'affection de vous plaire ne me forcoit (3),
"j'aymeroye mieux mourir que de commettre ces
"choses (3); car le cœur me seigne (4) en icelles
"(3). Bref, il ne veut venir avec moy, sinon
"soubs ceste condition, que je luy promette d'user
"en commun d'une seule table, et d'une mesme
"lict, comme auparavant; et que je ne l'aban-
"donne (5) si souvent (6): et que, si je le fay
"ainsi (7), il fera tout ce que je voudray, et me
"suivra. Mais il m'a prié, que je l'attendisse encor
"deux jours (8)."

(1) "I," Scotch; "etiam ipsa," Latin; "je,"
French, from the corrected Latin.

(2) "And

(2) "And—almaift," Scotch; "ac tantúm non," Latin; and, from the ignorance of the Frenchman concerning the peculiar import of *tantûm non*, " veu " que vous me forcez de *ne* joüer pas *feulement*," French.

(3) " Gif it wer not to obey zow," Scotch; "nifi " tibi obfequendi defiderium me cogeret," Latin; " fi l'affection de vous plaire ne me forcoit," French. " It, it," Scotch; " hæc, hæc," Latin; " ces chofes, icelles," French.

(4) This is the fecond fit of remorfe. It is alfo a ftrong one. But it is gone almoft as foon as the other. It ends fuddenly, like that. And, like that, it fuddenly paffes off into a profecution of the very bufinefs, which is the fubject of the remorfe. Both remind one of the repentance of Falftaff, who declares that he will not be damned for ever a King's fon in Chriftendom, and then, the very next minute, goes " from praying to purfe- " taking."

(5) Whofe fault was it, that the King and Queen were not at bed and board before? The Queen's, fays the letter. *She* had left *him*. Thus does the forger contrive to tell us of his own impofture, by the force which he puts upon facts. And let us take the figns, which he has fo kindly been pleafed to give us, and add one more proof of the forgery to the many which we have feen already.

The King and Queen were at Stirling together, about the end of September before. Their conduct in parting there, let the French embaffadour, and the
privy

privy council of Scotland, tell us together. "On "the 22d of the last month," says the former in a letter of October 15th, "your brother—arrived "at Stirling,—where he found this Queen in good "health.—The Queen is now returned from Stir- "ling to Lisleburgh," Edinborough, "as being "vacation-season, which, as you know, continues "in this country from August until Martin-mas, "and during which the nobility are convened to "look after the public affairs of the Queen and her "realm. *The King however abode still at Stirling.*" "About ten or twelve days ago," says the council in a letter of October the 8th to the Queen Dowa- ger of France, "the Queen at our request came to "this towne of Lisleburgh," Edinborough, "to "give her orders about some affairs of state, which "without her personal presence could not be got "dispatched. *Her Majesty was desirous the King* "*should have come along with her;* but *because he* "*liked to remain at Stirling, and wait her return* "*thither,* she left him there, *with intention to go* "*towards him again* in five or six days." Yet IT WAS HER FAULT, says the letter-writer, that they were not at bed and board together. But *why* did the King "like to remain at Stirling," when the Queen was obliged to go to Edinborough upon public business? The embassadour and the council shall again tell us. "The King, however, abode "still at Stirling; and *he told me there, that he had* "*a mind to go beyond sea,* in a sort of desperation." Yet IT WAS MARY, says the letter-writer, that was

frequently

frequently or continually leaving *him.* " I said to
" him," adds the embassadour, " what I thought
" proper at the time, but still I could not believe
" that he was in earnest. Since that time, the Earl
" of Lenox, his father, came to visit him [at Stir-
" ling]; and he has written a letter to the Queen,
" signifying that *it is not in his power to divert his
" son from his intended voyage,* and prays *her Majesty
" to use her interest therein.*" " Meantime, while the
" Queen was absent," say the council, " the Earl
" of Lenox, his father, came to visit him at Stir-
" ling; and having remained with him two or three
" days, he went his way again to Glasgow.—From
" Glasgow my Lord Lenox wrote to the Queen,
" and acquainted her Majesty, that altho' *formerly,*
" both by *letters* and *messages,* and *now* also by *com-
" munication* with his son, he *had endeavoured to divert
" him from an enterprize he had in view,* he never-
" theless *had not the interest* to make him alter his
" mind. This project, he tells the Queen, was to
" *retire out of the kingdom beyond sea* ; and that *for
" this purpose he had just then a ship lying ready.*"
YET THE KING WOULD GLADLY HAVE LIVED WITH
THE QUEEN, the letter insinuates, if she would have
permitted him. " This letter from the Earl of
" Lenox the Queen received on Michaelmas-day
" in the morning; and that same evening the King
" arrived here [at Edinborough] about ten of the
" clock. When he and the Queen were a-bed to-
" gether, her Majesty took occasion to talk to him
" about the contents of his father's letter, and *be-*
" *sought*

"sought him to *declare to her* the *ground* of his
"*designed voyage*; but in this he would *by no means*
"satisfy her." "The Earl of Lenox's letter came
"to the Queen's hand on St. Michael's day; and
"her Majesty was pleased to impart the same in-
"continent to the lords of her council, in order
"to receive advice thereupon. And if her Majesty
"was *surprized* by this advertisement from the
"Earl of Lenox, these lords were no less *astonished*
"to understand, that the King should entertain any
"thought *of departing after so strange a manner out*
"*of her presence*, nor was it *possible* for them to
"form a *conjecture* from whence such an imagina-
"tion could take its rise.—The same evening the
"King came to Edinburgh, and then her Majesty
"entered calmly with him upon the subject *of his*
"*going abroad*, that she might understand from
"himself the *occasion* of *such a resolution*. But he
"would *by no means* give, or acknowledge that he
"had, any *occasion* offered him of *discontent*." Yet
it WAS THE QUEEN that would not permit him to
live with her. "Early the next morning the
"Queen sent for me, and for all the lords and
"other counsellors:—and the Queen *prayed* the
"King to *declare*, in presence of the lords, and be-
"fore me, the *reason* of his *projected departure*,
"since he would not be pleased to notify the
"same to her in private betwixt themselves. She
"likewise *took him by the hand*, and *besought him*
"*for God's sake* to *declare*, if *she* had given him
"any *occasion* for *this resolution*; and *entreated* he
 "might

" might *deal plainly*, and *not spare her*.—I likewise
" took the freedom to tell him, that his departure
" must certainly affect either *his own* or the *Queen's*
" honour; that if the Queen had afforded any
" ground for it, his declaring the same would affect
" her Majesty; as, on the other hand, if he should
" go away without giving any cause for it, this
" thing could not at all redound to his praise.—The
" King at last declared, the HE HAD NO GROUND
" AT ALL GIVEN HIM for such a deliberation."
" The lords of council being acquainted *early* next
" morning, that the King was *just a going* to re-
" turn to Stirling, they repaired to the Queen's
" apartment,—to understand from the King, whe-
" ther, according to advice imparted to the Queen
" by the Earl of Lenox, he had formed a resolu-
" tion to depart by sea out of the realme, and upon
" what ground, and for what end.—And here we
" did remonstrate to him, that his own honour, the
" Queen's honour, the honour of us all, were con-
" cerned.—And for her Majesty, so far was she
" from ministring to him occasion of discontent,
" that on the contrary *he had all the reason in the*
" *world to thank G O D for giving him so wise*
" *and virtuous a person, as she had shewed herself in*
" *all her actions*. Then her Majesty was pleased
" to enter into the discourse, and *spoke affectionately*
" *to him*, beseeching him, that seeing he would not
" open his mind in private to her the last night,
" *according to her most earnest request*, he would at
" least be pleased to declare before these lords,
" where she had offended him in any thing. But

VOL. II. M " though

"though the Queen, and all others that were pre-
"sent, together with Monf. du Croc, used all the
"intereſt they were able, to perſwade him to open
"his mind; yet he would not at all *own*, that he
"intended any voyage or had any difcontent; and
"declared *freely*, that the QUEEN HAD GIVEN
"HIM NO OCCASION FOR ANY." Yet he per-
ſiſted in it. Such was the ſpirit and underſtanding of this wayward child of fortune! He compleatly exculpated the Queen. But the letter-
writer will not take even *his* word in her favour.
He will be like his hero Darnly. He will perſiſt
when " he has no ground at all given him for
" fuch a deliberation." And Mary ſhall be condemned for not ſuffering Darnly to live with her,
even though Darnly himſelf ſays that he is refolved
to go abroad, though he tells it to Le Croc,
though he tells it to Lenox, and though he owns
before all the council he has no reafon for ſuch a
refolution.

But let us attend the farther account of this
extraordinary man. " Whereupon," adds the
council, " he took leave of her Majeſty, and went
" his way *." And, as the embaſſadour proceeds
to ſay, " thereupon he *went out of the chamber of*
" *prefence*, ſaying to the Queen, ADIEU, MADAM,
" YOU SHALL NOT SEE MY FACE FOR A LONG
" SPACE †." Yet, poor good man! THE QUEEN
WOULD NOT LET HIM STAY AT HOME.

Nor was he worfe than his word. He ſtill per-
ſiſted in his refolution of going abroad. Even

* Keith, 348—349.   † Ibid. 345—346.

when

when he abandoned this, he kept at a distance from the Queen. An order had been made by the privy council on the 24th of September, for summoning the nobles, gentlemen, and others, of some adjacent counties, to meet the King and Queen at Melrofs on the 8th of October following, in their progrefs to hold affizes at feveral places in perfon. But the King chofe not to attend, and fhe was obliged to go without him *.

In this progrefs fhe was feized with a malignant fever. On the 25th of October, at fix in the morning, fhe lay for a confiderable time as if fhe had been quite dead. And in a letter from the French embaffadour, dated the 24th, he fays, That the King was at Glafgow, that *he had been apprized of her illnefs*, that he had *had time enough to have visited her*, if he had been willing, and that yet he had never been near her. She had then been ill eight days. "This is a fault in the King," fays the embaffadour, "for which I can make no apology." And the Bifhop of Rofs adds in a letter of the 27th; "the King all this tyme remanis in Glafcow, and " zit is nocht cumm towart the Quenis Majeftie." He appeared at laft, when the crifis had been now three days over. This took place on the 25th. She then fell into a violent fweat, which was the termination of the fever. Yet fhe was left in a very weak condition. And it was not till the 28th that the King appeared. Even then he ftaid only one night with her †.

* Goodall, i. 302—303. † Keith App. 133—136, and Pref. vii.

In this third period of voluntary exile from the Queen, he continued about a month; though the Queen was all the while in an un-recovered state. But let us see Le Croc's account of her at this period. "The Queen," he says in a letter of December the 2d, "is for the present at Craigmillar.— "She is in the hands of the physicians, and I do "assure you is not at all well, and do believe the "principal part of her disease to consist in a deep "grief and sorrow: nor does it seem possible to "make her forget the same. Still she repeats these "words, *I could wish to be dead.* You know very "well, that the injury she has received is exceed- "ing great, and her Majesty will never forget it. "The King her husband came to visit her at "Jedburgh," where she lay ill, "the very day "after Captain Hay went away," who was sent with the Bishop's letter on Sunday October the 27th [*]. "He remained there but one single night; "and yet in that short time I had a great deal of "conversation with him. He returned to see the "Queen about five or six days ago: and the day "before yesterday he sent word to desire me to "speak with him half a league from this; which "I complied with, and found that things go still "worse and worse. I think, he intends to go away "to-morrow; but *in any event* I'm *much assured*, as "*I always have been*, that *he won't be present at the* "*baptism* [†]." Le Croc was right. Darnly *would* not be present at the baptism of the prince, his own

[*] Keith App. 135.   [†] Keith Pref. vii.

son;

son; which took place at Stirling a few days afterwards. Yet, with an absurdity which even Le Croc did not expect from him, he thought proper to take up his residence at that very time in Stirling; though he was previously determined not to come near the Queen, not to have any part in the baptism, and not to have any share in the entertainments. He thus exposed himself and her the more conspicuously by his conduct. The French embassadour was so shocked with his behaviour, that he absolutely refused to see him. But let the embassadour speak his own sentiments upon the occasion. " The King," he says in a letter of December 23, " had *still given out*, that
" he would *depart two days before the baptism*; but
" when the time came on he made no sign of re-
" moving at all, only he still *kept close within his*
" *own apartment*. The very day of the baptism he
" sent three several times, desiring me either to
" come and see him, or to appoint him an hour
" that he might come to me in my lodgings: so
" that I found myself obliged *at last* to signify to
" him, that seeing he was in no good correspond-
" ence with the Queen, I had it in charge from the
" most Christian King to have no conference with
" him. And I caused tell him likewise, that as it
" would not be very proper for him to come to my
" lodgings, because there was such a crowd of
" company there; so he might know that there
" were two passages to it, and if he should enter
" by the one, I would be constrained to go out by
" the

" the other *. His bad deportment is incurable,
" nor can there be ever any good expected from
" him.—The Queen behaved herself admirably
" well all the time of the baptism, and shewed so
" much earnestness to entertain all the goodly
" company in the best manner, that this made her
" forget, in a good measure, her former ailments.
" But I am of the mind, however, that she will
" give us some trouble as yet; nor can I be brought
" to think otherwise, so long as she continues to be
" so pensive and melancholy. She sent for me
" yesterday, and I found her laid on the bed *weep-
" ing sore*, and she complained of a grievous pain
" in her side. And for a surcharge of evils, it
" chanced that the day her Majesty set out from
" Edinbourgh for this place," Stirling, " she hurt
" one of her breasts on the horse, which she told
" me is now swelled. I am much grieved for the
" many troubles and vexations she meets with †."

In this mode of acting, adding absurdity to absurdity, and heaping one insult upon the head of another, did the King continue till the 26th or 27th of December. He then received a letter from his father, of whom he inherited all his folly and perverseness. " For that the extremitie of this stormy
" weather," says Lenox, " causes me to dout of

---

* To this it is that Buchanan alludes, in his wild way of writing history, *à la mode de Gibbon*, when he says, that " ye
" forane ambassadouris wer warnit not to talk with him,
" quhen zit the maist part of the day thay wer all in the same
" castell quhair he was." 15. Anderson, ii. and 242. Jebb i.
† Keith Pref. vii.

" zour fetting forward fo foon on zour journey
" [to Peebles], therefore I ſtay till I heir farther
" from zour Majeſtie; which I ſall humbly befeech
" zow I may, and I ſall not fayle to wayt upon zow
" accordinglie *." On the receipt of this, the King,
notwithſtanding " the extremitie of this ſtormy
" weather," ended his refidence at Stirling juſt as
he had continued it before. He ſat off, without
taking the leaſt notice of the Queen. He retired
to Glaſgow. And there he was taken ill †.

I have gone over this hiſtory of the King's conduct towards the Queen, for the laſt four months
before his illneſs; in order partly to fix upon its
proper foundation, which I think has never yet
been done, the King's non-appearance at the baptifm ‡; and principally to lay open, in a ſatisfactory
manner, another proof of the general forgery.
Theſe little incidents in the letters have not been
ſufficiently attended to before. Yet they are deci-

---

* Keith Pref. vii. † Knox, 401. Goodall, i. 321.

‡ The abfence of the King from the baptifm and the entertainments, has been accounted for differently by the friends
and the enemies of Mary. The latter have referred it to the
unkindneſs of the Queen (Detection, 15, and Robertſon, i. 389).
The former have afcribed it to Elizabeth's private inſtructions
to her embaſſadour, not to give the appellation of King to
Darnly (Keith, 360. Goodall, i. 319. Guthrey's Scotch Hiſt.
vi. 373, and Stuart, i. 175—176). But both are plainly miſled
by a ſpirit of refinement. The abſence was occaſioned by the
King himſelf. *He choſe to be abſent.* This Le Croc's letter
decifively ſhews. He had determined to be abfent, weeks before the baptiſm. And he adhered to his determination at
it.

M 4 five

five evidences againſt them. And they ſhould all of them be dwelt upon particularly, as they ariſe.

(6) I now wiſh to point out a new evidence of the forgery, in a new ſpecies of variation. The letters, as I have ſhewn in the former volume, were exhibited in Scotch at York and at Weſtminſter. Both theſe MSS have been tranſmitted down to us, the one in a number of extracts made by the commiſſioners, and the other in the printed copy. But then there are ſome different readings in the two MSS, which have never been noticed. Thus a paſſage before, "he is not over mekle *deformit*," as it ſtands in the CODEX WESTMONASTERIENSIS, appears thus in the CODEX EBORACENSIS, "he is "not oer meikle *ſpilt*." The words immediately following too, "zit he has *reſſavit* verray mekle," are read thus, "*bot* he has *gottin* verray mekill." The ſucceeding words alſo are a little different, "he has almaiſt ſlane me with his braith, it is "*worſe than* [York MS *war nor*] zour un- "cle's, and zit I cum na neirer *unto him* [left out "in York MS], bot [*ſat*, York MS] in ane," &c. And in the next extract made by the com- miſſioners, we have the following variations thrown into the paſſage now before us: "Remember "[*how*, Weſtm. MS *yow*, York MS] he will "not cum with me, except upon conditioun "that I will promeis to him, that I ſall be at bed "and buird with him as of befoir, and that "I ſall leif him *na ofter*" [*na efter*, York]. "Na ofter," Scotch, has "ne ſæpius," Latin, and

and " si souvent," French. There is some sense in the French providing, that the Queen should not leave the King *so often*. But there is absolutely none at all, in the Latin charging her not to leave him *oftener*. Yet the Latin copy reading " sæpiús," the Frenchman, with more judiciousness than he generally exerts, retained the word, and furnished a meaning. And the reading of the York copy removes all the absurdity at once, gives us the true word, and shews us the true meaning. The Queen was not to leave the King afterwards.— With such variations, were the very copies delivered to the commissioners at Westminster and at York! At the *first* appearance of Mary's letters, she had written " spilt," " gottin," and " na efter;" but, at the second, the words were changed into " de-" formit," " ressavit," and " na ofter." And this little circumstance alone would have been sufficient, to disclose the whole forgery.

(7) " Upon my word," Scotch, omitted in the Latin and French.

(8) " Quhil uther morne," till the next day but one. This shews the second half of the letter to be written on January 25th; as January 27th was actually the day, on which she set out with the King [*].

[*] See Rebel Journal in Appendix, N° x.

§ II.

§ II.

LETTER THE FIRST continued.

XXV.—" He spak verray bravely at ye begin-
"ning, as yis beirer will schaw zow, upon the pur-
"pois (1) of the Inglismen, and of his depart-
"ing (2): bot in ye end he returnit agane to his
"humilitie (3).

XXVI.—" He schawit, amongis uther purpo-
"sis (4), yat he knew weill aneuch, that my bro-
"ther had schawin me yat thing, quhilk he had
"spoken in Striviling, of the quhilk he denyis ye
"ane half, and abone all yat ever he came in his
"chalmer (5). For to mak him traist me,"

XXV.—" Valde ferociter ab initio loquebatur,
"uti qui has fert tibi narrabit, de colloquio (1)
"cum Anglis, de suo discessu (2): sed tandem re-
"versus est ad suam humanitatem (3).

XXVI.—" Inter alia consilia quæ mihi retuli
"(4), se satis scire, quód meus frater ad me detu-
"lisset, quæ ipse cum eo egisset Sterlini; quarun
"rerum dimidium negavit, ac maximé illud, quó
"fratris mei cubiculum esset ingressus (5). U
"ego faciliús fidem apud eum"·

XXV.-

XXV.—" Au commencement il parloit fort
" aſprement, comme vous recitera celuy qui porte
" les preſentes, du devis (1) eu avec les Anglois,
" et de ſon depart (2); mais enfin il revint a ſa
" douceur (3).

XXVI.—" Entre autres ſecrets qu'il me recita,
" il dit (4), qu'il ſcavoit bien, que mon frere
" m'avoit rapporté ce qu'il avoit fait avec luy a
" Stirling; des quelles choſes il a nié la moytie,
" et principalement, qu'il fuſt entré en la chambre
" de mon frere (5). Et afin"

(1) " Purpois," Scotch; " colloquio," Latin;
" devis," French. But the tranſlations are both
wrong. " Purpois of the Ingliſmen and of his de-
" parting," can mean only the *point* concerning the
Engliſhmen and his departure.

(2) He ſpoke very bravely at the beginning,
ſays the letter, concerning the plan of departing in
an Engliſh veſſel. But let us turn to the former
part of the letter, and there ſee how very bravely
he ſpeaks. The letter-writer neglected to do this,
and ſo plunged into a contradiction. " I aſkit
" quhy he wald pas away in ye Inglis ſchip; he
" DENYIS IT, and SWEIRIS THAIRUNTO; bot he
" *grantis* that *he ſpak with the men*." All his
bravery lay in *denying* the fact, and in denying it
with an *oath*. So little was he reſolute, at the beginning or at the end of the converſation, about
his departure in an Engliſh ſhip; that he denied he
ever

ever had any such intention, and he swore he had not. And so gross is the contradiction here! Indeed the line of conduct *here* assigned him, would have suited much better with his character, than what was assigned before. The letter also would then have agreed with history. But Lethington first makes him deny the intention, then thinks it best to make him talk very bravely about it at first, but forgets to eraze the former when he has inserted the latter. And thus both stand together in the same letter, the one to shew a forgery from its opposition to history, and both to shew it again from their opposition to each other.—" And," Scotch, omitted in the Latin, but preserved in the French from the corrected Latin, " et."

(3) " Humilitie," Scotch ; " humanitas," Latin ; " douceur," French. The Miscellaneous Remarker observes *, that, as " it would have " been absurd to have made Mary praise the in- " nate and characteristical civility of Darnly, *sua* " *humanitas*, hence we may conclude that the La- " tin translator used the word *humilitas*, and that " *humanitas* is an error of the press." Yet " the " faithful French translator says—*sa douceur*." The word *humanitas* was an error of the press or pen. But it was altered into *humilitas* in the corrected Latin. *For that reason*, the Frenchman says " *sa* " *douceur*." He does not mean *humanity*, but *humility*, by the word. And he actually uses the same word in the same sense, a few pages before ; " ze

* P. 10.

" saw

" saw him never fpeik mair *humbler*," being rendered " nunquam vidi eam—loqui *humiliûs*," and " je ne l'ay jamais veu—parler fi *doucement*."

(4) " Purpofis," Scotch, difcourfes, not " confilia," Latin, or " fecrets," French. *Dixit* is omitted in Latin, and yet " il dit" appears in French from the corrected Latin.

(5) What this alludes to, I know not. " His," Scotch ; " fratris mei," Latin ; " mon frere," French.

" it behovit me to fenzé in fum thingis with him
" (1) : thairfoir, quhen he requeiftit me to promeis
" unto him, that quhen he was haill we fuld have
" baith ane bed ; I faid to him fenzeingly, and
" making me to beleve his promifis (2), that gif he
" changeit not purpois (3) betwix yis and that tyme,
" I wald be content thairwith : bot in the meane
" tyme I bad him tak heid, that he let na body wit
" thairof, becaus, to fpeik amangis ourfelfis, the
" lordis culd not be offendit, nor will evill thairfoir
" (4) ; bot thay wald feir in refpect of the boifting
" he made of thame (5), that gif ever we"

" affequerer, neceffe mihi erat quædam fingendo ei
" obfecundare (1). Quamobrem cúm rogaret ut ei
" pollicerer, cúm primúm revaluiffet, communem
" nobis fore lectum ; ego diffimulanter dixi, ac fin-
                                                " gens

" gens me bellis (2) ejus pollicitationibus fidem
" habere, me confentire, nifi ille interea propofitum
" mutaret (3) : fed interea videret ne quifquam
" id refcifceret, proptereâ quód proceres noftris col-
" loquiis offendi non poffent, nec ideó (4) malé
" velle ; fed in timore futuros, quód comitatus
" fuiffet (5), fi aliquando inter nos concordes effe-
" mus, fe daturum"

" qu'il me creuft pluftoft, j'eftoye contrainte de luy
" accorder quelque chofe en diffimulant (1) : par-
" quoy, lors qu'il me priaft, que je luy promiffe,
" qu'incontinent qu'il feroit guery, nous ne faifions
" plus qu'un lict ; je luy dy par diffimulation, en
" faingnant que je croyoye a fes belles (2) pro-
" meffes, que je l'y accorderoye, pour veu qu'il ne
" changeaft d' advis (3) : mais cependant qu'il
" regardaft que perfonne n'en fceuft rien, parce que
" les feigneurs ne pourroient eftre offenfez de nos
" propos, ny confequemment (4) nous en vouloir
" mal. Ains feroint en crainte de ce qu'il m'auroit
" fuivy (5). Et fi nous pouvions eftre d'accord
" enfemble."

(1) " Fenzé in fum thingis with him," Scotch ;
" quædam fingendo *ei obfecundare*," Latin ; " *de
" luy accorder* quelque chofe en diffimulant," French.

(2) " Promifis," Scotch ; " *bellis* pollicitationi-
" bus," Latin ; " *belles* promeffes," French.

(3) This is a ftroke at the *real* character of
Darnly. Truth breaks out through the cloud of fiction.

fiction. And he, who has been hitherto reprefented as a forced exile from his Queen and his family, is here intimated to have been, as he was, a voluntary one. We have a fimilar ray of truth flashing out juft before, concerning his refoluteness about the Englifh fhip, and his own departure in it; another ftill nearer, concerning Murray's enmity to Darnly; and others again, concerning the enmity of the lords in general to him.

(4) "Thairfoir," Scotch; "ideó," Latin; "confequemment," French. The Frenchman applied "ideó" to the lords being offended, when it relates to the King and Queen converfing together; and fo rendered it, as he does. But what poor and petty exertion of mind is here! The Queen gravely informs the King, that the lords could not be difcontented, and would not form plots,—though he and fhe did *talk*, that is, *live*, together. Was ever fuch impertinence of words?

(5) "Boifting," Scotch, fignifies threatening. So Mary's nobles fay, " in cais" they " had raifit " ane armie" to releafe her from Lochlevin, " it " was menafit and *boiftt*, that thay [the rebels] " fould fend hir heid to thame *." And this fenfe the Latin intended to exprefs, the *comitatus* of it being plainly a mif-print only for *comminatus*. Yet the Frenchman finding *comitatus*, and having no Scotch to direct him, he was obliged to follow it. And he followed it with fome judgment,

* Goodall, ii. 355.

giving

giving a new turn to the paſſage, and refining the blunder into ſenſe.

But we have here another contradiction to the former part of the letter. Mary before "inquyrit "him,—yat he was angrie with ſum of the lordis, "and wald *threittin thame:* HE DENYIS that, and "ſays *he luifis thame all*, and prayis me to give "traiſt to nathing aganis him." Yet now it appears, that Mary believes, and Darnly does not deny, he *had* threatened them *much*, even *ſo* much, that they would be alarmed with any proſpect of union betwixt him and the Queen. This is a plain contradiction.

But let me go on to obſerve, that this threatening, thus mentioned twice, is undoubtedly real; and that the alarm ſure to be taken by the lords, on a proſpect of an union between the King and Queen, was proved to be dreadfully ſo in the event. The reconciliation took place, in conſequence of this ſickneſs and this viſit; and the deſtruction of Darnly followed inſtantly afterwards. This paſſage, therefore, becomes very remarkable. It is pregnant with meaning. And it involuntarily betrays the grand ſecret of the King's murder.

" we aggreit togidder, he ſuld mak thame knaw
" the lytill compt thay tuke of him (1); and that
" he counſallit me not to purchas ſum of thame
"by

" by him (2). Thay for this caus wald be in
" jelofy (3), gif at anis (4), without thair know-
" ledge, I fuld brek the play fet up in the contrair
" in thair prefence (5)."

" operam ut intelligerent quám parvi eum æftimaf-
" fent (1); item, quód mihi confuluiffet, ne gra-
" tiam quorundam feorfum a fe expeterem (2).
" Has ob caufas eos in magnâ fufpicione futuros
" (3), fi ego (4) faciem fcenæ ad contrariam huic
" fabulam inftructæ, in præfentiâ, eis infciis, tur-
" barem (5)."

" qu'il pourroit donner ordre, qu'ils entendroient
" combien peu ils l'avoient eftimé (1). Item, de
" ce qu'il m'avoit confeillé, que je ne recerchaffe
" la bonne grace d'aucuns fans luy (2). Et pour
" ces raifons qu'ils feroient en grand foupcon (3),
" fi (4) je troubloye ainfi maintenant la face du
" theatre, qui avoit efté apprefté pour joüer une
" autre fable (5)."

(1) Such threats, no doubt, Darnly had thrown
ut; and they would ferve to haften his fate. The
efign of the letter-writer in mentioning them
ems to be this, that Darnly's character fhould be
iifed, as it ftands oppofed to the Queen's, but kept
own in its real ftate, as it fets itfelf againft the
rds. And, as this was a very natural mode of
ting in a forgery made by thofe very lords, and
ems peculiarly apparent here; fo will it account
r the great opening, which is here given us, into
e caufes of the King's murder. Where two fuch
irpofes were to be profecuted at once, one of them

was

was sure to injure the other, and some truths to be betrayed betwixt them.

(2) This counsel was probably true also. But it could only have been true, just after the murder of Rizzio; when the Queen pardoned Murray, Glencairn, Rothes, &c. These she "purchased" over to her side, by a pardon for all their treasons, a permission to continue in the country notwithstanding their exile, and a re-instatement in offices of trust and authority about her. Accordingly, that gaunt and grim assassin Ruthven, in his own cool account of the murder of Rizzio, represents the King as declaring " to the Queen's majesty, that he had " sent for the lords to return again; whereunto she " answered, that she was not to blame that they " were so long away, for she could be content to " have them home at any time, *but for angring him;* " and to verify the same, when the Queen gave re- " mission to the Duke, *he was miscontented there-* " *with* *." And the allusion in January 1567 to a fact that happened the March preceding, as if it had very recently happened, and was still a strong ground for jealousy, is a full proof of the forgery.— " Sum of thame," Scotch; " quorundam," Latin, for *quorundam de iis*; " d'aucuns," French. And the use of the word " by" appears very singular to us; " seorsum a se," Latin; " sans luy," French: but was common in the Scotch at that time †.

(3) " For this caus," Scotch; " has ob causas," Latin; " pour ces raisons," French: " in jelosy,"

* Keith, App. 125.   † See Goodall, ii. 287, 315, 319.

Scotch;

Scotch; " in *magnâ* fuspicione," Latin; " en *grand* foupcon," French.

(4) "At anis," Scotch, omitted in the Latin and French.

(5) "In thair prefence," Scotch; " in præfen-"tiâ," for *in eorum præfentiâ*, Latin; and fo rendered, as *in prefentiâ* properly fignifies, " mainte-"nant," French. " Without thair knowledge," Scotch; " eis infciis," Latin; omitted in French. And " I fuld brek the play fet up in the contrair," Scotch, is very well tranflated into Latin thus, " ego faciem fcenæ ad contrariam huic fabulam in-" ftructæ—turbarem;" and very clofely copied by the French, "je troubloye la face du theatre—qui " avoit efté apprefté pour joüer une autre fable."

This paffage implies the King and Queen to have agreed at the meeting, that their reconciliation fhould not be fhewn to the world at prefent, for fear of incenfing the lords, Murray mentioned before, and others who were equally minifters to Mary and enemies to Darnly. Yet fuch an implication is contrary at once, to the truth of hiftory, and to the general defign of the author. Hiftory fhews the reconciliation to have taken place; and the moft ftriking proofs of it to have been given, in the Queen's offices of tendernefs about him. And the defign of the author is, to make thofe offices appear all infidious, the refult of adultery, and the leaders to murder. Dr. Robertfon accordingly tells us, that " fhe not only vifited ' Henry, but by all her words and actions endea-
" voured

"voured to express an *uncommon affection* for him."
Yet all this was hypocrisy, he says. For " two [he
" should have said, four] of her famous letters to
" Bothwell were written during her stay at Glas-
" gow, and fully lay open this scene of iniquity *."
With such gross disingenuity does the Doctor act,
concerning the letters. When they contradict
history, he does not follow them, but *he still believes them to be genuine*. He shews he *observes* the
contradiction. Yet he *retains his implicit faith
in them*. His judgment is not warped. But his
probity is corrupted.

XXVII.—" He said, verray joyfully, And think
" zow thay will esteme zow the mair of that?
" Bot I am verray glaid that ze speik to me of the
" lordis; for (1) I beleve at this tyme ze desyre
" that we suld leif togidder in quyetnes (2); for
" gif it wer utherwyse, greiter inconvenience
" micht come to us baith than we ar war of (3):
" bot now I will do quhat ever ze will do, and
" will lufe all that ze lufe (4); and desyris zow to
" mak thame lufe in lyke manner: for, sen thay
" seik not my lyfe (5), I lufe tham all equallie.
" Upon yis point (6), this"

XXVII.—" Tum ille vehementer lætus subjecit,
" Et tu putas-ne quód pluris illi te æstimabunt ob
" hanc causam ? Sed valdé gaudeo quód sermonem

* Hist. i. 396—397.

" de

"de proceribus injecisti; nunc quidem (1) credo
"te cupere, ut uná concorditer vivamus (2): nam
"ni ita esset, majora quám uterque timemus in-
"commoda utrique possent evenire (3): sed nunc,
"quod tu vis volo, et quod amabis amabo (4); et
"cupio ut eorum similiter concilies amorem: quia,
"postquam non petunt vitam meam (5), omnes
"amo ex æquo. Circa hoc caput (6),"

XXVII.—"Alors estant grandement joyeux, il
"adjousta, Et pensez-vous que pour cela ils vous
"en estiment d'avantage? Mais je suis bien aise
"que vous avez fait mention des seigneurs; main-
"tenant (1) je croye, que vous desirez que nous
"vivions ensemblement en paix (2): car s'il estoit
"ainsi, beaucoup plus grandes fascheries nous
"pourroient advenir a tous deux, que nous ne
"craignons (3); mais a present je veux ce que
"vous voulez, et aimeray ce que vous aimerez (4);
"et desire que pareillement vous acqueriez leur
"amitie: car puis qu'ils ne pourchassent a m'oster
"la vie (5), je les aime tous esgalement. Tou-
"chant ce chef (6), le"

(1) "For," Scotch; "quidem," Latin; omitted in French.

(2) This, so far as it intimates that the separation of the King and Queen was occasioned by her, and not by him, I have already shewn to be contrary to fact, and consequently to be an evidence of the forgery. Dr. Robertson also acknowledges,

that the separation was occasioned by his absenting himself from court. He informs us, that " Henry " sometimes attended at court *," that he and the Queen " passed two nights together †," that he " soon after took a resolution, equally wild and des- " perate, of embarking on board a ship, which he " provided, and of flying into foreign parts ‡;" that he afterwards " refused to accompany the " Queen from Stirling to Edinburgh," and was " absent from court §;" and that, in short, " by his " folly and ingratitude he lost the heart of a woman " who doated on him ‖." But let us particularly see his account of the King's behaviour, on his return to court the 29th of September 1566. " He ar- " rived there," he adds, " on the same day she re- " ceived the account of his intended flight. But he " was more than usually wayward and peevish; and " scrupling to enter the palace, unless certain lords " who attended the Queen were dismissed, Mary " was obliged to meet him without the gates. At " last he suffered her to conduct him into her own " apartment. She endeavoured to draw from him " the reasons of the strange resolution which he had " taken, and to divert him from it. In spite, how- " ever, of all her arguments and intreaties, he re- " mained silent and inflexible. Next day the " privy council, by her direction, expostulated with " him on the same head. He persisted notwith- " standing in his sullenness and obstinacy; and

* Hist. i. 372. † i. 373. ‡ i. 375.
§ Ibid. ‖ i. 400.

" neither

" neither deigned to explain the motives of his
" conduct, nor signified any intention of altering it.
" As he left the apartment, he turned towards the
" Queen, and told her that she should not see his
" face again for a long time *." This last account
is *instar omnium*, in shewing to which side the separation is to be attributed. The Doctor indeed has not done Mary full justice, because he has suppressed *her taking him by the hand* in the council, *her double address* to him, the *address of the lords*, the *address of the French embassadour*, the *declaration of Darnly* that he had had no reasons given him for such a resolution, and *his instantly walking out of the council-chamber*; which are circumstances of great moment in this transaction. His suppression of these must reflect much upon his integrity, as an historian. But he has said enough to convict Darnly, as the most unreasonable of all unreasonable husbands. And his so plainly attributing the separation to Darnly, when the letters attribute it to Mary; and yet his adherence to the authenticity of those letters, when they contain acknowledged falshoods; form one of those glaring contrarieties of conduct, which are too common indeed in life, but which always denote the conflicts of principle with passion, and betray the shameful victories that the latter occasionally obtains over the former.

(3) This tells us an important truth, which is plain upon the face of the history; that Murray and his accomplices took advantage of the King's

* i. 375—376.

foolish

foolish and froward behaviour to the Queen, and endeavoured to prosecute their own purposes by the aid of it.

(4) This implies, that the King *had* acted frowardly before, and so far is inconsistent with various passages preceding. That he had, let us be once more shewn, and from a new authority, and from one that was peculiarly hostile to Mary. "All "honour," says Randolph to Leicester, in a letter of July 30th 1565, the very day after the marriage, "that may be attributed unto any man by a "wife, he hath it wholly and fully. All praise that "may be spoken of him, he lacketh not from her- "self. All dignities that she can endow him with, "are already given and granted. No man pleas- "eth her that contenteth not him. And what "may I say more? She hath given over unto him "her whole will, to be ruled and guided as himself "best liketh." Yet, notwithstanding all this kindness, "*she can so much prevail with him in any* "*thing that is against his will*, as your lordship "may with me, *to perswade that I should hang my-* "*self**."

"Quod amabis amabo," Latin, is intimated by Mr. Goodall †, and agreed to by Miscellaneous Remarker ‡, to be the printer's or copier's error of *quod* for *quos*; and yet to have been followed, says

---

* Goodall, i. 222. and Robertson, ii. 347.—This letter is dated "the last day of July;" but from the mention of " this " day, Monday," appears to have been written on the 30th.
† i. 96. ‡ P. 10.

the latter, "with his wonted fervility" by the Frenchman, in his "j'aimeray *ce que* vous " aimerez." And the reafon affigned for their opinion, is the immediate appearance of " eorum." But the obfervation is more nice than juft. " I " will do *quhatever* ze will do, and lufe *all that* ze " lufe," Scotch, is naturally and properly rendered, " *Quod* tu vis volo, et *quod* amabis amabo," and " je veux *ce que* vous voulez, et aimeray *ce* " *que* vous aimerez." Nor does " eorum," Latin, and " leur," French, follow more ftrangely afterwards, than " thame," Scotch. And it is the very impertinence of criticifm, to think of reducing fuch a compofition as this to the precifeft rules of language.

(5) This forms one of the various hints in the letter, that fome of Mary's minifters were plotting againft the life of Darnly. We are very fure that this is true, by the legal proofs againft Bothwell and Morton, and by that which is paramount to all legal proofs, the full and ftrong voice of facts againft Murray and Lethington. But how the letter-writer could be fo abfurd as to mention it, is furprizing. Yet the truth *would* intrude upon him, it is plain from this and other inftances, and mingle with his mafs of fiction. Thus, in the prefent letter, Mynto told him that fome of the council had brought an order to Mary for her fignature, to fend Darnly to prifon, and to flay him if he made refiftance. Thus alfo he fays afterwards, that Mary refufed to fubfcribe this order, and that, as to the others who wanted to purfue his life, he would

fell

fell it at a dear rate to them. Thus again, he intimates Murray to have told a great falshood of him; and she speaks of the threats which he had thrown out against the lords, that, if ever he and she became reconciled, he should make them suffer for the slights which they had put upon him. And now he himself hints again, that they had been seeking his life. A train of plots had been formed against him by Murray probably, the engaging him in the murder of Rizzio, the plan of a divorce, the poison perhaps administered to him, and this order for his commitment, though never presented to Mary. " O good pitiful men," says the Bishop of Ross, with a pointed sneer at Murray and Murray's associates, pretending to take up the cause of the murdered King, " who for the very tender love
" and singuler affection, which you did ever beare
" to the L. Darley (the which truly was so ve-
" hement, that for your exceeding hot and fervent
" love towards him, *ye ever fought his hart's blood),*
" do now so pitifully bewaile him *!"

(6) " Upon yis point," Scotch; " circa hoc caput," Latin; " touchant ce chef," French.

" beirer will schaw zow mony small thingis. Becaus
" I have over mekle to wryte, and it is lait (1); I
" give traist unto him upon zour word (2). Summa,
" he will ga upon my word to all places (3).

* Defence, 25.

XXVIII.—

XXVIII.—" Alace! I never diſſavit ony body:
" bot I remit me altogidder to zour will (4). Send
" me advertiſement quhat I ſall do, and quhatſaever
" thing ſall cum thairof, I ſall obey zow (5). Ad-
" viſe tó with zourſelf, gif ze can find out ony
" mair ſecret inventioun by medicine (6); for he
" ſuld tak medicine"

" hic tabellarius multa minuta tibi declarabit; quia
" nimis multa ſuperſunt ſcribenda, et jam ſerum
" eſt (1). Huic adhibebis fidem juxta tuum ver-
" bum (2). Breviter, meo juſſu quóvis ibit (3).

XXVIII.—" Hei mihi! nunquam quenquam
" decepi; ſed ego me in univerſum tuæ voluntati
" ſubjicio (4). Fac me certiorem quid faciam, et
" quicunque ſequatur eventus, tibi obſequar (5).
" Etiam tecum perpende, an comminiſci queas ali-
" quam occultiorem rationem per medicinam (6);"

" porteur vous recitera pluſieurs particularitez;
" d'autant qu'il y a trop de choſes qui reſtent a eſ-
" crire, et qu'il eſt deſia tard (1): vous adjouſterez
" foy ſelon voſtre parole (2). En ſomme, il ira ou
" vous voudrez par mon commàndement (3)."

XXVIII.—" Helas! je n'ay jamais trompé per-
" ſonne; mais je me ſubmets en toutes choſes a
" voſtre volonté (4). Faiĉtes moy ſçavoir ce que
" je doy faire; et quoy qu'il en puiſſe advenir je
" vous obeiray (5). Et penſez en vous meſme, ſi
" pouvez trouver quelque moyen plus couvert que
" par breuvage (6);"

(1). This

(1) This shews the second half of the letter to be written in the night of the second day after the arrival, January 25th.

(2) This is also one of the noted instances, by which Mr. Goodall discovered the unknown original of the letters in the disguise of a translation, that it had now worn unobserved for nearly two hundred years; and pointed it out decisively to the reason of all mankind. "Paris had been an old "servant to the Earl of Bothwell, and had lately "been taken into the Queen's service." She therefore says she trusted him upon the earl's recommendation. But Buchanan overlooking the pronoun of the first person, he necessarily translated the sentence, " huic adhibebis fidem juxta " tuum verbum;" and the French translator, having no other original but the Latin, followed it closely, " vous adjousterez foy selon vostre pa- " role *." This adds one more to the many instances that we have already had, of the wonderful negligence with which Buchanan made his translation. The same took place, no doubt, in forming the original Scotch. We have even seen some astonishing proofs of it, in the contradictoriness of parts to parts. And in this manner was cooked up that celebrated composition, which the faction and the folly of succeeding times was to raise into consequence, to exalt into authenticity, and to engraft upon the stock of history.

* Goodall, i. 89—90.

(3) " He

(3) " He will ga upon my word to all places," Scotch; " meo juſſu quóvis ibit," Latin; and, " il ira ou vous voudrez par mon commandement," French; the Frenchman miſtaking " quóvis " for *quo vis.* This was another of Mr. Goodall's deciſive proofs *."

(4) This is a third touch of remorſe. But it is more ridiculous than either of the two before. It is ſhorter. It goes off ſooner into iniquity again. And it acts in oppoſition to every principle of nature, in repreſenting one, who is expreſsly declared to have " never diſſavit ony body" before, as deceiving Darnly in the higheſt manner, as mounting at once to the very height of hypocriſy, as becoming by one exertion a very prodigy of malignity.

(5) What does this mean? Did not the Mary of the forgers know full well what ſhe was to do, when ſhe went to Glaſgow? If ſhe did not, why did the forgers write this letter? But this very letter ſhews, that ſhe came to Glaſgow in order to draw him to Edinborough. So the commiſſioners of York underſtood it, as I have noticed before; when they ſaid in their account of it to Elizabeth, that " ſhe toke her journey from Edinburghe to Glaſco, to viſite him [the King], being theare ſicke, and *purpoſely of intent to bring him with her to Edenburghe.*" And this they notice, as they tell us themſelves, " for the declaration of the conſpiracie, and her procurement and conſent to the murder of her ſaid huſ-

* i. 96—97.

" band."

" band *." But is not her *particular* intention very plain? It is. " I anſwerit," ſhe ſays, " that " I wald tak him with me to Cragmillar, quhair " the mediciner and I micht help him, and not be " far from my ſone." " Bot he hes prayit me," ſhe adds in another place, " to remane upon him " quhil uther morne." And in the next letter ſhe ſubjoins thus: " howbeit I have na farther newis " from zow, according to my COMMISSIOUN I bring " the man with me to Cragmillar upon Monoun- " day." She therefore had her commiſſion, before ſhe ſet out. And theſe repeated calls for directions are mere impertinence, the oſtenſible reaſons for writing the letter, but in direct contradiction to the deſign and contents of it.

(6) This is a very remarkable paſſage. It carries a murderous tendency in the very tone of it. And it is accordingly pointed out twice to Elizabeth, by her commiſſioners at York †. But how are we to underſtand it? The word *by* we have juſt ſeen to ſignify, not *with*, but *without*. Does it ſo ſignify here? The authority of Buchanan is, that it *does*, and—that it *does not*. This is extraordinary. From a *written* copy of his Detection, which is thought to be the very copy that he preſented to Elizabeth, he appears to have originally tranſlated the words, " occultiorem rationem *quàm* per medi- " cinam." The French remains accordingly at preſent, " moyen plus couvert *que* par breuvage." But he afterwards altered his verſion, leaving out

* Appendix, N° vi.   † Ibid. N° vi. and vii.

the word *quàm*, and so making the whole to stand as it does now, " occultiorem rationem per medi-" cinam." He did this likewise in a passage of his Detection itself, in which he quoted the letters. And there he reasoned slanderously against Mary, upon the credit of his *new* version *.

This exhibits Buchanan to us in a singular view, correcting his own Latin version in the interval, betweeen writing out a copy for the eager curiosity of Elizabeth, and publishing it in print to the world. This also proves the French version to have been made, not from the printed copy, but from the MS; not after the publication of the Latin, but before, though the Latin was published about the end of October 1571; and the French in the middle of February afterwards †. I have historically proved the French copy, to have been formed long before the publication of either. But it here appears to have been so, from a slight incident in the language of it; even before the publication of the letters in any language, and when they were merely in MS, in the hands of Elizabeth, or in the hands of Murray. And the French translation was left, by this extraordinary double in the Latin, differing from it even where it had adhered to it; the corrected Latin here following Buchanan's closely, even when Buchanan himself had deserted it.

Which then are we to follow, the original, or the corrected, Buchanan? If we consider the words,

---

* Goodall, i. 326—327. Detection, xi. 51. Anderson, ii. and Jebb, i. 255.   † Goodall, i. 37—38.

" ony

"ony mair secreit inventioun *by* medicine," to mean *without* medicine; then the passage must be supposed to intimate, that the King had been poisoned already in some medicine, and that the next attempt should be without the use of medicine, and in a way which would not shew itself so openly. But if we consider the words as they sound to *our* ears, then Bothwell is desired to think of some mode of dispatching the King, that should be more secret than that of gun-powder, and that might be given him in his physic. Mr. Goodall adopts the former sense; " for the words,—in the Scots "language in Buchanan's days, signified *without* "*medicine**." But the commissioners of England plainly took them in the latter †. Buchanan himself also, upon revisal, took them in this view. And the context plainly confines them to this. "Advise "with zourself," it says, " gif ze can find out ony "mair secreit inventioun," than what had been already projected, " by medicine; FOR *he suld tak me-* "*dicine* and the bath at Cragmillar, he may not "cum furth of the house this long tyme."

But why was this hint concerning poisoning him in his medicines thrown out? No calumny was ever started by the rebels, of Mary's attempting to poison him *posteriorly to this period*. It was thrown out therefore, to give the stronger credit to their slander, of her *having poisoned him before*. Yet it wholly refutes it. If poison was *now* to be tried by her and Bothwell, it had not been tried

* i. 326—327. † Appendix, N° vi. and vii.

before

before by them. And the paſſage preceding, that hints at his *having been* poiſoned by them, is as much oppoſed to this, which inſinuates that he *was to be* poiſoned; as it is to the other, which intimates that he was *not* poiſoned, but poxed. So ſtrangely contradictory is the letter to itſelf!

" and the bath at Cragmillar. He may not cum
" furth of the hous this lang tyme (1)."

' ſumpturus eſt enim et medicinam et balneum ad
" Cragmillarium. Non poteſt domo egredi ad multos dies (1)."

' car il doit prendre medicine et eſtre baigné à
' Cragmillar. Il ne peut ſortir du logis d'icy a
.' pluſieurs jours (1)."

(1) The meaning of the words " he may not
' cum furth of the hous this lang tyme," is this;
hat the King cannot leave his confinement, and
ningle with the world again, for a long time. But
ne Frenchman, reſtraining the meaning to the
Ling's houſe at Glaſgow, ſays he cannot leave *that*,
' d'icy," for a long time. He left *that* two days
fterwards. But he was confined to his houſe at
irk-a-field, for many afterwards.

This being noticed, let me here aſk, What was
Iary's view, in the opinion of her ſlanderers, for
ringing Darnly to Edinborough. The vulgar
herd

herd have always supposed it to be, in order to murder him there. With this the letters agree. And murdered he certainly was, in a few days after she brought him to Edinborough. But Dr. Robertson has found out a better reason. It was *to prevent his going abroad.* " She was assured, that " he resolved instantly to leave the kingdom ; that " a vessel was hired for the purpose, and lay in the " river Clyde ready to receive him, Keith, Pref. " viii." This " was what Mary *chiefly* dreaded.— " While he resided at Glasgow, he might with " more facility accomplish his designs. In order, " therefore, to prevent his executing any such wild " scheme, it was necessary to bring him to some " place, where he would be more immediately un- " der her own eye *." This is a passage astonishingly replete with folly. The design of going abroad, I have already shewn to have existed long before. The very author whom he cites for it, Keith, proves it plainly; though not in the place to which he refers, " Pref. viii." but in Hist. 345— 351. The very intelligence referred to in Keith, was received by Mary so long ago as September 29th, very nearly FOUR months before. Nay Dr. Robertson has even acquainted us with it before; telling us, that " soon after" Darnly's writing to the Pope, &c. " he took a resolution equally wild " and desperate, of embarking on board a ship, " *which he provided,* and of flying into *foreign* " *parts* †." This was in September. He had

---

* Hist. i. 398—399.   † Ibid. 375.

therefore

therefore provided a ship in September. Had he also in January? He had, according to Dr. Robertson. Yet it is one and the same ship, provided at one and the same time; though the Dr. has so strangely split it into two. He refers to Keith for his January vessel. But this is the same vessel that was provided in September. " He commu-
" nicated the design," says Dr. Robertson, " to
" the French embassador Le Croc, and to his father
" the Earl of Lenox.—Lenox instantly communi-
" cated the matter to her [the Queen] by a let-
" ter.—Henry arrived there [at court] on the same
" day she received the account *." This, Le Croc himself assures us, was on September 29th †. But the Dr. has, with more judgment than integrity, suppressed all the dates and some circumstances; particularly one which appeared from Lenox's letter, that *then* " he had a ship lying ready to sail," or, as the privy council expresses this part of the letter, " he had *just then* a ship lying ready;" in order to give himself the liberty, with a better air, of producing the intelligence again at a new period, and with a new gloss upon it. He has also suppressed another circumstance, or rather a train of circumstances, which equally appears in Le Croc's letter; that the latter had since seen the King, that he had used every argument which he could think of to dissuade him from his project, that now he believed the King would not go, and that he had acquainted the Queen with the whole ‡. This, if

* Hist. i. 375. † Keith, 346. ‡ Ibid. 347.

noticed,

noticed, would have precluded his re-mention of the project and the ship; and was therefore kept under cover. He chose to follow Buchanan and flander, even when he had Le Croc and the truth before him. Buchanan (as I have previously noticed) has just made the same anachronism, for *he* also has engrafted history upon the letters; and so brought down what happened in September, to the January following. " Ibi," at Holyrood-house, " cûm rescitum esset," he says, " Regem convales- " cere, ac vim veneni ætatis vigore et corporis " firmitate naturali superatam, novum de eo tol- " lendo consilium initur; cûm interea ad Reginam " delatum esset, Regem de fugâ in Galliam aut " Hispaniam cogitare, eâque de re cum Anglis, " qui navem in æstuario Glottæ stantem habebant, " collocutum:—consulunt omnes festinandum, an- " tequam planè convalesceret*." This was plainly the authority, upon which Dr. Robertson proceeded; though he formally refers to Keith. *That* coincides with him. *This* is directly against him. Only the Doctor has enhanced the wilful misrepresentation of Buchanan, by giving us the truth (in part at least) before, and then giving us the falshood afterwards. And he has also heightened the absurdity of all, by assigning such a boyish reason for Mary's drawing Darnly from Glasgow, That he might not embark there.

On the 30th of September Darnly went out of the council-chamber, and told the Queen, that she

* Hist. xviii. 350.

should

should not see his face again for a long time. After this, says the council, " by a letter which " the King has since wrote to the Queen in " a sort of disguised stile, it appears that he still has " it in his head to leave the kingdom; and there " is advertisement otherwise, that he is secretly " preparing to be gone*." Le Croc also adds thus: " he is not yet embarked; but *we* receive adver- " tisement from day to day, that he still holds on " his resolution, and keeps a ship in readiness." Yet all this time Mary never goes to *him* when he was gone from *her*; and never tries to bring him back to Edinborough, though he was then at Glas- gow, at that very port so formidable to Mary, and so close to his ready-prepared vessel. Then Darnly sent to Le Croc to confer with him. " The King, " who had gone to Glasgow," says Le Croc, " sent " me word to come and meet him half way, betwixt " Lislebourgh," Edinborough, " and Glasgow. I " obeyed him, and found his father, the Earl of " Lenox, with him. We had much communing to- " gether; and I remonstrated to him every thing that " I could think of: and now I believe he will not " go out of the kingdom, though I can perceive, " that he still entertains some displeasure †." Mary still went not to him at Glasgow, to draw him from thence. She even went another way, towards Berwick. And, while he was holding his confe- rence with Le Croc, she was residing at Jed- borough.

* Keith, 349—350. † Ibid. 347.

I am surprized, however, at the reprefentation of this wild project in all our hiftorians. It is confidered by them as a ferious one. But it appears to me nothing more than a feint, a low act of cunning to extort the matrimonial crown from Mary, by the fear of his going abroad. Hence Lenox went to him at Stirling, *immediately on the Queen's fhort abfence*. Hence he himfelf came back to Holyrood-houfe, *the very evening* of the day on which fhe had received *his father's letter of intelligence concerning it*. Hence he would not, becaufe he could not, tell her, either in private or in public, the *grounds* of his intended departure. Hence he went out of the council-chamber fo abruptly in his manner, and with fo rude a menace on his lips, that fhe fhould not fee his face again for a long time. Hence he wrote the letter to her afterwards " in a fort of difguifed ftile," intimating his refolution to go. Hence fhe received advertifements from day to day, of his intending to go, and of his preparing to depart. And hence alfo, when he and his counfelling father found that the Queen fo little heeded his intentions, as never to attempt to ftop him, to draw him from the port and the veffel, and to fecure him " immediately under her own eye" at Edinborough; as even to leave him to the execution of his own devices; and even to give him ftill greater opportunity for it, by her ftill greater diftance from him: then, then, his father and he fought a conference with Le Croc; he wanted to be diffuaded, from what he had never intended in earneft; and he fuffered himfelf at laft to be brought,

brought, apparently, very near to a conviction. Accordingly I find the whole privy-council of Scotland at the time, concurring with me in this idea; though it has been so little attended to by our historians. After a full narration of all that passed at the council-table, on September the 30th; they speak of the King's departure, and say, " so that " we were *all* of opinion, that this was but *a false* " *alarm* the Earl of Lenox was *willing* to give her " Majesty *."

Yet, more than three months after this, Buchanan and Dr. Robertson; and the latter with a spirit (I fear), that would have made him half a Buchanan in times less civilized, and less inquisitive, than the present; represent Darnly as still persisting in his project, and as persisting in it, even when he was reduced by sickness to the utmost extremity of weakness. And Dr. Robertson adds to all, by describing the Queen, who had never gone near the King from the day of his departure to Glasgow, September 30th, till nearly the end of January following; who had particularly not gone all the time, that she received *daily* intelligence of his preparing to embark; as now going, when she received no such intelligence at all; when she had been fully certified above three months before, that in all probability he had given up the design; when the length of time, elapsed since, had fully proved that he had; and when his super-added

* Keith, 349.

illness

illness rendered it impossible for him to go, for some time to come. But it is hardly worth the labour, to discredit such impertinencies as these. Only they serve to shew the imposition that has been put upon the publick, when histories, so little founded on truth, and so little conducted by judgment, have taken advantage of the factious madness of the times, and raised themselves to an high degree of authority among us. Yet I shall just pursue the subject, to shew the Doctor equally contradicting himself and the letters at once.

He has already told us, that Mary drew Darnly from Glasgow to Edinborough, to prevent him from embarking, and to keep him under her own eye. He tells us however in a few lines afterwards, that this was *not* the design in drawing him, that she meant to *murder* him, and that for this purpose she lodged him in a lonely house at his arrival. " In order to prevent his executing any such
" wild scheme, it was necessary to bring him to
" some place where he would be more immediately
" under her own eye. *For this purpose*, she first
" employed all her art to regain his confidence, and
" then proposed to remove him to the neighbour-
" hood of Edinburgh.—The King was weak enough
" to suffer himself to be persuaded" [*not* dissuaded from staying at Glasgow, and embarking on board a ship, as the chain of ideas requires us to suppose at first; but, from a new set of ideas that have here started up suddenly in the author's mind, persuaded to go to Edinborough in order to be murdered];
" and was carried—to Edinburgh. The place pre-
" pared

"pared for his reception was" such, as "the soli-
"tude of the place rendered—*extremely proper for*
"*the commission of that crime*, WITH A VIEW TO
"WHICH IT SEEMS MANIFESTLY TO HAVE BEEN
"CHOSEN *." What was only an innocent and
ridiculous purpose at first, that of preventing
Darnly from embarking at Glasgow, as if this was
the only port in the kingdom, or as if he could
not elope from Edinborough to Glasgow again;
becomes at last a serious and important plan of
concerted murder. The transition from the one to
the other is totally unmarked. And to our asto-
nishment we find ourselves engaged in a murderous
project, when we thought we were only employed
in preventing a voyage. So strangely does the
Doctor contradict himself! It is no wonder therefore, that he contradicts the letters. They, with
as much consistency as such self-repugnant writings
can have, intimate the visit to be for drawing
Darnly to Edinborough, in order to be murdered.
This is indeed the plan, upon which the Doctor
himself has ultimately proceeded. But then the
other plan, of preventing the embarkation by
keeping him in her own eye, cannot be reconciled
with this or with the letters. In these, as we have
already seen, the King is even made expressly to
deny, that he ever had any scheme of embarking.
This undoubtedly is false in fact. But then this, and
the general drift of the letters, concurring together,
do doubly and trebly preclude in those who believe

* i. 399.

the

the authenticity of the letters, all possibility of supposing, that Mary came to Glasgow in order to prevent the scheme, and to hold him directly under her own inspection. If the scheme never existed, it could not be prevented. If she fetched him from Glasgow in order to murder him, she did not mean to confine him within the immediate sphere of her own observance. And to Dr. Robertson the argument is decisive. Yet the good Doctor has shewn us in some instances before, and will perhaps shew us in others hereafter, how little he minds the letters at times, though he professes his firm belief of their genuineness. He treats them, as Papists treat their legends. He reveres them in general as true. Yet he is obliged by the power of truth, to leave them at one time. He is induced by the solicitations of slander, to desert them at another. He thus treats them repeatedly as false. And yet he still believes them to be true.

§ III.

LETTER THE FIRST CONTINUED.

XXIX.—" Summa, be all that I can leirne, he
' is in greit fufpicioun (1), and zit, notwithftand-
' ing, he gevis credit to my word (2); but zit not
' fa far that he will fchaw ony thing to me (3):
' bot nevertheles I fall draw it out of him, gif ze
  will that I avow all unto him (4). Bot I will
  never rejoyce to diffaive ony body that traiftis in
  me: zit, notwithftanding, ze may command me
  in all thingis (5). Have na evill opinioun of
  me for that caus, be reffoun ze ar the occafion of
  it zourfelf; becaus, for my awin particular re-
  venge, I wald not do it to him."

XXIX.—" Breviter, quantum intelligere poffum, in magnâ fufpicione verfatur (1), nihilo
'tamen minús magnam habet fidem orationi
'meæ (2); nec tamen ufque adeo, ut quicquam
'mihi effutiat (3): nihilo minús ego ex eo, fiqui-
'dem tu vis, omnia apud eum profitear et agnof-
'cam (4). Sed nunquam gaudebo in quovis ho-
'mine, qui mihi fidit, decipiendo; nihilo minús tu
'mihi potes omnibus in rebus imperare (5). Noli
'ideo finiftram opinionem de me concipere; quia
'tu ipfe hujus rei mihi author es; nunquam enim
                                            " iftud

" istud in eum committerem, meæ propriæ ultionis
" causâ."

XXIX.—" Brief, à ce que j'en puis entendre, il
" est en grand soupcon (1); neantmoins il adjouste
" beaucoup de foy a ma parole (2); mais non en-
" cores tant, qu'il n'en descouvre quelque chose (3):
" toutesfois je confesseray et recongnoistra tout de-
" vant luy, si vous le trouvez bon (4). Mais si ne
" m'esiouiray-je jamais a tromper celuy qui se fie en
" moy: neantmoins vous me pouvez commander en
" toutes choses (5). Ne concevez donc point de
" moy aucune sinistre opinion, puis que vous-
" mesmes estes cause de cela; car je ne le feroye ja-
" mais contre luy pour ma vengeance particuliere."

(1) The " *greit* suspicioun" of this passage is
directly contrary to another before, in which the
King himself says, that " he suspectit na body, nor
" zit wald not."

(2) His " suspicioun" cannot be " griet," when
" he gevis credit to her word," " *magnam* fidem,"
says the Latin, and " *beaucoup* de foy," says the
French.

(3) *He is in great suspicion, yet he believes her
word, and yet he will not shew her any thing*
These are three clauses, following successively in
order, and contradicting one the other.

(4) What did Mary want Darnly to shew her
even upon the plan of the letters? *Nothing surely*
What then was she to draw out of him? *Nothing
surely*. And what is the *all*, that she asks Bothwell'
leav

leave to avow to him? *Nothing surely.*—" Draw it out of him," Scotch; " ex eo," Latin, *exsculpam* or *expiscabor* being omitted by the pen or press; and all therefore being omitted by the French. This was one of Mr. Goodall's famous proofs *. " Avow," Scotch; " profitear et agnoscam," Latin; and " confesseray et recongnoistray," French.

(5) These fits of remorse are so petty and so frequent, that they appear plainly to be *acted*.

XXX.—" He gives me sum chekis of yat quhilk I fear, zea, evin in the quick (1). He sayis this far, yat his faults wer publeist (2): bot yair is that committis faultis, that belevis thay will never be spokin of (3); and zit thay will speik of greit and small (4). As towart the Lady Reres (5), he said, I pray God that scho may serve zow for zour honour: and said, it is 'thocht,"

XXX.—" Interim me attingit in loco suspecto; 'idque ad vivum (1) hactenus proloquutus 'est, sua crimina esse palam (2): sed sunt qui 'majora committant, et opinantur ea silentio tegi '(3); et tamen homines de magnis juxta ac par'vis loquuntur (4). D. Reresia ait (5), Deum

* i. 97.

" precor,

" precor, ut officia quæ tibi præstat sint tibi ho-
" nori : ait etiam quosdam credere,"

XXX.—" Cependant il m'a donné attainte du
" lieu suspect; et a jusques icy discouru bien au
" vif (1), que ses fautes sont congneües (2):
" mais qu'il y en a qui en commettent de plus
" grandes, encores qu'ils estiment qu'elles soient
" cachées par silence (3); et toutesfois que les
" hommes parlent des grands aussi bien que de
" petits (4). Quant a Reres (5), il dit, Je prie
" Dieu que les services qu'elle vous fait, vous
" soient a honneur."

(1) This means the adultery. Concerning this, he gave her (she says) some pointed strokes. " For " certanetie," she says almost immediately afterwards, " he suspectis of the thing ze knaw," the adultery, " and of his lyfe : bot as to the *last*, " how sone that I spak twa or thré gude wordis " unto him, he rejoysis, and is out of dout." As to the adultery therefore, he still suspected ; and so gave her some severe checks about it. Yet how is this to be reconciled with other passages? Had he suspected the adultery; had he even so strongly suspected it, as to intimate his suspicions to her, and touch her to the very quick about it; could he have been imposed upon by her, as the whole tenour of the letter implies he was? Accordingly, Dr. Robertson represents him as unsuspecting and credulous. " This," her kindness, " made impres- " sion on the credulous spirit of her husband."

She

She " first employed all her art to regain his con-
" fidence, and then proposed to remove him to the
" neighbourhood of Edinburgh;" though the pro-
posal appears before, to have been made *the very
evening of her arrival*, and *very early in the conversation then*. And " the King was weak enough to
" suffer himself to be persuaded *."—" Interim,"
Latin, and " cependant," French, are both added
to the Scotch.

(2) The Latin not observing the full stop at
" vivum," the French has altered the sense materially. " Publeist," Scotch; " palam," Latin, instead of *publicata*; and so " congneües," French,
instead of *publié*.

(3) " Is, committis, belevis," Scotch; " sunt
" qui committant, et opinantur," Latin; " commet-
" tent, estiment," French. " Faultis," Scotch;
" majora," Latin; and " plus grandes," French.
" Never be spokin of," Scotch; " silentio tegi,"
Latin; and " cachées par silence," French.

(4) " Thay," Scotch; " homines," Latin; and
" les hommes," French.

(5) The Latin leaves out *de* before " D. Rere-
" sia." But the French preserves it, reading the
initial letter for *Domina* into *de*, " quant a Reres,"
and so omitting *madamoiselle*.

* i. 396 and 399.

" and he belevis it to be trew, that I have not the
" power of myſelf into myſelf, and that becaus of
" the refuſe I maid of his offeris (1). Summa,
" for certanetie he ſuſpectis of the thing ze knaw,
" and of his lyfe (2). Bot as to the laſt, how ſone
" that I ſpak twa or thré gude wordis unto him,
" he rejoyſis, and is out of dout (3).

XXXI.—" I ſaw him not this evening for to end
" zour bracelet (4), to the quhilk I can get na
" lokkis (5). It is reddy to thame (6): and zit I
" feir that it will"

" ac ſe id verum exiſtimare, me non habere poteſ-
" tatem mei intra me, idque quia recuſaverim con-
" ditiones a ſe oblatas (1). Breviter, certum eſt
" quód de eo quod ſcis ſuſpicetur, ac de vitâ
" etiam (2). Quod ad poſterius, cúm primúm
" ego duobus aut tribus bonis verbis eum compello,
" gaudet, ac timere deſinit (3).

XXXI.—" Non vidi eum hâc veſperâ, quia tuam
" armillam conficiebam (4), cui nullam poſſum
" ceram invenire (5), id enim unum ad perfectio-
" nem ei deeſt (6); et adhuc vereor ne aliquod ſe
" offerat infortunium, et"

" Il dit auſſi, qu'il y en a qui croient, et que de ſa
" part il l'eſtime veritable, que je n'ay point en
" moy

" moy la puissance de moy-mesme, d'autant que
" j'ay refusé les conditions qu'il avoit offertes (1).
" Brief, il est certain qu'il se doute de ce que sca-
" vez, et de sa vie mesmes (2). Quant au reste,
" soudain que je luy propose deux ou trois bonnes
" paroles, il se resiouit, et n'a point de crainte (3).

XXXI.—" Je ne l'ay point veu ceste apres-
" disnée, parce que je faisoye vostre brasselet (4),
" auquel je ne puis accomoder de la cire (5);
" car c'est ce qui defaut a sa perfection (6); et
" encor je crain qu'il n'y survienne quelque incon-
" venient,"

(1) That he made no such offers as are here hinted at, has been already shewn. Dr. Robertson himself does not pretend that he did. And yet *the letters are genuine.*—" Offeris," Scotch; " conditiones oblatas," Latin; " conditions offertes," French.

(2) " His life," Scotch; " vitâ etiam," Latin; "*sa* vie *mesmes*," French, from the corrected Latin.

(3) " Last," Scotch; " posterius," Latin; ' reste," for *posterieur*, French. " Dout," Scotch; ' timere," Latin; " crainte," French.

(4) This aggravates the absurdity of the letter, in the conduct of Mary. She is come to see the King in his sickness, and to nurse him. This is acknowledged by all to have been done by her. Dr. Robertson says, that " she not only visited ' Henry, but, by all her words and actions, endea- " voured

" voured to exprefs an uncommon affection for
" him*." Yet, *by the letters*, this is not true. She
is employed a great part of her time in abfences
from him. She is writing a very long letter to her
adulterer. She is making a pair of bracelets for
him. She could not fit up late with Darnly the
firft night, becaufe fhe was tired with her journey.
She could not the fecond night, becaufe fhe was
writing to Bothwell. She could not the third
night, becaufe fhe was making bracelets for Bothwell. And fhe fpent all the morning of this day
till two, in the fame employ. So ridiculoufly has
the letter engaged her, on this vifit to her fick hufband; in order to give fcope to its own flanders!
—" Evening," Scotch; " vefpera," Latin; " apres-
" difnée," for *foir*, French.

(5) This is an amazing contradiction to a preceding paffage, which runs thus: " I wrocht this
" day quhill it was twa houris upon this bracelet,
" for to put the key of it within the lock thairof,
" quhilk is couplit underneth with twa cordounis;
" I have had fa lytill tyme, that it is evill maid."
Then the bracelet was " maid," yet it is *now* to be
" ended." *Then* it had a " key" and a " lock"
to it, but *now* fhe can get " na lokkis" for it.
Then the " key of it" was " put within the lock
" thairof," and " couplit underneth with twa cor-
" dounis;" but *now* the bracelet is only " reddy to
" thame." This is fuch a grofs and maffy contradiction, in fo plain a point, and at fo little a dif-

* i. 396.

tance,

tance, as speaks out loudly the infinite negligence of the author in this work of forgery.—" Lokkis," Scotch; " ceram," a mis-print for *feram*, Latin; and yet followed implicitly by the French in " cire." This is one of the proofs, which Mr. Goodall used so succesfully for the investigation of the true original *. And surely this and the other blunders of the French translation, must have given a strange appearance to that pretended original, at its exhibition to the commissioners in Westminster.

(6) " It is reddy to thame," Scotch ; " id enim " unum ad perfectionem ei deest," Latin ; and " car c'est ce qui defaut a sa perfection," French.

" bring some malheur, and may be sene gif ze " chance to be hurt (1). Advertise me gif ze will " have it (2), and gif ze will have mair silver (3), " and quhen I sall returne (4), and how far I may " speik (5). He inragis when he heiris of Le- " thingtoun, or of zow, or of my brother (6). Of ' zour brother (7) he speikis nathing. He speikis ' of the Erle of Argyle (8). I am in feir quhen I ' heir him speik; for he assuris himself yat he ' [Argyle] has not an evill opinioun "

' et conspici possit, si te contingat lædi (1). Fac ' me certiorem num eam velis habere (2), et si

* i. 96.

" pluscu-

" plufculum pecuniæ velis habere (3), et quando
" debeam redire (4), et quem in loquendo modum
" mihi ftatuam (5). Infanit ad mentionem de Le-
" thintonio, de te, de fratre meo (6). De tuo
" fratre (7) nihil loquitur. De Comite Argathe-
" liæ (8) in timore verfor, quóties eum audio lo-
" quentem; pro certo habet "

" et qu'il foit recogneu, s'il advenoit que vous fuf-
" fiez bleffé (1). Faictes moy entendre fi vous le
" voulez avoir (2), et fi avez affaire de quelque peu
" plus d'argent (3), et quand je doy retourner (4),
" et quel ordre je tiendray a parler a luy (5).
" Il enrage quand je fay mention de Lethington,
" de vous, et de mon frere (6). Il ne parle point
" de voftre frere (7). Quant au Conte d'Ar-
" gathley (8), je fuis en crainte, toutes les fois
" qu'il en devife ;"

(1) When the letters were *firſt* projected, on the 24th of July 1567, hopes were entertained of feizing and flaying Bothwell immediately. On the 11th of Auguft 1567, Sir William Murray of Tullibardin, and Sir William Kirkcaldy of Grange, were commiffioned to purfue him by fea and land, with fire and fword *; though one of thefe very gentlemen, Kirkcaldy, on Mary's preparing to pafs with him to the rebels upon the fatal 15th of June before, " *tuik the Erle Boythwell be the band*, and " *baid him depart,* promifing *that na man fhould*

* Keith, 442.

" *folow*

" *folow nor perfew him*; and fwa by thair awin con-
" fent he paft away *." *For the fame reafon* now,
if Bothwell fhould be taken alive, they had power
to hold courts, to condemn, and to execute immediately. Well therefore might it be remarked in
the Memoirs of Crawford, that " if Grange had
" taken him, it is more than probable (left he had
" betrayed his accomplices) that he had been fa-
" crified on the fpot †." Then this pair of bracelets, *fo particularly defcribed in the letter*, would
have been produced as found upon him. And this allufion to the expected fact, at once evinces the general forgery of the letters, and fhews the prefent
part of them to have been forged in the original
moments of projection. Lethington fat down, it
feems, while the new ideas were fhooting ftrong in
his mind; and fketched out fome parts of the letters immediately. Thefe fketches he naturally laid
before him, when he entered upon the completion
of the work in the winter following. And he as
naturally incorporated them all into it; and, in the
hurry and negligence with which the whole was
finifhed, inferted this temporary expectation along
with the reft.

(2) Here is another contradiction concerning
his ill-fated bracelet. Mary now afks Bothwell, *if
he will have it*. She had previoufly informed him,
that fhe fhould fend it to him by the bearer of the
letter. " I wrocht this day, quhill it was twa houris

* Goodall, ii. 164—165.   † Crawford, 54.

" upon

"upon *this* bracelet:—I have had fa lytill tyme "that it is evill maid; bot *I fall mak ane fairer*. In "THE MEANE TIME," &c. All this plainly implies her to fend it with the letter. Yet now, before she clofes the letter, she directly contradicts herfelf, and afks him if she shall fend it. And the hint concerning the "evil making" was thrown in plainly, to account for the inelegance of the work from fo elegant a workwoman as Mary, when the bracelet should come to be produced. We have the fame hint, and with the fame view, concerning the penmanship of the letters.

(3) This implies that she had given Bothwell some money before. Accordingly Paris is made to fwear, that on the road betwixt Kalendar and Glafgow, and confequently on January 23d, she fent Bothwell a purfe with three or four hundred crowns in it*. It has been afked, why she did not give it to Bothwell himfelf, who left her at Kalendar only that very day†. For this plain reafon, that *Paris might carry and tell of it afterwards*. But having given him three or four hundred crowns on the 23d, would she afk him on the 25th if he wanted more? She certainly would not! With fuch profufion, Mary's treafury would have been drained to the bottom, in a few days only.—"Silver," Scotch; "pecuniæ," Latin; "argent," French. This concurs with other inftances to shew, that many coincidences between the French and the Scotch are

* Goodall, ii. 76.   † Keith, 366, and Tytler, 138—139.

purely

purely casual, the result of a similarity between the two languages.

(4) But the return was already fixed. " The " King," she says before, " hes prayit me to re- " mane upon him quhil uther morne." And at " uther morne," or on January the 27th, she actually set out. But, even if this had not been the case, what *could* Bothwell advise about the day of her return ?

(5) Concerning *what* does she want to know how far she may speak ? This is like her desire to know, whether she might " avow all" to Bothwell. A mysterious air is thrown round some undiscernible points, in order to lend a consequence to nothing.—" How far I may speik," Scotch; " quem in loquendo modum mihi statuam," Latin; " quel ordre je tiendray a parler a luy," French.

(6) " Or," Scotch, omitted in Latin; " et," French, from the corrected Latin. But this shews plainly, who the lords were that he considered as hostile to him. Murray he has even noticed before, as an enemy.

(7) This means Huntley, whose sister had been married to Bothwell.

(8) The Latin omitting by accident one word, ' De Comite Argatheliæ [loquitur] ;" the French omits it too, and the two clauses are run into each other in both. " Argatheliæ," Latin ; " Argathley," French, for " Argyle."

"of him. He speikis nathing of thame that is
"out (1), nouther gude nor evill, bot fleis 'yat
"point (2). His father keipis his chalmer (2), I
"have not sene him.

XXXII.—" All the Hammiltounis are heir,
"that accompanyis me verray honorabilly. All
"the friendis of the uther [the King] convoyis me,
"quhen I gang to se him. He defyris me to cum,
"and se him ryse the morne betyme (3). For to
"mak schort, this beirer will tell zow the rest.
"And gif I leirne ony thing heir, I will mak zow
"memoriall at evin (3). He will tell zow the oc-
"casioun of my remaning (4). Burne this letter,
"for it is ovir dangerous (5), and nathing weill
"said in it (6); for I am thinking upon nathing
"bot fascherie. Gif ze be in Edinburgh "

"eum nihil de se malé opinari. De eis qui extra
"sunt (1) nihil, neque boni neque mali, loquitur,
"sed semper hunc locum vitat (2). Pater ejus
"domi (2) se continet, nondum enim [eum]
"vidi.

XXXII.—" Omnes Hamiltonii híc adsunt, et
"me comitantur valdé honorificé. Alterius om-
"nes amici me comitantur quoties eum viso. Petit
"a me ut cras tempori adsim, ut eum surgentem
"videam (3). Ut paucis absolvam, híc tabella-
"rius reliqua tibi narrabit. Si quid novi híc dis-
"cam,

" cam, vesperi (3) faciam commentarium. Ille
" tibi explicabit meæ moræ causam (4). Crema
" has literas, sunt enim periculosæ (5), nec quic-
" quam bene in eis dictum (6); ego enim nihil
" cogito nisi molestias. Si fueris Edinburgi cúm"

" Il s'asseure qu'il ne pense point de mal de luy.
" Quant a ceux qui sont de dehors (1), il n'en
" parle ny en bien ny en mal, seulement il a evité
" tousjours ce lieu (2). Son pere se tient tous-
" jours au logis (2), et ne l'ay point encores veu."

XXXII.—" Tous les Hambletons sont icy, qui
" me sont compagnie assez honorable. Tous les
" amis de l'autre me suivent lorsque je le visite.
" Il me prie, que je voye demain (3) assez a temps
" pour le voir lever. Afin que le face court, ce por-
" teur vous dira le surplus. Si j'appren icy
" quelque chose le soir (3), je le mettray en me-
" moire. Il vous declarera la cause de mon re-
" tardement (4). Bruslez ces lettres, car elles sont
" dangereuses (5), et s'il n'y a rien qui soit bien
" couché; je ne pense que choses fascheuses (6). Si
" vous estes a Edinbourg "

(1) " Thame that is out," means the men that
had been banished the kingdom, for their share in
the murder of Rizzio the March before. So Ruthven calls Murray and his associates in exile, " the
" lords which were fugitive *." So Buchanan,
with a nearer approach to the language of the

* Keith, 332.

letter,

letter, stiles them the lords that were absent, "nobi-
"litas quæ aberat*;" and, with an approach still
nearer in another place, denominates them those
that are absent, "absentibus †." So likewise the
Earl of Bedford, in a letter of August the 3d 1566,
speaks of some of these very rebels in the letter, as
those "who were *abroad* with Morton ‡." And
this serves, as almost every allusion to known facts
has hitherto served, to detect the forgery. With so
careless a hand was this idol of Dr. Robertson's
put together. The banished conspirators had been
pardoned and restored, a little while *before* the period of this letter. Upon Christmas Eve preceding,
the Queen had granted a pardon to the Earl of Morton and seventy-five of his accomplices, for that
horrible fact §. But the forger, writing the letters
in the November and December afterwards, with
his usual carelessness confided in his memory, and
was deceived by it.

(2) "Fleis yat point," Scotch; "*semper* hunc
"locum vitat," Latin; "il a evité *tousjours* ce
"lieu," French. "Chalmer," Scotch; "domi,"
Latin; "logis," French.

(3) This means the morning and evening of the
next day, January 26th.

(4) This is another of the mysterious involu-
tions of nothing, so frequent in this letter. The

---

* Hist. xvii. 344.   † Ibid. 345.   ‡ Goodall,
i. 305.   § Ibid. i. 321, Robertson, ii. 434, Keith, 429,
Pref. xi. and Melville, 76 and 77.

reason of her stay, as she has told us already, was the King's desire. And the reason of his desire must have been his weakness of body.

(5) What a ridiculous precaution to Bothwell, when she sends this very letter, " ovir dangerous " as it is, *unsealed*, by the hands of Paris!

(6) This is thrown in to account for Mary, the accomplished and the lively Mary, writing such a dull and stupid fardle of folly, under the name of a love-letter. And Buchanan has inflamed the absurdity of the precaution, by asserting it to have been given in almost every one of the letters, " Pene in singulis scriptum erat," he says, either wildly inattentive to the letters, or boldly daring to foist any thing into them, " ut lectæ statim cremarentur *."

" at the ressait of it (1), send me word sone.

XXXIII.—" Be not offendit, for I gif not ovir
" greit credite (2). Now seing to obey zow, my
" deir luse, I spair nouther honour, conscience, ha-
" sarde, nor greitnes quhatsumevir (3); tak it, I
" pray zow, in gude part, and not efter the inter-
" pretatioun of zour fals gude-brother (4), to
" quhome, I pray zow, gif na credite aganis the
" maist faithful luiser that evir ze had, or ever sall
" have.

* Hist. xviii. 364.

XXXIV.—

XXXIV.—" Sé not hir, quhais fenzeit teiris fuld
" not be fa mekle praifit nor eftemit, as the trew and
" faithful travellis (5) quhilk I fuftene for to merite
" hir place. For obteining of the quhilk, aganis
" my natural I betrayis thame that may impefche
" me (6). God forgive me, and God give zow,
" my only lufe, the hap and profperitie (7)
" quhilk zour humble and faithful lufe defyris
" unto zow, quha hopis to be fchortly ane uther
" thing to zow (8), for the reward of my irkfum
" travellis."

" cúm has accipies (1), fac me certiorem.

XXXIII.—" Noli offendi, quia non nimium
" fido (2). Nunc poftquam ob ftudium tibi obfe-
" quendi, mi chare amice, neque honori, neque
" confcientiæ, nec periculis, neque quantævis mag-
" nitudini parco (3); rogo in bonam partem acci-
" pias, ac non juxta interpretationem fallacis fra-
" tris uxoris tuæ (4), cui rogo nullam adhibeas fi-
" dem adverfus fideliffimam omnium quas aut ha-
" buifti, aut habebis, amicam.

XXXIV.—" Noli eam intueri, cujus fictæ la-
" chrymæ non debent tanti effe, quanti fidi la-
" bores (5) quos ego perfero, ut merear in ejus
" locum fuccedere; quem ut obtineam, ego eos
" prodo, idque adverfus ingenium meum, qui im-
" pedimento effe poffent (6). Deus mihi det ve-
" niam, et Deus tibi det, mi unice amice, eum fuc-
" ceffum, et felicitatem (7.), quam tua humilis et
" fidelis

" fidelis amica tibi optat, quæ brevi sperat aliud
" de te in (8) præmium mei molesti laboris."

" quand vous recevrez ces lettres (1), faictes le
" moy sçavoir.

XXXIII.—" Ne vous offensez point, si je [ne]
" me fie par trop (2). Maintenant donc, mon cher
" amy, puis que pour vous complaire je n'espargne
" ny mon honneur, ny ma conscience, ny les dan-
" gers, ny mesmes ma grandeur quelle qu'elle
" puisse estre (3); je vous prie, que vous le pre-
" niez en la bonne part, et non selon l'interpreta-
" tion du faux frere de vostre femme (4), auquel
" je vous prie aussi n'adjouster aucune foy contre
" la plus fidele amye, que vous avez euë, ou que
" vous aurez jamais.

XXXIV.—" Ne regardez point a celle, de la-
" quelle les feinctes larmes ne vous doivent estre de
" si grand poix, que les fideles travaux (5) que je
" souffre, afin que je puisse meriter de parvenir en
" son lieu. Pour lequel obtenir, je trahi, voire con-
" tre mon naturel, ceux qui m'y pourroient empes-
" cher (6). Dieu me le vueille pardonner, et vous
" doint, mon amy unique, tel succez et feli-
' cité (7), que vostre humble et fidele amye le
' souhaitte, laquelle espere en brief autre recom-
' pense de vous, pour ce mien facheux labeur."

(1) But how *could* he be in Edinborough at the
eceipt of this letter, when he appears from the

rebel

rebel journal itſelf, to have left Edinborough on the evening of January 24th, and not to have returned *towards* it till January 28th *.

(2) "*For* I give not ovir greit credite," Scotch; "quia non nimium fido," Latin, very erroneouſly; and ſtill more erroneouſly, "*ſi je me ſie* par trop," French. I have added the loſt negative.

(3) The French here has added "mon, ma, les," and "meſmes," to the text.

(4) Huntly; called here in French, by a literal tranſlation from the Latin, "frere de voſtre femme," but hereafter, with more preciſion, "beau-frere."

(5) "Sa mekle praiſit nor eſtemit," Scotch; "tanti," Latin; "ſi grand poix," French. "Trew and faithful," Scotch; "fidi," Latin; "fideles," French.

(6) "Natural" and "impeſche me," Scotch; "ingenium" and "impedimento," Latin; "naturel" and "me impeſcher," French.

(7) "Hap and proſperitie," Scotch; "ſucceſſum et felicitatem," Latin; "ſuccez et felicité," French.

(8) "Hopis to be—ane uther thing to zow," Scotch; "ſperat aliud de te in præmium," Latin; "and eſpere—autre recompenſe de vous," French.

* Appendix, N°. x.

XXXV.—

XXXV.—" It is lait (1); I defyre never to
" ceis fra wryting unto zow; zit now, after the kif-
" fing of zour handis, I will end my letter. Ex-
" cufe my evill wryting (2), and reid it twyfe over.
" Excufe that thing that is fcriblit, for I had na
" paper zifterday quhen I wrait that of the memo-
" riall (3). Remember upon zour lufe, and wryte
" unto hir, and that verray oft (4). Lufe me as I
" fall do zow."

XXXV.—" Serum eft (1); tamen nunquam
" cupio ceffare a fcribendo ad te; tamen nunc,
" poft ofcula manuum tuarum, finem meis literis
" imponam. Excufa meam in pingendo imperi-
" tiam (2), eafque relege. Excufa curfionem cha-
" racterum, quia heri chartam non habebam, cúm
" id quod in commentario erat fcriberem (3). Re-
" minifcere tuæ amicæ, ac fæpe ad eam refcribe (4).
" Redama me, uti ego te amabo."

XXXV.—" Il eft tard (1); neantmoins je ne
' defire jamais ceffer de vous efcrire; et touftes
' fois, apres vous avoir baifé les mains, je feray fin
' a mes lettres. Excufez mon ignorance a efcrire
' (2), et relifez mes lettres. Excufez la brief-
' ueté des characteres, car hier je n'avoye point de
' papier, quand j'efcrivi ce qui eft au memoire (3).
' Ayez fouvenance de voftre amye, et luy refcri
' uez fouvent (4). Aimez moy, comme je vous
' aime."

(1) This

(1) This shews the second half of the letter to be pretendedly written in the night of the second day, as the first pretends to have been in that of the first day.

(2) This is thrown in a second time, to account more strongly for the diffimilarity of the forger's writing to Mary's.—" Evill wryting," Scotch ; " in " pingendo imperitiam," Latin ; " ignorance a " escrire," French.

(3) This whole clause shews " the memoriall " or *memorandums* about the middle of the letter, to have been written " zisterday," or the day before the second half of the letter was; and to have been written in a particular manner, because her paper failed, as she actually mentions at the time that it was failing. And it concurs with that mention to prove, that the first half of the letter terminates with those memorandums.—" Erat," Latin, wrong ; and " est," French, right, from the corrected Latin.

But there is another point to be confidered here. That " the memoriall " means the *memorandums* preceding, is plain from what I have just noticed, and from the use of the word *memorial* before in the fame sense. " Gif I leirne ony thing heir," she fays, " I will mak zow *memoriall* at evin." These *memorandums* were written, it appears, " scriblit," Scotch ; " curfione characterum," Latin ; " brief- " ueté des characteres," French ; or in words shortened and abbreviated, *because* her paper begun to fail. Yet *are* the *memorandums* in contracted terms at present ? No ! They are not, in the

Scotch.

Scotch *. They are not, in the Latin †. They are not, in the French ‡. They are at full length in all. They are even at more than full length. Each *memorandum* makes a diftinct paragraph in all. So different are the copies at prefent, from what the originals pretend to have been!

(4) " *Verray* oft," Scotch; " fæpe," Latin; " fouvent," French. But how *could* Bothwell write to her either " oft," or " verray oft ?" This letter could not be difpatched till the next morning, and could not reach Edinborough before the day afterward. And that day, as fhe has told us already and will tell us again, fhe intends to fet out, and actually does fet out. The words are plainly thrown in from a wanton imitation of a real love-letter, without confidering the particular circumftances of the cafe. But they ferve ufefully at prefent, to expofe the abfurdity of thefe fictitious epiftles. And they add one more to the many proofs which we have noticed already, concerning that abfurdity.

XXXVI.—" Remember zow of the purpois of the Lady Reres (1).
" Of the Inglifmen (2).
" Of his Mother (3).

* See Anderfon, ii. 138.   † See Jebb, i. 273, and Goodall, ii. 16—17.   ‡ See Jebb, i. 337, and Goodǝ, ibid.

" Of the Erle of Argyle (4).
" Of the Erle of Bothwell (5).
" Of the ludgeing in Edinburgh (6)."

XXXVI.—" Reminiscere sermonis de Rere-
" siâ (1).
" De Anglis (2).
" De Matre ejus (3).
" De Comite Argatheliæ (4).
" De Comite Bothueliæ (5).
" De hospitio Edinburgi (6)."

XXXVI.—" Et ayez memoire du propos Ma-
" damoiselle Reres (1).
" Des Anglois (2).
" De sa Mere (3).
" Du Conte d'Arghley (4).
" Du Conte de Bothwel (5).
" Du logis d'Edimbourg (6)."

(1) This relates to the immediately preceding half of the letter, in which Lady Reres is mentioned. " *Lady* Reres," Scotch ; " Reresiâ," Latin ; " Madamoiselle Reres," French, from the corrected Latin.

(2) This relates both to the first and the second half of the letter, in both which the design of embarking on board an English vessel is mentioned.

(3) This refers to neither the first nor the second half. The Countess of Lenox, mother to the King is noticed in neither.

(4) The

(4) This Earl is spoken of in the second half. "Argyle," Scotch; "Argathelia" again, Latin; "Arghley," a mis-print for "Argathley," French.

(5) In the former volume I have marked the strangeness of mentioning Bothwell as a third person, when the letter is supposed to be addressed to him. Nor does the strangeness consist merely in the form. It is equally in the substance. The Earl of Bothwell is desired to remember about — the Earl of Bothwell. This is so excentric and unnatural in itself, as could never come from the pen of Mary. And the forger appears from this stroke, as I have previously observed, to have originally addressed the letter to some person different from Bothwell, and to have left the stroke unaltered when he altered the address.

(6) How strongly does *this* set of *memorandums* prove the absurdity of Dr. Robertson's and Mr. Hume's respective hypotheses, concerning the preceding! *These* cannot be hints for the *subsequent* parts of her letter, because they are absolutely at the end of the whole. *These* cannot be the contents of the letter *preceding*, because they refer to some points which are not in the letter at all; that concerning his mother, and this concerning the lodging at Edinborough.

But how comes the latter point to be mentioned? The King by this letter is to go to Cragmillar, not Edinborough. By the next also he is. How comes then a hint to intrude here, about his lodgings at Kirk-a-field; for those are plainly meant?

From

From this circumstance only. The rebel journal shews the letter originally to have carried the King, by Kalendar and Linlithgow to Kirk-a-field. This route was afterwards changed into another for Cragmillar. But a solitary reference to the original route, was accidentally forgotten to be altered. It had been originally answered by this passage of the journal: " Bothwell this 24th day [of Ja-" nuary] wes found verray tymus weséing the " Kyng's *ludging*, that *wes in preparing for him* *." And it still remains at the tail of the whole, to confirm the account of the journal, to betray the alteration made in the letter, and to demonstrate the forgery in the clearest manner.

* Appendix, N° x.

CHAPTER THE THIRD.

§ I.

LETTER THE SECOND (1).

I.—" It appeiris, that with zour abfence thair is alfwa joynit forzetfulnes, feand yat at zour departing ze promyfit to mak me advertifement of zour newis from tyme to tyme (2). The waitting upon yame zifterday (3), caufit me to be almaift in fic joy as I will be at zour returning, quhilk ze have delayit langer then zour promeis was (4)."

I.—" Videtur cum tuâ abfentiâ conjuncta effe oblivifcentia, præfertim cúm in tuo difceffu promiferis, quód me certiorem faceres, fi quid incidiffet novi, per fingula propé momenta (2). Eorum exfpectatio (3) propemodum in tantam lætitiam me conjecit, quam [quantam] in tuo reditu fim acceptura, quem diftulifti ultra quám promiferas (4)."

I.—" Il femble, qu'avec voftre abfence foit joinct l'oubly, veu qu'au partir vous me pro-
" miftes.

"miſtes de vos nouvelles, et toutesfois je n'en puis
"apprendre (2); de quoy l'eſperance (3) m'a
"quaſi jetté en auſſi grande joye, que celle que je
"doy recevoir a voſtre venue, laquel vous avez
"differée plus que ne m'aviez promis (4)."

(1) *When* this letter pretends to be written, will appear hereafter. But it may be proper to remark, at preſent, that, plainly as this ſhews itſelf to be one in ſucceſſion to another, yet it was publiſhed in Buchanan's Engliſh Detection, as the firſt of all *. The title of it ran thus; " ane letter writtin
" be hir from Glaſgow to Bothwell, proving hir
" hait to hir huſband, and ſum ſuſpiciounis of
" practiſing his deith, quhilk letter was writtin in
" French, and heir enſewis tranſlatit worde for
" worde." Then comes the firſt letter, which is ſo apparently the firſt from the contents of it, publiſhed as the ſecond, and with this title to it, " ane
" *uther* letter to Bothwell, concerning the hait of
" hir huſband, and practice of his murther †." The eighth letter is put third, with this inſcription to it,
" ane letter to Bothwell concerning certane takinis
" that ſcho ſent him ‡." The third ſucceeds in the fourth place, called " ane uther letter to Bothwell,
" of hir luſe to him §." And then we have the real fourth. So negligently are they arranged, even under the eye of Buchanan himſelf! Yet the three firſt were arranged in their natural order, by the

* Anderſon, ii. 129.   † Ibid. 131.   ‡ Ibid. 144.
§ Ibid. 147.

Latin

Latin edition of them. And the seven first were equally arranged so, by the French.

(2) This it was impossible for Bothwell to have done. He left her at Kalendar on January 23d, and returned to Edinborough. The next day in the evening, he set out for Lydisdale. And on January 28th, and not before, he set out from Lydisdale on his return *. He was gone therefore in the evening of January 24th, when she wrote the former half of her letter preceding. He was absent in the evening of January 25th, when she wrote the latter half. He was absent, when she wrote the present and the two next letters. They were all written, says the journal, on the 24th—26th of January. " 24. The Quene remaynit at Glascow, " lyck as she did the 25th and the 26th,—and in " this tyme wrayt hir BYLLE [the former letter] " and uther letteris to Bothwell." Nor let it be suspected, that his departure from Edinborough was sudden, unexpected by himself, and unknown to the Queen. She peculiarly knew of it. This appears from several strokes in the very letters themselves. Thus in the preceding she says; " gif ze " be in Edinburgh at the ressait of it," her letter, " send me word, &c." Thus also in the present she wants to know what she shall do, " in cace ze " be not RETURNIT quhen I am cum thair," to Edinborough. This is a plain intimation concerning his journey to Lydisdale. But soon afterwards

* Appendix, N° x.

she speaks of it in direct terms. "I pray zow," she says, "to send me gude newis of zour voy-"AGE." She therefore knew of his "voyage" or journey. She was doubtful, whether he would be returned from it or not, by the time of her arrival in Edinborough. And she was previously doubtful, whether he could be at Edinborough at the coming of her letter. He therefore could *not* have promised her, and she could *not* have expected him, "to mak her advertisement of his newis from tyme "to tyme." Hence also she could not have charged him now with forgetfulness. Those repeated addresses too, which we have seen before and shall see hereafter, in which Mary requires advice and requests intelligence from him, are as impossible to have been made, as I have previously shewn them to be absurd in the making. And all concur to make Murray's letters, for the twentieth time, betray his and their own villainy.

Stat contra dicitque tibi tua pagina, PUR ES.

The Latin here is very strange. It interpolates "præsertim," but is not followed by the French. "Zour newis" it renders "si quid incidisset novi," in opposition to the whole tenor of the sentence. And "from tyme to tyme" it translates, in opposition to itself, "per singula propé momenta;" as if something new was to befall him, nearly every moment. For this reason perhaps, the French drops the last intimation entirely, and then gives us these words, "et toutesfois je n'en puis apprendre." Yet this is one of the three sentences, which Doctor Robertson, fighting in the very breach for his assaulted faulted hypothefis, fondly fancied to be the laft vifible remains of the real original in French, and to have a " fpirit" and an " elegance" in them, which neither the Scotch, the Latin, nor the prefent French, have attained *. The *proof* for this paffage is — what? That it has the words " et toutesfois je " n'en puis apprendre" in it, when neither the Latin nor the Scotch have them; and, as ought to have been added, that it leaves out the words " from tyme to tyme," which both the others have. And, if there is a " fpirit" and an " elegance" in the interpolation, there muft be a double " fpirit" and a double " elegance" in the fuppreffion. But indeed the claufe, " et toutesfois je n'en puis ap-" prendre," is not properly an addition at all. It is merely a blundering tranflation of a claufe in the Latin. It was intended by the Frenchman, to anfwer fome words which he did not underftand. For ' promiferis—fi quid incidiffet novi," we have ' promiftes de vos nouvelles ;" and for " quod me ' certiorem faceres," we have " et toutesfois je n'en ' puis apprendre." He underftood not the latter. He gueffed at the meaning. He was unhappy in his guefs. And by fupplying the negative which he thought to be wanting, and fhaping the whole to his own conceptions, he produced the prefent fentence.

(3) " Zifterday," an important note of time ftrangely omitted in Latin and in French, could

* Diff. 32 and 34.

not

not be the day in which she wrote the second half of her letter, because of the joy which she says she felt in expecting a letter from him. Had she *then* been in this expectation and this joy, it would have appeared in what she then wrote. "Zis-"terday" therefore was the day afterward, or January 26. And consequently the day, on which she wrote this, was January 27. Accordingly in this very letter she says thus; "gif Paris bringis me "that quhilk I send him for, I traist it sall amend "me." If "send" here means the present time, she sent him off the morning after she had finished *the letter*, and this must then be January 26th. But if it means the past, as it stands equally for our *send* and *sent*; then it refers to what she had done the morning before, and this must then be the 27th. And that it does mean the past, Buchanan is a strong witness; he rendering it "miseram," and the French accordingly, "j'avoye envoyé."

(4) This is also impossible to be true. He had gone into Lydisdale on the evening of the 24th. It was a long journey, through the worst of roads, and in the worst of seasons. She knew he was to take it. He went, no doubt, upon some business of his office. He was lord-warden of the marches[*]. An object, that required such a journey in such a season, would be important enough to detain him a day or two. In fact it did detain him till the 28th[†]. And yet Mary is most absurdly made to

---

[*] Goodall, i. 303.   [†] Appendix, N° x.

complain,

complain on the 26th or 27th, whichever day we fix the date of this letter, that he had *then* delayed his return (not to Edinborough, but to Glafgow) longer than he had promifed; when in fact he *could* not have gone and returned, by *either* of thofe days.

II.—" As to me, howbeit I have na farther
" newis from zow, according to my commiffioun, I
" bring the man with me to Craigmillar (1) upon
" Monounday (2), quhair he will be all Wednef-
" day (2); and I will gang to Edinburgh to draw
" blude of me, gif in the meane tyme I get na newis
" in ye contrary fra zow."

II.—" Quod ad me attinet, quanquam nihil
" audiam præterea ex te novi, tamen, juxta partes
" mihi commiffas, hominem adduco mecum ad
" Cragmillarium (1) die Lunæ (2), ubi erit toto
" die Mercurii (2); ego autem ibo Edinburgum,
" ut mittam ex me fanguinem, fi nihil interea novi
" in contrarium de te audiam."

II.—" Quant a moy, encor que je n'oye rien de
" nouveau de vos, toutesfois, felon le charge que j'ay
" receuë, j'ameine l'homme avec moy Lundy (2) a
" Cragmillar (1), ou il fera tout le Mecredy (2);
" et j'iray a Edimbourgh pour me faire tirer du
" fang,

" fang, fi je n'enten [entend] rien de nouveau de
" vous au contraire."

(1) To fhew again the important alteration which has been made in this and the preceding letter, concerning the defigned route of the Queen towards Edinborough; let me once more produce the words of the journal. " The Quene (conforme " to hir commiffion, as fhe wryttis) broucht the " King from Glafcow to the *Kalendar*, towards " Edynbrough;" as the next day " the Quene " broucht the King to *Linlythquow*," and on the third day " remained all day in *Linlythquow* with " the King." And on the fourth " the Quene " broucht the King to *Edynbrough*, and put him in " his ludging qubair he endit," that very " ludgeing " in Edinburgh" noticed at the end of the laft letter *.

(2) This paffage points out the days of the week, as the date at the bottom of the letter alfo does, " From Glafgow this Setterday in the morning." Let us appropriate the days of the month to them. And then we fhall gain from both, one of the ftrongeft marks of forgery that we have yet feen.

The Queen, by the Rebel Journal, reached Glafgow on January 23d, 1566-7. Now January 23d in that year was a THURSDAY †. On THURSDAY

---

* Appendix, N° x. † Goodall, i. 120; Robertfon Diff. 40; Goodall, ii. 249, Rebel Journal, for April 12th being Saturday; and Goodall, ii. 244, compared with ii. 248, for February 5th and 7th being Wednefday and Friday.

evening she sat with him after supper. On FRIDAY evening, January 24th, she wrote the former half of the first letter. And on SATURDAY evening, January 25th, she wrote the other half. The evidences for this have been produced again and again before. There is no error possible in them. The *first* letter could not be finished till SATURDAY night. It could not be sent off before SUNDAY morning. And yet the *second* letter is dated on SATURDAY MORNING. This is exceedingly gross indeed.

But let us trace some of the principal notes of time once more, to pin down conviction more strongly on the mind.

In the *former* half of the letter preceding, she speaks of something that happened " the morne " efter my cumming." This again shews the *former* half to be written on FRIDAY January 24. Nor let disingenuity pretend to take shelter in a supposed interpolation *. Interpolations must be proved, before they are allowed. And, if arguments were to be answered by suppositions, all reasoning would be at an end, and the human mind left to drivel on in the chimæras of a dream.

All the other notes of time also coincide with this. They all concur with it, to prove *that* half of the letter to have been written, in the *evening* of *the day after her arrival.* Thus, the first or THURSDAY evening, January 23, he " desyrit," she says, " yat I suld walk," that is, wake, " with him;—I

* Robertson, Diss. 28.

" excusit

"excufit myfelf for this nycht that I culd not
"walk." *This night therefore fhe retired to bed*,
as fhe well might after her journey. The *next*
day, being "the morne efter her cumming," he
confeffed fomething concerning Willie Hiegait,
which he had not confeffed in the converfation the
night before. And in the *evening* of that day fhe is
employed in writing, what fhe calls her "firft jor-
"nay," which fhe "fall end the morne" or next
day; being now "ganging to fleip." So plainly
was the *firft* half of the preceding letter, written in
the *night* of FRIDAY January 24th. The *other* half,
we fee, was intended to be written "the morne," or
next day, SATURDAY January 25th. So alfo fhe
fays in another part of this former half; "I am
"gangand to feik myne [repofe] till the morne,
"quhen I fall end my bybill," bylle, or long letter.
But when does fhe end it? On the morrow, or SA-
TURDAY January 25. "I wrocht this day," fhe
fays, "quhill it was twa houris," or two o'clock,
"upon this bracelet." She alfo adds afterwards,
"I faw him not *this evening*, for to end zour brace-
"let." And fhe finally adds, that "it is *lait*."

All this demonftrates the falfe chronology of the
letters, in the plaineft manner. Their own notes of
time refute them. They carry their own paper of
infamy difplayed upon their breafts. And yet they
have been believed to be genuine, by a manly and
thinking nation. They have been defended by a
Hume. They have been admitted as hiftory by a
Robertfon.

III.—

III.—" He is mair gay then ever ze saw him (1);
" he puttis me in remembrance of all thingis yat
" may make me beleve he lufis me (2). Summa,
" ze will say yat he makis lufe to me (3) : of the
" quhilk I tak sa greit pleisure, yat I enter never
" where he is, bot incontinent I tak ye seiknes of
" my fair syde (4), I am sa troubillit with it (5).
" Gif Paris bringis me that quhilk I send him for,
" I traist it sall amend me (6)."

III.—" Est hilarior ac vegetior, quám unquam
" eum videris (1); subjicit mihi in memoriam (2)
" omnia, quæ efficere queant ut me credam ab eo
" amari. In summâ, diceres quód me cum summâ
" observantiâ colat et ambiat (3); quâ de re ita
" magnam capio voluptatem, quód nunquam ad
" eum ingredior, quin dolor lateris mei infirmi (4)
" me invadat, ita me malé habet (5). Si Paris ad
" me afferet id cujus causâ eum miseram, spero me
" meliús habituram (6)."

III.—" Il est plus joyeux et dispos, que vous ne
" l'avez jamais veu (1); il me reduict en memoire
" (2) toutes les choses, qui me peuvent faire enten-
" dre qu'il m'aime. En somme, vous diriez qu'il
" m'honnore et recherche avec grand respect (3):
' en quoy je pren si grand plaisir, que je n'entre
' jamais vers luy, que la douleur de mon costé
' malade (4) ne me saisisse, tant il me fasche (5).
' Si Paris m'apportoit ce pourquoy j'avoye envoyé,
' j'espere que je me porteroye mieux (6)."

(1) This

(1) This is extraordinary. The King is yet very weak. He was to rise, as she tells us in the second half of her letter written in the evening of Saturday January 25th, " the morne betyme," early on Sunday January 26th. This was the first time of his leaving his bed. He therefore desired the Queen " to cum and sè him ryse." Yet now, on *Saturday* morning, he is very gay. But let us suppose it to be the morning, on which he was to rise; and let us suppose him, on finding himself risen from the bed of dangerous sickness, full of spirit, full of courtesy, full of gallantry. Yet he could not possibly " be mair gay," than ever Both well had seen him. He had however *saluted every body, even to the lowest persons,* and had *made piteous caressing unto them, to draw down their pity upon him*; at a time when he kept his bed and saw no one. And in the same strain he is now " mair gay then ever;" when he is so weak, as to be carried to Edinborough in a litter.—" Mair " gay," Scotch; " hilarior ac vegetior," Latin; " plus joyeux et dispos," French.

(2) "He puttis me in remembrance of," Scotch; " subjicit mihi in memoriam," Latin; " il me re- " duict en memoire," French. " The word *me-* " *moire*," says the Miscellaneous Remarker*, " has " enabled THE SCOTTISH TRANSLATOR to give the " general meaning of this sentence. It is plain, " however, that he did not comprehend the particu- " lar import of the phrase, "' il me reduict en me- "' moire,'" which means to draw up a list or inven-

* P 9.

" tory.

"tory. The expression, as here used, is highly
'sarcastical and insulting. He makes out for my
" use a *catalogue* of all the circumstances in his con-
"duct, which may make me understand that he
"loves me." I have cited this passage, merely to
hold up the author of it once more to the merited
ridicule of the public. " Mr. Goodall," he acknow-
edges, " has proved beyond possibility of cavil,
' that the *first* letter, as we now have it, was tran-
' slated into French from the Latin copy*." This
acknowledgment was surely sufficient to have set-
led the gentleman's faith. If one letter is proved
to be a translation, when it pretended to be an original; then an imposture is detected. If one letter
asserted itself to have been written by Mary in the
French language, and yet appears from its own internal evidence to be merely a translation from the
Scotch at second hand; then a forgery is proved.
And if one of the letters is proved to be a forgery
" beyond possibility of cavil," he must be a caviller
indeed, who will still maintain the authenticity of
the others. Yet this gentleman does maintain it.
Ile suppoſes it. He speaks of the Scotch as a translation, in direct contradiction to his own confession.
He says, that this translation has not given us the
precise import of the French original here. And
thus any difference between the two copies, without
proof that the French is the original, and even
against proof that the Scotch is, is to be ascribed to
the inaccuracy of the Scotch as a translation. I

* P. 34.

have already confirmed the internal arguments of Mr. Goodall, by an hiſtorical evidence, that goes to *all* the letters, and that proves *all* to have been Scotch many months before they were French. But to what I have ſaid I wiſh to ſubjoin one brief remark, on this gentleman's reaſoning concerning the French of this paſſage. "Reduire en memoire," he ſays, ſignifies " to draw up a liſt or inventory." This is not true. Nor would it be available, if it was. "Reduire en memoire" ſignifies to make a memorandum of a thing. So "memoire" is uſed for "memorial," in Let. 1. Sect. XXXV. And " mettre en memoire" is uſed for " making me-"morial" in Sect. XXXII. Yet even this is only the *ſecondary* ſenſe of the expreſſion. The *primary* is ſimply " to recall into memory." So we have " ayez memoire" in Let. 1. Sect. XXXVI. for " remember zow." Indeed " reduire en memoire" is purely the Latin " reducere in memoriam," retained in the French. And, as we *know* the French of *all* theſe letters to be merely the Latin tranſlated, we know " il me reduict en memoire" here to be merely the " ſubjicit mihi in memoriam" of the Latin, or, as the corrected Latin perhaps ran, " re-" ducit mihi in memoriam;" and both to be a tranſlation of the Scotch, " he puttis me in re-" membrance." Biſhop Leſley ſays, in preface to his Negotiations, " I have reduced to theyr remem-" brance *."

(3) At York the words were theſe, " ſumma, ye "will ſay he makis *the court* to me †." And the

* P. xix. Anderſon, iii.   † Appendix, N° vii.

Latin

Latin verſion appears to have been formed upon this reading, " cum ſummâ obſervantiâ colat et " ambiat," ſo faithfully retained in the French, " honnore et recherche avec grand reſpect." And a variation of a ſingle word only, in a letter pretending to be an original of Mary's, evinces the forgery of the whole.

(4) Dr. Robertſon was imprudent enough, to dwell upon this as a mark of authenticity. The pain in her ſide, he ſays *, " is mentioned—in a 'manner ſo natural, as can ſcarce belong to any ' but a genuine production." An argument of this kind, from its very feebleneſs of nature, can never be of any conſequence. But let us examine t. Such a writer, even in his weakeſt eſſays of reaſon, is not unworthy of a refutation.

" The Queen," ſays Le Croc, " behaved her-' ſelf admirably well all the time of the baptiſm; ' and ſhewed ſo much earneſtneſs to entertain all ' the goodly company in the beſt manner, that this ' made her forget in a good meaſure her former ' ailments. But—ſhe continues to be—penſive and ' melancholy. She ſent for me yeſterday," December 22d, " and I found her laid on the bed ' weeping ſore, and ſhe complained of *a grievous* '*pain in her ſide.* And, for a ſurcharge of evils, it ' chanced that the day her Majeſty ſet out from ' Edinburgh for this place," Stirling, " ſhe hurt ' one of her breaſts on the horſe, which ſhe told ' me is now ſwelled †." The intimation in the

* Diſſ. 27.   † Keith, pref. vii.

text

text was plainly intended, as a kind of burlesque upon this incident in Mary's life; and, as a burlesque is sure to be, is greatly overcharged. She was "weeping sore" at the strange conduct of the King. And the strong anguish of her spirit, which she had thrown off during her appearance before her splendid guests, and which, for that very reason, returned with the greater force upon her in retirement, had occasioned, as strong anguish frequently did in her [*], and frequently does in others, a violent pain in her side. But what parallel can there possibly be, between such a cause for the pain, and the present; between the mere sight of her husband, *whom she went to see*, whom she *knew* she should find sick, whom she has *repeatedly* seen in his sickness already, and to whom she wished to shew every mark of attention; and this great burst of confined sorrow? None surely. And nothing, but the monster-making spirit of forgery, could have thought of ranking them as equivalent. Mary appears *not* to have been generally "subject to a vio-" "lent pain in her side," as Dr. Robertson infers she does from the embassador's letter [†]. He might as well have concluded from it, that she was generally subject to "pensiveness and melancholy," to a habit of "weeping sore," or to "a hurt and "swelled breast." These were complaints all equally incidental. The weeping, from the sharpness of the paroxysm, occasioned the pain. And the letter-writer, willing to catch at any circum-

---

[*] Diss. 27.   [†] Guthry's Scotch Hist. vii. 211.

stance

tance that should seem to *appropriate* his forgeries, and acting under the *peculiar* promptitude of forgers to *generalize* incidents, took up an occasional pain, made it an habitual one, and even gave it to the Queen at a time, when the most habitual could never have been given. He has thus made the pain in the side completely farcical. He has thus betrayed the over-doing hand of imposition in the work. He has thus turned Dr. Robertson's mark of authenticity, into a full proof of forgery *.

(5) " I am sa troubillit with it," Scotch; " ita me malé habet," Latin; " tant il me fasche," French. This is brought as another instance by Miscellaneous Remarker †, of *the Scottish translation missing the sense of the French original*. " The Scotch," he observes, " says with *it*, the French *il*; the sense is, *he* so troubles or vexes me." But the real sense in both is, that *it*, French *il*, troubles me. " He makis lufe to me," says this *transformed* Mary, " of the *qubilk* I tak sa greit pleisure, yat I enter never where he is, bot incontinent I tak ye seiknes of my fair syde, I am sa troubillit with *it*."

But here let me notice another proof of the forgery, in another variation of the text. " I am sa *troubillit* at it," as Mary writes in the *Westminster*, original of this letter, was primarily written by her

---

*. To shew the eternal shiftings of falshood, Buchanan has seen this intimation, and varied it thus; " quhais *stomach turnit* at the ficht of him, quha is suddanely taken with pangis at his presence." 144. Anderson. ii. and 252. Jebb, i.
† P. 39.

in the *York* original, "I am foe *faſchit* with it *."
And the French " tant il me *faſche*," which could
not be derived from the Scotch, becauſe it is not in
the Scotch of the Weſtminſter letters, ſhews very
plainly the caſual coincidences betwixt the Scotch
and the French of the letters.

(6) This is one more of the anachroniſms, that
betray the whole. Paris, the bearer of the laſt letter,
could not go with it before it was finiſhed. But it
was not finiſhed till late in the night of Saturday,
January the 25th. He therefore could not ſet out
till Sunday morning, January 26th. Yet "ziſter-
" day" ſhe was in full expectation of an anſwer, and
to-day ſhe thinks an anſwer would cure her of her
ſickneſs. And yet to-day, by the date of this
very letter, is only "Setterday in the morning." She
therefore expected an anſwer to her letter—before
it was ſent, and even—before it was written. Even
if we overlook this, and ſuppoſe this to be the
morning *after* ſhe had finiſhed her letter; the
bearer *can be but juſt gone with it*, as the letter
could not be ſent before the morning. Even if we
paſs over this too, and again ſuppoſe one whole
day to have elapſed between diſpatching the
firſt letter and writing the ſecond; ſhe could expect no anſwer yet, and ſtill leſs could ſhe expect
one "ziſterday." Even if we once more addreſs
ourſelves to the work of *creating* time, and throw
in two whole days betwixt the firſt and ſecond letters; ſtill no anſwer could be expected to-day, none

* Appendix, N° vii.

could

could be expected yesterday, and none could come in less than one whole day more. And when we consider further, that all this is said upon the supposition of Bothwell being then at Edinborough, though he was actually at Lydisdale all the while; and reflect also, that the letter-writer knew he was; we see the difficulties increasing upon us in spite of all our endeavours. We see the chronology hanging like a mill-stone around the neck of the letters. And we behold them sinking under the weight,

> With louder ruin to the gulphs below.

The fact is, that the letters suppose the Queen to have continued longer at Glasgow, than the journal allows her to have done. That such a variation should have been introduced into letters, which were to be modelled upon the dates of the journal; is most extraordinary. The very existence of the journal, the very discovery of it among the other papers of Cecil's, shews it to have been intended as the key and the companion of the letters. On that, no doubt, were they formed at first. But from that were they made to deviate afterwards, by those alterations and corrections, of which we have seen so many in the preceding parts of this work, and of which I have shewn an additional one at the end of the last letter. And thus mention was incidentally made of a variety of days in the letters, while here were only three, and one evening besides, in the journal. Thus, the first letter is written in *two* days after the day of arrival. A *third* day is referred to in these words of it, " he desyris me to " cum and sè him ryse *the morne* betyme;—gif I
" leirne

"leirne ony thing heir, I will mak zow memoriall
" at *evin*." On this third day, the firſt letter is diſpatched. An anſwer could not return, even from Edinborough only, under three days. Murray actually makes Paris to be three days, in bringing back this very anſwer*. "Ziſterday" therefore, when Mary expected an anſwer, muſt have been the *fifth* day at leaſt. And *to-day* muſt be the *ſixth*. This is very like Falſtaff's " eleven buck-
" ram men grown out of two," and reſults from the very ſame ſpirit, the careleſs confidence of habitual falſhood. It is certainly very wonderful, that the rebels ſhould have ſo far indulged their confidence and their falſhood, as to depart boldly from the very line which they had preſcribed to their conduct. But it is certainly more wonderful, that, after they *had* departed, they ſhould either not ſee or not mind their own anachroniſms; and ſtill give in to the commiſſioners of England that very journal, by which, of all poſſible papers in the world, thoſe anachroniſms were moſt ſure to be detected. And all ſerves to ſhew, what cannot be too often inculcated, the amazing infatuation of ſucceeding times, in catching up with profound reſpect this haſtily and clumſily carved block of wood, fancying it " an
" image that fell down from Jupiter," and ſo giving it a moſt honourable niche in the temple of hiſtory.

* Goodall, ii. 77—78.

IV.—

IV.—" I pray zow, advertife me of zour newis
" at lenth, and quhat I fall do in cace ze be not re-
" turnit quhen I am cum thair (1); for in cace ze
" wirk not wyfely, I fé that the haill burding of this
" (2) will fall upon my fchoulderis. Provide for
" all thingis, and difcourfe upon it firft with zour-
" felf. I fend this be Betoun (3), quha gais to ane
" day of law of the Laird of Balfouris (4). I will
" fay na farther, faifing that I pray zow to fend me
" gude newis of zour voyage (5). From Glafgow
" this Setterday in the morning."

IV.—" Oro, fac me certiorem de tuis rebus pro-
" lixé, et quid mihi fit faciendum, fi tu non eris re-
" verfus cúm ego illuc veneró (1); quia, nifi tu
" rem geras prudenter, video totum onus (2) in
" meos humeros inclinaturum. Profpice omnia, ac
" priús tecum rem expende. Hæc tibi mitto per
" Betonem (3), qui proficifcitur ad diem dictum
" D. Balfurio (4). Non dicam plura, nifi quód te
" rogo ut de tuo itinere me certiorem facias (5).
" Glafcua hôc Sabbato mané."

IV.—" Je vous prie, faiƈtes moy fcavoir bien
" au long de vos affaires, et ce qu'il me faut faire,
" fi vous n'eftes de retour quand je feray là ar-
" rivée (1); car fi vous ne conduifez la chofe fage-
" ment, je voy que tout le faix (2) retournera
" fur mes efpaules. Regardez a tout, et premiere-
" ment

" ment efpluchez le faict en vous mefmes. Je vous
" envoye ceci par Beton (3), qui s'en ira au jour
" affigné au Sieur Balfurd (4). Je ne vous en di-
" ray d'avantage, finon pour vous prier que me fa-
" ciez entendre de voftre voyage (5). A Glafcow
" ce Samedy matin."

(1) This is one of thofe many addreffes for intelligence, which could not poffibly be granted, even upon the forger's *own* chronology. *By this very letter* it was now Saturday in the morning. *By this very letter,* fhe was to fet out on Monday. And he was to fend her a long letter of news, betwixt the one and the other. But where was he *then?* Not at Edinborough. This is plain. He might not be returned thither, even by the time fhe reached the city. From whence then was he to write her this long letter? From Lydifdale, very plainly. And betwixt Saturday and Monday morning he was to receive her letter from Glafgow, and to write a long anfwer from Lydifdale, containing a full account of himfelf, and inftructing her how fhe was to act in cafe he fhould not be returned at her arrival. So wonderfully do the impoffibilities multiply upon us, at every furvey of the chronology!

(2) "Of this," Scotch, omitted in Latin and French.

(3) This is "Archibald Betoun," as Thomas Nelfon's depofitions inform us, " quhilk—wes ef-
" cheare of the Quenis chalmer-door *."

* Goodall, ii. 244.

(4) " Day

(4) "Day of law," Scotch; "diem dictum," Latin; and "jour assigné," French. The Frenchman, not underſtanding the peculiar import of the expreſſion "dies dictus," tranſlated it literally, and therefore unmeaningly. When "day of law" occurred before, the Latin rendered it paraphraſtically, "in eum ipſum diem ut cauſam diceret accerſitum," and the French, "ce jour-la meſme il eſtoit adjournée." And the Miſcellaneous Remarker appears to have been as ignorant of the Scotch, as the Frenchman was of the Latin. "'A day of law of the laird of Balfouris,'" he ſays, "is an unintelligible phraſe: the meaning of the French ſeems to be, who will go on the day appointed to Mr. Balfour.'" "We know not to what circumſtance this alludes*." And thus the very Mary, who ſays ſhe ſends this letter by a bearer that *goes* to one of the Lord of Balfour's courts, is made by the Frenchman and the Remarker to ſend it by a man, that *will go* on ſome future day with it, and to *Mr. Balfour* inſtead of Bothwell. "A day of law" is an expreſſion, which was very common formerly for a court-day. The Earl of Lenox deſires Mary "to differ this *day of law*" for Bothwell's trial †, and points out ſome ridiculous inconvenience, "gyf your Majeſtie ſuffer this ſchort *day of law* to go forwart ‡." And "the *day of law*," ſays the Engliſh embaſſadour Randolph to his Queen, "againſt the four burgeſſes, men of this

* P. 39.   † Anderſon, i. 53.   ‡ Ibid. 54.

"town,

"town, is like to hold, for any thing that she," Mary, " can be persuaded to the contrary *." The term *law-day*, also, appears in all the old charters within our own kingdom. It appears even in Sir Nicholas Throgmorton's dispatches to Elizabeth from Scotland; he saying in one of them, that " the *law-day* for the murder of the late King doth " hold †." And " the laird of Balfouris" was the well-known Sir James Balfour, called by our Walsingham " Sir James Baford ‡," as he is here called by the French translator " Sieur Balfurd."

(5) The mention of the " voyage" here confirms the hint above, of Bothwell's being gone to Lydisdale, and of the Queen's knowing it. Yet she still continues her clamours for news from him; when from that very " voyage" they were doubly impossible to be gratified. " Send me *gude* newis," Scotch; " me certiorem facias," Latin; and " me " faciez entendre," French. She wanted not merely to hear *news* of his journey, but *good* news. Yet Miscellaneous Remarker, with a strange turn of thought, objects to the Scotch for—being wiser in its meaning than the French §.

* Goodall, i. 246—247. † Keith, 451. ‡ Robertson, ii. 463. § P. 39.

§ II.

§ II.

LETTER THE THIRD.

I.—" I have walkit [waked] laiter thairup then
" I wald have done (1), gif it had not bene to
" draw fum thing out of him (2), quhilk this beirer
" will fchaw zow; quhilk is the faireft commoditie
" that can be offerit to excufe zour affairis (3). I
" have promyfit to bring him [the bearer] to him
" [the King] the morne (4). Put ordour to it, gif
" ze find it gude (5).

I.—" Diutiús illic morata fum quám volebam
" (1), nifi id factum fuiffet ut aliquid ex eo ex-
" fculperém (2), quod hic tabellarius tibi indica-
" bit; quæ eft belliffima occafio ad excufandum
" noftra negotia (3). Promifi me ipfum cras ad
" eum adducturam (4). Tu rem cura, fi tibi com-
" moda videtur (5)."

I.—" J'aye veillé plus tard là-haut, que j'en euffe
" fait (1), fi ce n'euft efté pour tirer (2) ce que ce
" porteur vous dira; que je trouve la plus belle
" commodité pour excufer voftre affaire, qui fe
" pourroit prefenter (3). J'ay promis, que je luy
" meneray demain ceftuy-la (4). Vous aiez en foin,
" fi la chofe vous femble commode (5).

(1) Buchanan read the words, as they feemingly
ought to be read, " walkit up there," not " walkit
" thair-up,"

"thair-up," as Dr. Robertson reads them *. But he carelessly rendered " walkit up," by " mo-rata sum." And so the whole became " illic morata sum." The corrected Latin saw the error, amended it, and made another. It turned " morata sum" into *vigilavi*, and " thair-up," as it read the words with Dr. Robertson, into *illic sursus*; and so produced in its reflection, the French, " j'aye veillé plus tard là-haut." And thus the passage, as I shall shew more at length hereafter, implied Mary to be, as she is actually said in the rebel journal to have been, when she wrote the non-apparent letter concerning " the abbot of Haly-ruid-house," writing in a room below the King's. Yet she now lodged in a different house. " All the freindis of the uther," the Stuarts, the adherents of Darnly, " convoyis me quhen I gang to se him," she says in her first letter. And there she " wrayt hir *bylle* and uther letteris to Both-well."—This passage, however, shews the third letter, like the two parts of the first, to be written late at night. On what night, will appear hereafter.

(2) " Out of him," Scotch; " ex eo," Latin, omitted in French.

(3) " Fairest occasioun," Scotch; " bellissima occasio," Latin; and " la plus belle commodité," French. " Zour," Scotch; " nostra," Latin; " vostre," French, from the corrected Latin. Miscel-

* Diss. 35.

laneous

laneous Remarker suspects, "that the French has "been erroneously transcribed, and that the origi- "nal word was *executer* *." But has the Scotch also been "erroneously transcribed?" This however he will presume to be only a version from the French, and so to copy the erroneous reading there. He may *presume* it was. But others have *proved* it was not. And was the Latin also transcribed erroneously, or will he *presume* the Latin to be equally a version from the French? The word being the same in all the three copies, and good sense in all; every conjectural reading surely is precluded for ever.

This is the last of the three sentences, from which, as connoisseurs in statuary pretend to judge of an Apollo by a finger or a toe, Dr. Robertson attempts to prove the existence of a French copy, different from that very copy in which these very sentences are found. But what is the *proof* from the present passage? It lies, according to the Doctor himself, in " j'aye veillé plus tard là-haut" being plainly no translation of "diutius illic morata sum," and ' pour excuser *vostre* affaire" being "very" different from " ad excusandum *nostra* negotia †." The whole therefore is reduced to two variations betwixt the French and the Latin. Are such variations, then, *confined* to the *first* sentence of each of these three letters? Are they not extended to other sentences? And are they not diffused all over the

* P. 40. † Diss. 33.

letters?

letters? They are. I have shewn them to be so, in the two letters preceding. I shall shew them to be so in this. And the Doctor's argument will thus, in *his* mode of proving, demonstrate the *present* French, and *every* sentence in it, to be that very original, which it primarily pretended to be, which Mr. Goodall has so powerfully proved it not to be, and which even the Doctor dares not assert it is. The truth is, as I have already shewn and shall shew still farther, that from those posterior corrections of the Latin, which we have even seen Buchanan himself making, from inattention at one time, and from ignorance at another, the French and the Latin vary frequently; though they are still so close in general, and the French still adheres so particularly even to the blunders of the Latin, that the confession of the French translator was hardly necessary to shew he translated from the Latin. He confessed however, that he did. Nor does he make the ridiculous exceptions, which Dr. Robertson chuses to make for him; and say he translated all from the Latin, *except the first sentence in each of the letters*, which he took from—the French original. He says that he translated *all*, all of the first three letters, and all of the other four too. Let him come, and speak for himself again. "Au reste," he tells us, "epistres mises sur la fin," which *were all but the eighth,* " avoient esté escrites par la Royne, partie " en Francois, partie en Escossois, et depuis tra- " duictes ENTIEREMENT en LATIN: mais, n'ayant " cognoissance de la langue Escossoise, j'ay mieux

"aimé

"aimé exprimer TOUT ce que j'ay trouvé en LA-
"TIN, que," &c. This confession takes a comprehensive sweep. It makes *all* the seven letters, and the *whole* of *each* of the seven, to have been translated into Latin, and from thence to have been rendered into French. It starts no piddling objections about sentences or half-sentences, at the head or at the tail of any. It embraces all within its wide-spread arms. And it proves the fancied existence of a French copy at the time, to be all a fairy vision, the creation of minds that have subjected their judgments to their imaginations, the invited dreams of self-delusion. Nor let this be thought too severe upon a very respectable writer. He is here, I believe, all that I insinuate. He has noticed two variations in this very passage, of the French from the Latin. But he *omits* a third, because it is a variation from the *Scotch* as well as the Latin, and because it makes *nonsense* of the clause. ' To draw sum thing *out of him*, quhilk this beirer ' will schaw zow," Scotch; " ut aliquid *ex eo* ex-' sculperem, quod hic tabellarius tibi indicabit," Latin; " pour tirer [*hors de luy*, should have ' been added] ce que ce porteur vous dira," French. And the Doctor ought, in honesty, to have produced *this*, as a *third* proof of the originality of the French here; or, as he saw the absurdity of that, to have given up his hypothesis entirely, to have owned his convictions, and to have remitted the letters to the scorn and detestation of mankind.

VOL. II. S (4) " The

(4) "The morne," Scotch. What day this was, I shall endeavour to shew hereafter. At present I remark, that this letter was not to go away, before the bearer had been carried by the Queen to the King the next day.

(5) What this was, we know not. It was never intended, that we should know. It is only one of the many nothings, which are veiled up in a mysterious obscurity, in order to rise into consequence; as a hill, seen through a fog, swells up into a mountain.—"Put ordour to it," Scotch, that is, put the matter in a train for action; "tu rem cura," Latin; and "vous ayez en soin," French.

———

II.—" Now, Schir, I have brokin my promeis;
" becaus ze commandit me nouther to wryte nor
" send unto zow (1). Zit I have not done this to
" offend zow (2). And gif ze knew the feir yat I
" have presently, ze wald not have so many con-
" trary suspiciounis in zour thocht (3); quhilk
" notwithstanding I treit and chereis (4), as pro-
" ceeding from the thing in the warld (5) that I
" maist desyre, and seikis fasteft to haif (6), quhilk
" is zour gude grace; of the quhilk my behaviour
" sall assure me (7). As to me, I sall never dis-
" pair of it; and prayis zow, according to zour
" promeis, to"

II.—

II.—" Nunc, Domine, ego pactum violavi;
" quia tu vetuisti ne vel scriberem vel mitterem ad
' te (1). Non tamen hoc feci quo te offenderem
' (2). Et si scires quanto in metu ego sum in
' præsentiâ, non tot in animo haberes contrarias
' suspiciones (3); quibus tamen ego faveo, et boni
' consulo (4), tanquam profectis ab eâ re, quam
' ego omnium quæ sub cœlo sunt (5) maximé
' cupio et diligentissimé persequor (6), qui est tuus
' favor; de quo mea me officia certam et securam
' facient. Quod ad me attinet, nunquam de eo
desperabo; ac te rogo,"

II.—" Maintenant j'ay violé l'accord; car vous
aviez deffendu que je n'escrivisse, ou que je n'envoyasse, par devers vous (1) : neantmoins je ne
l'ay faict pour vous offenser (2). Et si vous
scaviez en quell crainte je suis a present, vous
n'auriez point tant de soupçons contraires en vostre esprit (3), lesquels toutesfois je supporte, et
pren en bonne part (4), comme provenans de la
chose que je desire le plus de toutes celles qui
sont soubs le ciel (5), et que je poursuy avec extreme diligence (6), a scavoir, vostre amitié,
dont tant de devoirs que je fay me rendent certaine et assurée (7). Quant a moy je n'en desespereray jamais; et vous prie,"

(1) Mary now appears to have made a " promeis," because Bothwell required one from her,
' nouther to wryte nor send unto" him. This is
most amazing. She has never mentioned it before.

fore. Yet she has actually written TWICE. And this gives the very stamp of absurdity itself to these ill-contrived forgeries. Nor let it be said, in order to evade the censure, that he so "comman-"dit" her in a *letter* since his departure. She speaks not merely of his "command," but of her own "promeis." This could not be given by *letter*, even if the "command" could; as to give it so, would be to break the command in promising to obey it. And the stamp must still remain fixed, in one of its deepest impressions, upon the face of the forgeries.—"Schir," Scotch; "Domine," Latin, omitted in the French.

(2) Why then did she write at all? She has nothing particular to say. Even if she had, she was commanded, and had promised, neither to write nor send unto him. But when both reasons concur to keep her hand from the pen, in the name of propriety why does she write at all?—*She was obliged to write.*

> Is it in equilibrio,
> Whether the Gods descend or no?
> Then let th' affirmative prevail,
> As requisite to form my tale.

(3) What suspicions were these? Of Mary's fidelity to Bothwell, I suppose. But *why* should Bothwell entertain such? And *how* comes Mary to know, that he does entertain them? Neither appears. She *cannot* have heard from him, though she was so impatient for hearing in the last letter. He is in Lydisdale all this while. She does not say that she has heard from him, and yet has lost all

her

her impatience. How is all this? This letter indeed is apparently unconnected with the foregoing. All intimation concerning the King is nearly suppressed. There is no hint of Paris or the first letter. There is no hint of Beton or the second. And I take it, from all the features of it, to have been one super-added to the original number from Glasgow, super-added some time after the number was finished, but before the mention of the letters in the journal was finally settled. The journal speaks of Mary writing " hir bylle and uther letteris" from Glasgow; plainly implying her to have written two or three letters besides her bylle.

(4) " Treit and chereis," Scotch; " faveo et " boni consulo," Latin; " supporte, et pren en " bonne part," French.

(5) " The thing in the warld," Scotch; " om- " nium quæ sub cœlo sunt," Latin; " toutes celles " qui sont soubs le ciel," French.

(6) " Maist desyre, and seikis fasteft to haif," Scotch; " maximé cupio *et diligentissimé persequor*," Latin; " je *poursuy avec extreme diligence*," French, omitting the former clause.

(7) " My behaviour sall assure me," Scotch; " mea me officia *certam et securam facient*," Latin; " tant de devoirs que je fay me rendent *certaine et* " *assurée*," French. The wordiness of the French, and even of the Latin, compared with the Scotch, is very evident. And the French has additionally turned the future time of the Scotch and Latin into the present.

" difcharge zour hart unto me (1): utherwayis I
" will think that my malhure, and the gude hand-
" ling of hir (2) that hes not ye third part of the
" faithfull nor willing obedience unto zow that I
" beir (3), hes wyn, aganis my will, yat advantage
" over me, quhilk the fecond lufe of Jafon wan (4):
" not that I will compair zow unto ane fa unhappy
" as he was, nor zit myfelf to ane fa unpietifull ane
" woman as fcho (5)."

" ut juxta tua promiffa animum tuum mihi expo-
" neres (1): alioqui fufpicabor fieri malo meo fa-
" to et fiderum favore erga illas (2), quæ nec ter-
" tiam habent partem fidelitatis, et voluntatis tibi
" obfequendi, quam ego habeo (3); ut ipfæ, velut
" fecunda Jafonis amica, me invitâ, priorem apud
" te locum gratiæ occupaverint (4): nec hoc eó
" dico, quó te cum homine, eâ quâ ille erat infeli-
" citate, comparem, nec me cum muliere tam alienâ
" a mifericordia (5) quám"

" que fuivant vos promeffes, vous me faciez en-
" tendre voftre affection (1): autrement j'eftimeray
" que cela fe faict par mon malheureux deftin, et
" par la faveur des aftres envers celles (2), qui
" toutesfois n'ont une tierce partie de loyauté, et
" volonté que j'ay de vous obeïr (3); fi elles, comme
" fi j'eftoye une fecond amye de Jafon, malgré
" moy

" moy, occupent le premier lieu de faveur (4): ce
" que je ne dy, pour vous a comparer a cet homme
" en l'infelicité qu'il avoit, ny moy avec une
" femme toute efloignée de mifericorde (5), comme
" eftoit celle-la. Combien que vous"

(1) " Difcharge zour hart unto me," Scotch;
" animum tuum mihi exponeres," Latin; " me
" faciez entendre voftre affection," French. The
Mifcellaneous Remarker obferves, that it is difficult " to fay how fo plain a French phrafe fhould
" have been disfigured in a tranflation *;" he being
one of thofe logicians who choofe to *beg* the queftion, when they cannot make it their own by their
prowefs; and fo fuppofing the Scotch to be a
tranflation from the French. But are the Scotch
and the French then different? They certainly are.
And *the French is wrong*. Mary does not want
Bothwell to difclofe his affection to her. She
wants him to lay open his heart, and to tell her the
ground and reafon of his fufpicions. Accordingly,
the Latin renders the words, " animum tuum mihi
" exponeres." And the Frenchman, miftaking the
import of the Latin, turned " animum" into " af-
" fection."

(2) " My malhure, and the gude handling,"
Scotch; " malo meo fato, et fiderum favore," Latin;
and " mon malheureux deftin, et par la faveur des
" aftres," French. This is a very extraordinary
tranflation, in the Latin. It is fubftituting one

* P. 40.

thing for another. Yet how faithfully does the French adhere to the Latin, even when this departs most widely from the Scotch; marking carefully the print of its steps, and treading exactly in them! "Vestigia nulla *retrorsum*." But the Miscellaneous Remarker informs us, that "par la faveur des "astres" is certainly right, for "par mon mal- "heureux destin" goes before *. He might as well have said, that the Latin "siderum favore" is certainly right, for "malo meo fato" goes before. The French is derived entirely from the Latin. And both are wrong, because both are different from the Scotch, the true original. This has "the "gude handling of," &c. But the Miscellaneous Remarker adds, and in the same strain of unfortunate argumentation, "there must be some blunder here." He did not comprehend the meaning of the words. He therefore very naturally chose rather to impeach the sense of the text, than affront his own understanding. The meaning is this: Mary desires him to lay open his heart to her; or else she shall suspect, that her own evil fate, and Lady Bothwell's cunning management, have drawn Bothwell from her. "The gude handling of hir" plainly means the good management of Lady Bothwell. So we have in the sixth letter, "quhat he desyris for the "*handling* of himself;" meaning what instructions he wants, for the proper management of himself. And the same clause was actually in the letter, at its original appearance in York; with another

* P. 40.

word in it inftead of "handling," but precifely to the fame purport. "I pray zou," the fentence then ran,—"to difcharge your hart to me, uther-"wayis I will think, that my malheure, and the "guid *compofing* of," &c*.

But from this variation in the readings at the York and the Weftminfter conferences, and from the words of the Latin verfion, I fufpect another variation to have taken place in the paffage, and the *original* words to have been *as the Latin read them*. The Latin is too wide from the Scotch at prefent, to have ever proceeded from mif-printing, mif-reading, or mif-underftanding the terms of the latter. The Scotch alfo appears plainly to have undergone a change, fince the conference at York. And the Latin feems to ftand as a powerful witnefs at prefent, that the Scotch underwent a change preceding this, and that the Latin verfion was made from it in its primary ftate. This feems alfo to be confirmed by another inftance of the fame nature, but of which the evidence is more pofitive. "I cum na neirer unto him," fays our prefent copy, "bot in ane chyre at the bed-feit †." "I cum na neirar," faid the copy at York, "bot "sat in ane cheir at the bed-fute ‡." Yet the Latin was made from the York copy, running thus, "non accedo propiús ad eum, fed in cathedrâ "sedeo ad pedes ejus." And the French runs accordingly, "je n'approche pas pres de luy, mais je

* Appendix, N° vii.   † L. i. §. xx.   ‡ Appendix, N° vii.

m'assieds

"m'assieds en une chaire a ses pieds." These facts concur with others to point out a train of *verbal* variations, that were continually made in the letters, and that were much more numerous probably than the *substantial* alterations which I have noted before. On any supposition, however, THE FORGERY IS PLAIN. Mary could not write both " gude handling" and " gude composing." And still less could she write " gude favour of the stars," instead of both.

" Hir," Scotch; " illas," Latin; " celles," French. Mr. Goodall observes, that the Latin has rendered " hir" by " illæ," as if it read *thir* for *their*; and subjoins to his observation, that " there " are writings of those times still extant, in which " here and there it is hard to distinguish betwixt the " *h* and the *th*." And the Miscellaneous Remarker concurs so far with him, as to say, that " *them*—in " the Scottish dialect would be *thir* *." But this is a mistake in both. *Thir* in old Scotch does not mean *them*, but *these*. Accordingly, in these very letters we have always *thame* for *them*. And in the fifth letter we have *thir* twice for *these*. " I dar not " traist zour brother," says the mis-represented Mary, " with *thir* [these] letteris." And " judge " ze," she adds, " quhat amendment *yir* [these] " new ceremonies have brocht unto me." But the *original* word in the Scotch of this clause was not " hir," but " thame." So it was at the exhibition of the letters in York. " Utherwayis," says this oldest of all existing MSS concerning the letters, " I will think that my malheure, and the guid

---

* Goodall, i. 90 and 91; and Remarker, 37.

" composing

" compofing of *thame* that hes not," &c. It was this reading, which made the Latin run equally in the plural number, and drew the French after it. And, as this word concurs with the word adjoining it, to prove other variations in the very *terms* of thefe pretended originals of Mary's writing, and thus to convict them of forgery at every variation; fo the exiftence of " thame" in the original, at York, and when Buchanan made his tranflation, and the appearance of " hir" in the copy prefented at Weftminfter, and afterwards publifhed by Cecil, prove Buchanan to have made his tranflation *before the exhibition at Weftminfter*. He accordingly prefented his tranflation in MS to Elizabeth and her commiffioners, at the very time the letters were exhibited in Weftminfter [*]. The letters were determined to be publifhed, at leaft three of them; and the infamous *Detection* was actually drawn up, with three of them in it; AT THE VERY MOMENT when Murray, and his compartners in villainy, were by a folemn proteftation to the commiffioners declaring their unwillingnefs to accufe the Queen, the backwardnefs which they had hitherto fhewn to do it, and the neceffity which now forced them upon it at laft [†]. The preceding half of this note even implies Buchanan to have made his verfion, of the firft three at leaft, *before* the conference at York. A determination had probably been *then* formed for the publication. And with a view to this I fuppofe it was, that Buchanan was named an

[*] Camden tranf. 117, and orig. 144. 203—206. [†] Goodall, ii.

affiftant

affistant to the commiffioners, and so made to rank with persons much superior to himself in consequence.

(3) "Faithfull nor willing obedience unto zow that I beir," Scotch; "fidelitatis, et voluntatis tibi obsequendi, quam ego habeo," Latin; and "loyauté et volonté que j'ay de vous obeïr," French.

(4) "Hes wyn yat advantage over me," Scotch; "priorem apud te locum gratiæ occupaverint," Latin; and "occupent le premier lieu de faveur," French. How does every instance serve to demonstrate the great point laid down by Mr. Goodall, that the French is only a translation from the Latin! I have not *urged* the evidence upon the reader. I have left it to speak for itself. It has spoken loudly. And the point is clear, beyond a possibility of being obscured by all the powers of sophistry. History shews the French to be a *translation*. The language of the letters shews it to be a translation *from the Latin*. And the translator himself, the best witness in the world for such a fact, acknowledges expressly that he made it from the Latin, *because* he was *ignorant of the Scotch*.

The instances then, that incidentally occur in the French version, of a deviation from the Latin, and a correspondence with the Scotch, can never be attributed to the Frenchman himself. He who had no knowledge of the Scotch, " n'ayant cognoiffance " de la langue Escoffoise," could not catch any expression from it. He might take names, but he
could

could not borrow words. He could not even *consult* what he did not at all understand. He expressly tells us, indeed, that he made his translation from the *Latin*, and *entirely* from the Latin, " *tout* ce " que j'ay trouvé en *Latin.*" And the few correspondences that are not merely accidental between the Scotch and the French, when opposed to the thousand between the French and the Latin, can be referred only to the hand of a reviser; who went over the French version, just as another or the same went over the Latin, to make it more conformable to the Scotch; but went with a wanton and careless step, and made some slight and random corrections of single words, while he left an infinite variety of words and of combinations of words, to stand as they stood before, all different from the Scotch, and all similar to the Latin.

(5) " Not that," Scotch; " nec hoc eó dico," Latin; " ce que je ne dy," French. " Ane sa *unhappy as* " *he was*," Scotch; " homine, *eâ quâ ille erat infelici-* " *tate*," Latin; " homme en *l'infelicité qu'il avoit*," French. " Sa *unpietifull* ane woman as scho," Scotch; " muliere tam *alienâ a misericordiâ* quám " illa erat," Latin; and " une femme toute *es-* " *loignée de misericorde*, comme estoit celle-la," French.

———

" Howbeit, ze caus me to be sumthing lyke unto " hir in ony thing (1) that tuichis zow, or yat may " preserve

" preferve and keip zow unto hir, to quhome only
" ze appertene (2); gif it be fa (3) that I may ap-
" propriate (4) that quhilk is wyn throch faithfull,
" zea, only luifing of zow (5), as I do, and fall do
" all the dayis of my lyfe (6), for pane or evil that
" can cum thairof (7). In recompenfe of the
" quhilk, and of all the evillis quhilk ze have bene
" caus of to me, remember zow upon the place
" heir befyde (8)."

" illa erat: quanquam tu me cogis aliquâ ex parte
" ut illi fim fimilis omnibus in rebus (1) quæ ad te
" pertinent, aut quæ te fervare et cuftodire queant
" illi, cujus unius jure totus es (2): fiquidem (3)
" id tanquam meum mihi vindicare poffum (4),
" quod paravi, te unum fideliter, imó unicé aman-
" do (5), quod et facio, et faciam dum vixero (6),
" fecura omnis laboris et periculi, quæ illinc im-
" pendere poterunt (7). Et ob hæc omnia mala,
" quorum tu mihi caufa fuifti, hanc repende gra-
" tiam, ut loci memineris qui hîc vicinus eft (8)."

" me contraignez eftre en aucune partie femblable a
" elle, en toutes les chofes (1) qui vous concernent,
" ou qui vous peuvent garder et conferver a celle,
" a laquelle feule vous eftes entierement de droict
" (2): car (3) je vous puis m'attribuer comme
" mien (4), qui vous ay acquis feul loyaument,
" en vous aimant auffi uniquement (5), comme je
" fay, et feray tant que je vivray (6), me rendant
" affurée contre les travaux et dangers qui en pour-
" ront

" ront advenir (7). Et pour tous ces maux, def-
" quels m'avez efté la caufe, rendez moy cette fa-
" veur, que vous ayez fouvenance de lieu qui eft
" prochain d'icy (8)."

(1) " One thing," Scotch; " omnibus in re-
" bus," Latin; " toutes les chofes," French.

(2) " To quhome only ze appertene," Scotch;
" cujus unius jure *totus* es," Latin; " a laquelle
" feule vous eftes *entierement* de droict," French.

(3) " Gif it *be fa* that," Scotch, was thus when
the letters made their firft appearance upon Englifh
ground, " yf it *may be fuer* that *." The Latin
renders this by " fiquidem," and the French abfurdly fubftitutes " car" for " fiquidem."

(4) " Appropriate," Scotch; " tanquam meum
" mihi vindicare," Latin; " m'attribuer comme
" mien," French. The Scotch " verfion," fays
Mifcellaneous Remarker, " is incorrect, and does
" no more than aim at the fenfe of the French †."
This gentleman has thrown all his ideas into confufion, by embracing the ridiculous hypothefis of Dr.
Robertfon concerning a double copy in French,
one an original, and the other a tranflation; and by
embracing it without attending to *his* diftinctions.
The *prefent* French, except only a few claufes at
the *head* of the letters, the Doctor himfelf allows to
be all a tranflation, and a tranflation from the
Scotch through the Latin. Yet the Mifcellaneous

* Appendix, N° vii.   † P. 40.

Remarker,

Remarker, without knowing it, overleaps all the bars and bounds, that the Doctor had set up; and speaks of those passages in Scotch as a version from the French, which the Doctor himself allows to have been an original, a 'mediate original to the French, and an immediate one to the Latin. So thoroughly confounded and lost is he in the mazes of his own indistinctness! And thus the French here, which is apparently nothing more than the Latin reduced into French, he sets up for the original itself. The deviation of the French from the Scotch, particularly in translating " siquidem" by " car," which makes nonsense of the whole, he attributes to the departure of the Scotch from the French; just as children, moving in a coach, attribute their progress to the fields and the houses flying backward from them. And he overlooks entirely the interposition of the Latin, betwixt the Scotch and French; which shews demonstrably to our very senses, the level by which the French was fabricated.

(5) " That quhilk is wyn throch faithfull, zea, " only luifing of zow," Scotch. She means this: if she may appropriate to herself, without any rival in Lady Bothwell, that heart of Bothwell's, which she herself had gained by a faithful love of him, and of him only. Accordingly the passage is rendered thus in the Latin, " quod paravi, te unum " fideliter, imó unicé amando." But the French has made strange work of the Latin, " qui vous ay " acquis seul loyaument en vous aimant aussi
" uniquement

" uniquement comme je," &c. The words should have run thus, " qui vous ay acquis, en vous aim- ant auſſi loyaument et uniquement, comme," &c.; making a new arrangement, and throwing out the superfluous " seule." The tranſlator was perplexed by the native obſcurity of the clauſe.

(6) " All the dayis of my lyfe," Scotch ; " dum vixero," Latin; " tant que je vivray," French.

(7) " For pane or evill that can cum thairof," Scotch; " ſecura omnis laboris et periculi quæ illinc impendere poterunt," Latin; " me rendant aſſurée contre les travaux et dangers qui en pourront advenir," French. The brevity and force of the Scotch is ſtrikingly apparent in this, and ſome preceding paſſages; when contraſted with the laxity of the Latin and French.

(8) What evils had Bothwell *now* drawn upon Mary? None certainly. This is therefore a proof of forgery, ſpeaking from *poſterior* ideas.—" Ob hæc omnia mala—hanc repende gratiam," Latin; " pour tous ces maux—rendez moy ceſte faveur," French; both different from the Scotch in the turn of the words.

III.—" I craif with (1) that ze keip promeis to me the morne (2); but that we may meit togidder (2), and that ze gif na faith to fuſpiciounis without the certanetie of thame (3). And I craif na " uther

" uther thing at God, but that ze may knaw that
" thing that is in my hart, quhilk is zouris (4);
" and that he may preferve zow from all evill, at
" the leift fa lang as I have lyfe; quhilk I repute
" not precious unto me, except in fa far as it and I
" baith ar agreabill unto zow. I am going to bed,
" and will bid zow gude nicht (5). Advertife me
" tymely in the morning how ze have fairin (6);
" for I".

III.—" Non (1) poftulo ut cras (2) mihi pro-
" miffa ferves, fed ut congrediamur (2), et ut nul-
" lam fidem fufpicionibus adhibeas, nifi rebus ex-
" ploratis (3). Ego veró nihil aliud a Deo peto,
" nifi ut ea intelligas quæ funt in animo meo, qui
" eft tuus (4); et ut te præfervet ab omni malo,
" faltem dum mihi fupererit vita, quam et ego non
" duco mihi caram, nifi quatenus et ego et illa tibi
" placemus. Ego eo cubitum, et tibi valedico (5).
" Fac me certiorem fummo mane de tuâ valetu-
" dine (6);"

III.—" Je ne (1) demande pas que vous me te-
" niez promeffe demain (2); ains que nous nous
" affemblions (2), et que n'adjouftiez point de foy
" aux fufpicions, finon l'experience faicte (3). Je
" ne demande autre chofe a Dieu, fors qu'entendiez
" ce que j'ay en l'efprit, qui eft voftre (4); et
" qu'il vous garentiffe de tout mal, au moins pen-
" dant que je feray en vie, laquelle je ne tient
" point chere, finon en tant que moy et elle vous
" fommes agreables. Je m'en vay coucher, et
" vous

CHAP. 3. MARY QUEEN OF SCOTS.   275

" vous dy a Dieu (5). Faites moy certaine de bon
" matin de voſtre portement (6)";

(1) " With," Scotch, which is equally in Goodall's and Buchanan's editions, is plainly a miſ-print for " not." The ſenſe requires it. The context demands it. And the two tranſlations have it; " non," Latin, and " ne," French.

(2) This is the day after the evening of the preſent letter, and the day on which ſhe was to meet Bothwell. It was therefore the " Monounday," on which ſhe has already told us ſhe will ſet out, if ſhe does not hear to the contrary from him. She has not heard to the contrary. She therefore ſays nothing of having altered her intention. And ſhe acually ſet out, as the rebel journal itſelf ſhews us, on Monday the 27th of January. She ſet out agreeably to her previous reſolution. To this very reſolution the journal refers us. And on that very day of the week does it make her to ſet out *. This it is of conſequence to note.

(3) " Without the certanetie of thame," Scotch; " niſi rebus exploratis," Latin; " ſinon l'experience faiéte," French.

(4) " Hart," Scotch; " animo," Latin; " eſprit," French; both wrong, but the laſt peculiarly ſo. Her " ſpirit" could not be ſaid to be his. Her " mind" could not. But her " hart" might.

(5) This adds to the evidence before, that the

* Appendix, N°. x.

T 2   third

third letter pretends to be written late at night. And the night appears above to be that of Sunday, January 26th.

(6) This is very ſtrange. It is now late at night. She is going to bed inſtantly. Her letter therefore could not be ſent till the morning. And yet ſhe deſires him, in this very letter, and in the very next words of it, to apprize her " in the morning," and " tymely," or early in the morning too, how he is. This is ſuch a ſudden daſh of inconſiſtency in the letter, as is ſcarcely to be paralleled, I believe, within the regions of ſanity.

" will be in pane unto I get worde. Mak gude
" watch, gif the burd eſchaip out of the caige, or
" without hir mate. As the turtur I ſall remane
" alone for to lament the abſence, how ſchort yat ſa
" ever it be (1). This letter will do with ane gude
" hart, that thing quhilk I cannot do myſelf, gif it
" be not that I have feir that ze ar in ſleiping (2).
" I durſt not wryte this befoir Joſeph, Baſtiane, and
" Joachim, that did bot depart evin quhen I began
" to wryte (3)."

" ego enim ero in moleſtiâ donec intelligam. Si
" avis evaſerit é caveâ, aut ſine compare, velut
" turtur ego remanebo ſola, ut lamenter abſentiam
                                                " tuam

" tuam quamlibet brevem (1). Hæc epistola li-
" benter faciet quod ego ipsa facere non potero,
" nisi forté tu, quod metuo, jam dormias (2). Non
" sum ausa scribere præsentibus Josepho, Sebasti-
" ano, et Joachimo, qui nihil aliud [facerent] quám
" discesserant, cúm ego cæpi hæc scribere (3)."

" car je seray en peine jusques a ce que je l'entende.
" Comme l'oyseau eschappé de la cage, ou la tour-
" tre qui est sans compagne, ainsi je demeureray
" seule, pour pleurer vostre absence, quelque brieve
" qu'elle puisse estre (1). Ceste lettre fera volon-
" tiers ce que je ne pourray faire moy-mesmes, si
" d'adventure, comme je crain, vous ne dormez de-
" sia (2). Je n'ay osé escrire en presence de Jo-
" seph, Sebastian, et Joachim, qui ne faisoient que
" de partir quand j'ay commencé a escrire ces
" choses (3)."

(1) " He who fancies," says the Miscellaneous Remarker, " that there is here a Scottish original and a French copy, may enjoy his opinion in private, but he will hardly venture to expose it to the world *." Such is the confidence of confusion! But *mark how a plain tale shall put him down.* " Mak gud watch" is omitted in the Latin, and was therefore unknown to the French. It bids Bothwell to take good care of himself, for the reason suggested before and after it; that she should be in pain till she heard how he was, and that, without

* P. 40.

him, she should be a solitary turtle. This cautious admonition given, a new sentence commences, which goes to the end of the next. And, so pointed, the whole stands thus: " Mak gude watch. Gif " the burd eschaip out of the caige, or without " hir mate, as the turtur I sall remane alone for to " lament the absence, how schort yat sa ever it be." If I am separated from you, says the *actor* of Mary; I shall be like a bird escaped out of a cage, or like a bird that has lost her mate; and I shall remain solitary as the widowed turtle, to lament your absence from me, let it be as short as it will. This then is the " Scotch original." Let us now turn to the " French copy." But we must first look at the Latin, a copy which this gentleman is repeatedly forgetting, though the only original to the French." " Si avis evaserit e caveâ, aut sine com- " pare, velut turtur ego remanebo sola, ut lamenter " absentiam tuam quamlibet brevem." This, we see, is precisely just. The punctuation particularly is the very same, that I have introduced into the Scotch; and shews it to have been in the Scotch originally. But let us now see the French translation of the Latin. " Comme l'oyseau es- " chappé de la cage, ou la tourtre que est sans com- " pagne, ainsi je demeureray seule pour pleurer " vostre absence, quelque brieve qu'elle puisse " estre." This, we see, has retained the punctuation. It has also retained the general sense and imagery. But it has altered them in one circumstance. The words " velut turtur" it chose to read, as prefixed to " sine compare," in order, forsooth, footh, to preserve the unity of the allusion. And thus it came to be what it now is, plainly not an original, plainly a version of the Scotch, plainly a version of it through the medium of the Latin.

But let me add one more observation concerning this remarkable passage. It was obscure. It was particularly so. It carried a more " visible" kind of " darkness" in it, than most of the passages about it. And it contained a hint of caution o Bothwell. For these reasons the commissioners at York singled it out, as a part of the letters peculiarly charged with villainy. " Finally she wrote to Bothaill," they say, " that according to her commission she wolde bringe " the man with her; praying him to worke wisely, or " else the whole burden wolde lye on her shoulders, " and *specially* to make good watche, *that* the bird " escaped *not* owt of the cage*." This shews us very strongly, how lively and powerful their suspicions were, and how unfit they were to sit in impartial judgment upon the letters. Their imagination, " in a fine frenzy rolling," could " glance" from one letter to another, could see bloody spectres where a common eye can see only love, and could give " a body and a form" at once to these their " airy nothings."

(2) This passage undoubtedly imports, that the letter was to go to-night, and was to reach Bothwell, perhaps before he slept, but certainly before the morning. This therefore may seem to excuse

* Appendix, Nº vi.

the abfurdity preceding, of her defiring him to fend word early in the morning how he is. But let us confider all the circumftances; and then we fhall fee, that it is only an additional abfurdity. She has fat up late with the King. She has returned to her own lodgings. She has difmiffed all her attendants there. She has begun to write a letter to Bothwell. And at the clofe of it fhe says fhe is going to bed. Who then is to carry the letter? Nobody to-night. She has indeed a *particular* carrier. He is mentioned in the beginning of the letter. She there hints at fomething " quhilk this " beirer will fchaw zow." But then this bearer was not to fet out that evening. He was not to fet out till the next morning. He was even to wait upon the King firft. And " I have promyfit," fays Mary, " to bring him [the bearer] to him [the " King] the morne." Nor let it be fuppofed, that as " the morne" means not merely the morning, but the whole of to-morrow, the bearer was to go that night, to return the next day, and then be introduced by Mary to the King. The whole context reprobates the fuppofition. " I have walkit " laiter thair up," it fays, " then I wald have done, " gif it had not bene to draw fum thing out of him, " QUHILK THIS BEIRER WILL SCHAW ZOW; quhilk " *is the faireft commoditie that can be offerit to excufe* " *zour affairis*. I HAVE PROMYSIT TO BRING HIM " TO HIM THE MORNE. *Put ordour to it, gif ze* " *find it gude.*" The bearer was firft to fee the King upon the bufinefs, then to relate all that had paffed to Bothwell, and Bothwell was then to act

upon

upon his information, if he found it expedient. And all concurs to shew, that the requeft to hear early in the morning from Bothwell, when the requefting letter itfelf was not to go till the very morning, is as ridiculous as I have ftated it to be; and that the hint of the letter kiffing Bothwell that night, if he is not afleep before it reaches him, is even more ridiculous, if poffible, than the other. It was very ridiculous, even if the letter and the bearer were to fet off inftantly. At a late hour fhe had begun to write. At a later it was to be difpatched. It had to go fome way to him. Yet it might perhaps reach him, before he had gone to fleep. And the aftonifhing extravagance of the whole is heightened over and over by the confideration, that Bothwell was at this very time in the diftant region of Lydifdale, that this was Sunday January 26th, that he did not *fet out* on his return from Lydifdale till Tuefday January 28th, and that he did not meet her till Thurfday January 30th *.

" This letter will do with ane gude hart, that
" thing quhilk I cannot do myfelf, gif it be not that
" I have feir that ze ar in fleiping," Scotch.
" Here," fays Mifcellaneous Remarker, " the reader
" is entreated to try, whether he can make any fenfe
" of the Scottifh copy †." But is not the fenfe very obvious for one of thofe allufive fentences, in which the principal point is *underftood* and not expreffed? It certainly is. And now let us try the French. " C'eft lettre fera volontiers ce que je ne

* Appendix N° x.   † P. 41.

" pourray

" pourray faire moy-mefme, fi *d'adventure,* comme
" je crain, vous ne dormez defia." This is plainly
the fame in expreffion and in meaning. Only it
adds one word, " d'adventure." Shall " the
" reader" then be " entreated to try, whether he
" can make any fenfe of the *French* copy?" He
needs not. Every reader, except the Mifcellaneous Remarker, can make fenfe of both. Yet, " for
" my own part, I am perfwaded," fays the Remarker, " that the tranflator rendered into the
" Scottifh language words and phrafes, which he
" underftood when feparately taken, but not when
" taken altogether." But his own evidence fays directly the contrary. This very paffage fhews the
Scotch to be exactly as the French, one word ex-
cepted; and not merely in words " feparately taken,"
but in phrafes " taken altogether." And he totally forgets the Latin, though the French was derived from it, and though it betrays its derivation
by its additional word: " hæc epiftola libenter fa-
" ciet quod ego ipfa facere non potero, nifi *forté* tu,
" quod metuo, jam dormias."

(3) " Did bot depart," Scotch; " nihil aliud
" [facerent] quám difcefferant," Latin; and " ne
" faifoient que de partir," French. The prefs had
omitted " facerent" in the Latin. But it was in
the *MS.* And from *this* the French took it, as it
took " *que* par breuvage" from " *quàm* per medici-
" nam," when the printed copy was only " per me-
" dicinam."

Of the three perfons here mentioned as attendants
upon

upon the Queen, Joseph was brother to that David, whose murder must have fixed such a deep stain of disgrace upon the reputation of Scotland, in the eyes of all foreign nations, at the time. He entered Scotland the 20th of April after the murder, in the train of the French embassadour *. He first acted as secretary in his brother's place †. He afterwards became the Queen's goldsmith ‡. Hence Darnly is made to ask, whether Mary meant to dismiss Joseph from her service ‖; as if his Majesty had taken some dislike to him. And he, together with "Francis Bastiane" here mentioned, whose full name was Francis Sebastian de Villars, and with "John de Bourdeous [Bourdeaux]," the "Joa-" "chim" perhaps of the letter, as John was equally with Joachim one of the Queen's houshold; was accused on suspicion of the King's murder by Lenox, under the title of "Joseph, Dauryis [David's]" "brother §." He also appears, from Paris's second mock-confession, to have been frightened at a real or pretended summons to appear before the parliament; and, with a prudence that was quickened probably by the unhappy fate of his brother, to have left the regions of barbarism and of murder by a hasty flight ╪.

But, before I close my remarks upon the present letter, let me advert again to an expression at the head of it. "I have," says the mimicker of Mary there, "walkit laiter thair up then I wald have

* Keith, App. 129.   † Robertson, ii. 359.   ‡ Anderson, ii. 157.   ‖ L. i. §. 6.   § Anderson, i. 48; and Crawford 41. See also Spotswood, 200.   ╪ Goodall, ii. 84.

"done."

" done." These words carry a more than ordinary signification with them. They mean not, as at first we are apt to suppose they do, *I have waked up later there*, but with a sense much more emphatical, *I have waked there-up later*. THAIR-UP is the very same form of expression, with our UP THERE; when, with a reference to our own ideas, or to the conversation at the moment, we say of a place, that we have been *up there*. It therefore means not, that the Queen had " waked up" with the King in the King's apartment. It means more specifically, that she had " waked" with him in his apartment *above*. This the very arrangement of the words shews us; " I have *walkit laiter thair up* then I " wald have done." This therefore the corrected Latin, the French, and Dr. Robertson, all understand them to import. And the French, "j'aye " veillé plus tard *la-haut*," is particularly expressive. This then being the sense of the words, how are we to apply them? To the relative situation of the King's and Queen's apartments at Glasgow? But let us see, where they respectively lodged. I have already shewn, that they were not in the same house. The Queen, no doubt, lodged in the archi-episcopal palace; while the King certainly lay at Lord Lenox's. She was attended to Glasgow, as I have shewn before, by " all the Hamiltons." She was accompanied from Glasgow, as Buchanan shews, by the Hamiltons again, and by the archbishop of St. Andrew's, for one of them. She therefore lodged with her train in the palace at Glasgow, the archi-episcopal owner being at that time her embassador in France. This is upon the highest ground of the city,

city, being close to the cathedral; while the house, in which Darnly lodged, is still pointed out by tradition, and lies upon the descent from it. And therefore Mary could not possibly allude to the King's lodgings at Glasgow, by the words " thair " up;" as she could not possibly call them the apartments *above*. To what then does she refer by the words? She refers to this. The forger of the letter, with all that carelessness of confidence, which I have noted so frequently before, and shall note so frequently hereafter, laboured here under a confusion of ideas from the perplexities of his memory. He imagined himself to be writing a letter for her at *Kirk-a-field*, while he was actually writing one at Glasgow. He did write her one afterwards from Kirk-a-field. She *then* " ludged all " nycht *under the King*, in the chalmer quhairin," &c.; " and *from thence* wrayt that same *nycht*" to the King. *Then* therefore she might with the utmost propriety say, as she says here, that she had waked to a late hour " thair-up," *up there*, or in the apartments *above*. *Then* only *could* she point at the King's apartments, by such a relative allusion. And, as the forger has thus placed the Queen at Kirk-a-field, when by his own account she was at Glasgow; he has sufficiently betrayed his forgery by his forgetfulness again [*].

[*] Detection, 15 and 65, Anderson, ii. 242, and Jebb, i. 259; Keith, 330; and App. N° x. And Buchanan, Hist. xviii. 351, says of Kirk-a-field and Mary, " Ibi ipsa aliquot," " noc- " tus, *extracto in longum colloquio*, conquievit."

§ III.

§ III.

LETTER THE FOURTH (1).

I.—" My hart, alace! muſt the foly of ane wo-
" man, quhais unthankfulnes toward me ze do ſuf-
" ficiently knaw, be occaſioun of diſpleſure unto
" zow, conſidering yat I culd not have remeidit
" thairunto without knawing it (2)? And ſen that
" I perſavit it, I culd not tell it zow, for that I knew
" not how to governe myſelf thairin (3); for nou-
" ther in that, nor in ony uther thing, will I tak
" upon me to do ony thing without knawledge or
" zour will, quhilk I beſeik zow let me underſtand
" (4); for I will follow it all my lyfe, mair willingly
" than zow ſall declair it to me:"

I.—" Mon cœur, hélas! faut-il que la folie
" d'une femme, dont vous cognoiſſez aſſez l'ingra-
" titude vers moy, ſoit cauſe de vous donner deplai-
" ſir, veu que je n'y pouvoye mettre remede, ſans
" le donner a cognoiſtre (2)? Et depuis que je
" m'en ſuis apperçuë, je ne le vous pouvoye dire,
" pour ce que je ne ſçavoye pas comme m'y gou-
" verner (3). D'autant qu'en cecy, ny en autre
" choſe, je ne veux point entreprendre de rien
" faire, ſans que je cognoiſſe quelle eſt voſtre vo-
" lonté

" lonté (4); que je vous supplie me faire entendre,
" car je l'executeray tout ma vie, voire plus volon-
" tiers que ne me le voudriez declarez [declarer]:"

(1) *When* and *where* does this letter pretend to be written? It is one of the four from Glasgow. The rebel journal says, that Mary there " wrayt hir " bylle and *uther letteris* to Bothwell." The bylle we know to be the first. The " uther letteris" must be two or three at least. And as this letter shews itself to be one of the four, by mentioning something " quhilk micht be hurtfull to that quhairunto " baith we do tend," the marriage by means of the murder; so the next, or fifth, letter shews itself clearly to be written from another quarter. Yet when was it written at Glasgow? The Queen staid at Glasgow from Thursday January 23d, when she arrived there, till Monday morning January 27th, when she set out on her return. Of this time the *first* letter has occupied Friday and Saturday nights, January 24th and 25th. The second is perhaps written on Sunday morning, January 26th; though it pretends to be written on Saturday morning January 25th, which is impossible to be true. The *third* is written late at night, and on Sunday night, January 26th. And where then is there any room for the *fourth?* NOWHERE CERTAINLY. The rebels had once calculated their letters from Glasgow, to be three for the three days. Their own journal makes them only three or four. JUST THREE WERE ACTUALLY PRODUCED AT YORK. The intimation also in the third, of meeting Bothwell

well the next day, shews this to have been THE
CLOSER OF THE 'WHOLE. Thus the first was designed for Friday evening; the second for Saturday morning, as it still is dated; and the third for
Sunday evening, as in the evening it pretends to
have been written. And the letters appear, from
the rebel journal, to have actually been so once.
" January 24th [Friday]," it says, " the Quene re-
" maynit at Glascow, lyck as she did the 25th [Sa-
" turday] and 26th [Sunday];—and IN THIS TYME
" wrayt hir bylle and uther letteris to Bothwell."
But *Hyperion crossed the forgery* afterwards. He
blasted it with the humour of correction. Alterations were made in the original letters. The original plan was overlooked in the amendments. Even
a fourth letter was subjoined to the rest. And the
whole chronology was thrown into such confusion,
that the first letter extended itself into the place of
the second as well as its own; that the second was
apparently written on Sunday, while its date af-
signed it to Saturday; and that the fourth was
added—when there was no room for it in time. This
presents us with a fine picture of the natural confusedness of villainy. Confounded by the work-
ings of its own guilty fears, the clearest understanding becomes muddled. A Lethington sinks into a
driveler. And even the large intellect of an angel,
is shrunk up into the narrow comprehensions of a
devil.

(2) The story alluded to in this letter seems to
tell us the reason, why it was written. It hints at
one

one of the Queen's gentlewomen, who had been ungrateful to her, now proving pregnant by a gentleman of her train. And she intimates that she will make him *marry* her. Now Francis Sebastian, a Frenchman whom she mentions in her third letter as then present at Glasgow, was actually married the Sunday but one afterwards. His coming marriage is also hinted at in the first letter, when it is said of the King, that " he spak evin of *the mar-* " *riage of Bastiane.*" And what makes it the more memorable, and is, I apprehend, the leading clue to the fourth letter, he was married at Holyrood-house *that very night* in which *the King was blown up,* and the Queen gave a banquet and a masque *that night* in honour of the wedding. " Upon the Sounday " at nycht," says Thomas Nelson in his depositions before the commissioners of England, " efter sche " [the Queen] had taryd lang, and intertened the " King very familiarlie, sche tuk purpois (as it had " bene on the suddan) and departed, as sche spak, " *to gif the mask* to *Bastyane,* quha *that nicht wes* " *mareit* *." Mary confirms the substance of this account, in a letter which she wrote the next day; as she says, that she " of very chance taryit not all " night, be reason of *sum mask in the abbaye* †." And, after two such testimonies, I may venture to quote Buchanan, who says, that " this Sebastiane " was ane Arvernois, a man in greit favour with the " Quene for his cunning in musike and his merie " jesting, and was maryit the same day ‡." But

---

* Goodall, ii. 245.   † Keith, Pref. viii.   ‡ Anderson, ii. 22, and Jebb, i. 244.

whom did he marry? The last author will tell us, if we suppose Sebastian to be the *man* of this letter. The *woman* of it, says Buchanan*, was " Mar-" garet Carwood." And a fourth letter was added after the York conference, in order to dwell upon the incident which produced this marriage, and so lead the thoughts of all who recollected the transactions, and remembered their connection, to the very night of the murder at once.

The Latin version by Buchanan going no farther, I wish to observe concerning it, that the numerous errors in it coincide exactly with the historical evidence, which I have given in the former volume; and prove it impossible for Buchanan, however he has been almost invariably supposed to the present day, to have been the original author of the letters. He could not have mis-understood what he wrote himself. He peculiarly could not so repeatedly and so grossly have mis-understood it, as he does. And the blunders of the Latin letters concur directly with the testimony of facts, to lay the guilt of this most impudent of all impudent forgeries upon the head of another.

We have thus, however, lost the very beneficial assistance of the Latin. But we have made such use of it already, that we can very well spare it at present. It is made demonstrably clear from the very collation of the two versions, Latin and French, that the French is only a version of the Latin. It has *appeared* so in all the *three* letters

* Anderson, ii. 150, and Jebb, i. 342.

before,

before. It must be so therefore, in *the remaining five*. And the very translator himself acknowledges expresly, that it was so in *all*. Yet the Miscellaneous Remarker labours hard to prove, *he is mistaken*; to prove the translator *did not translate* from the *Latin*, as he said he did; to prove he *did not translate at all*; to prove he unknowingly *wrote down the original*, when all the while he thought he was translating. This is of all ridiculous hypotheses the most ridiculous. It is an extravagance beyond the flight of Moorfields. And yet it is literally such as I have described it to be. The author indeed overlooks entirely the Frenchman's confession. He seems to be ignorant of it. But he flies directly in the face of it. And he thus becomes chargeable with all the wildness of execution, that I have imputed to him. With this wildness has he gone over the second and third letters. With this does he also go over the remaining five. " There is no evi-
" dence," he says, " that *they* were ever translated
" into Latin at all; an important circumstance,
" which Mr. Goodall and the author of the En-
" quiry [Mr. Tytler] have in great measure over-
" looked *." That they *were* translated, however, has been decisively proved, I trust, in the antecedent parts of the present work. But, for greater satisfaction, I have lately produced the proving passage again. It is in that very confession of the Frenchman's, which is of so much consequence in itself. The letters, says this translator, were

* P. 25.

" traduictes

"traduictes *entierement* en Latin;" and he translated into French, he adds, "*tout* ce que j'ay trouvé en "Latin." And yet the Miscellaneous Remarker is so ignorant of this, that he says "there is no evi-"dence" the five last letters "were ever translated "into Latin." They were *all* translated. Had they *not* been, we *should not have had* this French translation at present, to contest the palm of originality with the Scotch. The translator owns himself to have been quite ignorant of the language, in which the *true* original was written. He had no knowledge of the Scotch, he says; "n'ayant cog-"noissance de la langue Escossoise."

Having stated this important point for the last time, I trust; I now trace the steps of the Remarker, with the same attention that I have shewn before. "Must the foly," Scotch; "faut-il que la folie," French. "Faut-il que," French, observes the Remarker, "does not mean *must* but *ought* or *should*; and "that is the sense of the writer*." If the French did not properly express the meaning of the Scotch original, the blame must be charged to the French translation. But it does express it sufficiently, *according to his own account*, and even in *opposition* to it. "Faut-il que" means "should," he says; and *must* in this connection means the same. And "il "faut" accordingly means either *must* or *should*. "Without knowing it," Scotch; "sans le donner "a cognoistre," French. The Scotch, says the Remarker, "is an expression altogether unintel-

* P. 26.

"ligible."

" ligible *." Yet the language is surely very plain. The Queen says, that she could not have remedied a misfortune in her houshold " without knowing " it." This is one of the plainest propositions, that ever were presented to the human mind. Yet the Remarker finds it " altogether unintelligible."

Not to know me argues yourself unknown.

But the French alters this into a proposition more intelligible to *him*, that she could not remedy it without disclosing it to others. This is certainly not *more* intelligible. And it is *less* true. The next words shew it to be absolutely false. " I culd " not have remeidit thairunto," says the writer, " without knawing it; and *sen* that *I persavit it*, I " culd not tell it zow."

(3) This presents us with a glorious flourish of the forger's pen. Mary has the misfortune to find, that one of her maids of honour is with child by a gentleman in her retinue. Bothwell hears of the fact, at the distance of Edinborough or of Lydisdale. Court-scandal *then* flew with rapidity, it seems, without the aid of a *Morning Post* or an *English Chronicle*. Bothwell is much *hurt* at the news. The *adulterous* Bothwell is hurt at an intrigue of *fornication* in the Queen's family, in the family of that very Queen *with whom* he is carrying on an adulterous intrigue. He is hurt too with an intrigue in that very Margaret Carwood, who (according to Buchanan) " was previe and ane helper " of all thair lufe †," and had even been con-

* P. 26.   † Anderson, ii. 150.

cerned

cerned with the Queen and Lady Reres in a kind of rape upon himself*. And the *plotting murderer*, even in the very moments of plotting, and nearly at the critical minute of the murder, writes in such sharp terms upon the fornication to his partner in adultery and in murder; as forces her to break out abruptly, at the very commencement of her letter, in these terms of anguish, " my hart, alace! must " the foly of ane woman be occasioun of displesure " unto zow?" This is certainly a note above *Ela*, in the scale of absurdity.

It appears however from this, that Mary has heard from Bothwell, while she resided at Glasgow. Yet how could she? He left her on Thursday January 23 at Kalendar. He returned that day to Edinborough. He set off the next for Lydisdale. And he is still there. So absurd upon every examination does the chronology appear! But this is not all. Mary has received this letter since her last. The last was written the evening before she was to meet him. It was written late at night. She was to meet him the next day. She had heard from him then, to fix the appointment for next day. She has now heard from him since. She has therefore heard on Monday, the day she was to meet him, and the day that she actually left Glasgow. And she is writing to him, at the time that *by the letters* she should be with him, and at the time when she was *actually* on the road to, or now arrived at, Kalendar. So much *more* absurd does the chronology appear, upon further examination!

* Anderson, ii. 8, and Jebb, i. 240.

But

But Mary fays, that she could not *tell* Bothwell of the intrigue, becaufe she did not know how to act concerning it. Yet in the letter immediately preceding she has informed us, that he had "commanded" and she had "promifed" neither to write nor fend to him. The two paffages are ftrangely at variance. He "commands" and she "promifes" not to write or fend. She adheres to the ftipulation,—in writing *two* letters to him, and one an exceedingly long one. But she had *then* forgotten the ftipulation perhaps. She *at laft* recollects it. She recollects it *to break it*. She mentions it in the very inftant she is breaking it. The *third* letter records at once the promife and the violation. Nor does she ftop there. She breaks it a *fourth* time. She writes *four* letters in three days, when she was commanded and had promifed not to write a line, and not even to fend a meffage. And she does all this, not to confult him upon any incidents that had emerged fince the command and the promife were given, but merely to proclaim the adultery, to infinuate the murder, and to difplay her wantonnefs, her wickednefs, and her ftupidity, at once, in an *unfealed* letter.

(4) Thus is Mary made refponfible to Bothwell, for the pettieft actions of her life. She cannot have the misfortune of an intrigue in her court, but Bothwell rates her for it. She is taxed for not remedying it. She is condemned for not apprizing him of it, even when he himfelf had charged her not to write or fend to him. She finds him in difpleafure

sure about it. She is much wounded in her feelings by all. And she deprecates his displeasure in the lowest terms of humility. Yet Dr. Robertson and Mr. Hume could see the real Mary in all this. They could see no difference between a *Caliban* and a *man*. And even though the representation had been charged with still greater absurdities, if it was possible to charge it with greater; they would still (I fear) have reconciled themselves to the sight, and have still discovered all the natural proportions of the man under the " gaberdine" of the monster.

II.—" And gif ze do not send me word this
" nicht (1) quhat ze will that I sall do, I will red
" myself of it, and hasard to caus it to be interprysit
" and takin in hand, quhilk micht be hurtfull to
" that quhairunto baith we do tend (2). And
" quhen scho sall be maryit (2), I beseik zow to
" give me ane (3), or ellis I will tak sic as sall
" content zow for thair conditiounis (4); bot
" as for thair toungis or faithfulness towart zow, I
" will not answer."

II.—" Que si vous ne me mandez des nouvelles
" ceste nuit (1), de ce que voulez que je face, je
" m'en depescheray, et me hazarderay de l'entre-
" prendre, ce que pourroit nuire a ce que nous des-
" seignons tous deux (2). Et quand elle sera
" mariée (2), je vous prie de m'en donner une autre
" (3),

"(3), ou bien j'en prendray quelqu'une, dont
" j'eſtime que la façon vous contentera (4); mais
" quant a leur langue et fidelité envers vous, je
" n'en voudroye pas reſpondre."

(1) This letter then pretends, like the two parts
of the firſt, and like the whole of the third, to be
written in the night. It thus enables us to detect the
impoſture, even more clearly than we have already
done. The firſt being written in the firſt two nights,
thoſe of Friday and Saturday; the third could not be
written before Sunday night, or the fourth before
Monday night. The laſt therefore was written from
Glaſgow, when by the *ſecond* letter ſhe was to be at
Cragmillar near Edinborough, and by the journal
ſhe was actually at Kalendar near Falkirk. And,
to enhance the folly, ſhe ſpeaks of the night as already come, in calling it " *this* nicht," and yet deſires Bothwell to ſend her word in " this *nicht*;"
when by the *third* letter he was to be with her at
this very time, and by the journal he was actually
in Lydiſdale.

(2) This alludes to the maid of honour, or her
corrupter, or both, being privy to the adultery now
carried on, and to the murder ſpeedily intended.
Margaret Carwood, ſays Buchanan, was deeply
concerned in the adultery. But as the maid of honour is ſaid before to have been one, whoſe un-
thankfulneſs to Mary was ſufficiently known by
Bothwell; and as the forced marriage could be of-
fenſive only to her corrupter; we muſt refer the

intimation

intimation to him. Accordingly, when Lenox, in his folly of relying upon anonymous accusations, specified some persons whom he suspected of the murder, he named "Seignior Francis Bastian *." And when the rebels, the very night of sending the Queen to Lochlevin, made a general search through the capital for the murderers of the king, Sebastian was seized among others, and committed to prison †.—" I will red myself of it," Scotch; " Je " m'en depescheray," French. The sense is, says the Miscellaneous Remarker, " *I will make haste to* " *do it*, that is, *I will instantly dismiss the wo-* " *man* ‡." And this is to be a probable proof, that the French is the original, and the Scotch a translation, against such an accumulation of evidence to the contrary. But the SCOTCH Mary says, that she will *rid herself* of the business, and the FRENCH Mary, that she will *dispatch* it. These are expressions too nearly alike, to found any criticisms upon a variation between them. Of the two, the Scotch is the most proper, as it is always used for a troublesome business. But the meaning of either is not, that she will instantly dismiss the woman; but that she will make the gentleman to marry her. The words immediately following, " and quhen scho sall be maryit," shew this to be the meaning. But she says, that she will " hasard " to caus it to be interpryfit and takin in hand," Scotch; " me hazarderay de l'entreprendre," French. " Where," exclaims the Miscellaneous

* Anderson, i. 48.   † Crawford, 41.   ‡ P. 26.

Remarker,

Remarker, " is the happy turn of phrase here?
" Let any reader, converfant in the two languages,
" pronounce which is the original, and which the
" tranflation.*." We already know the Scotch
to be the original, and the French the tranflation,
even a tranflation from the Latin. We are not
therefore left to fuch petty fpeculations as thefe,
for the proof of the point. But, knowing it already, we think it of fome ufe to fet thefe objections afide with an eafy hand. Mary fays that, if
fhe does not hear this night from Bothwell, fhe will
undertake the bufinefs at her own hazard, and *caufe*
the matter to be enterprifed and taken in hand. In
other words, and freed from that obfcurity which
pervades all thefe letters, and which is the natural
confequence of a forger's fears, willing to fpeak
out, and yet compelled to whifper; fhe fays fhe will
inftantly fend a meffage to Sebaftian, and infift
upon his marrying the maid of honour, even though
fhe offend him by doing fo, and lofe his fervices in
the projected murder. She would caufe *the marriage* to be enterprized and taken in hand. That
the fecond *it* refers to the marriage underftood, is
plain from the words immediately following, " and
" quhen fcho fall be maryit." And yet the French,
catching the real fignification as little as the Remarker, makes the Queen to " hazard the enter-
" prizing of it," to *hazard the marriage herfelf*.

(3) " Ane," Scotch; " une autre," French. The
addition here is noted by the Remarker †, as a

* P. 26—27. † P. 27.

proof

proof of the originality of the French; when the *deduction* was before. " Thy truth, most mighty " Lord," said a madman once in defence of contrary propositions, " is on *every* side."

(4) " Conditiounis," Scotch; " façon," French. This is another of the Remarker's proofs. The force of it lies only in his own prepossessions. He is to *prove* the French the original. Yet *even amidst his proofs* he will *suppose* it to be so. And then every variation is an error in the Scotch. Such is this gentleman's logic! " Façon" is erroneously translated " conditiounis:" ergo, &c. He was bred, I suspect, in the logical school of the Socinian PRIESTLEY, and in the very *Antipodes* of all true reasoning.

III.—" I beseik zow yat ane opinioun of uther
" persoun (1) be not hurtfull in zour mynde to my
" constancie (2). Mistrust me; bot (3) quhen I
" will put zow out of dout and cleir myself, refuse
" it not, my deir lufe (4), and suffer me to mak
" zow sum prufe be (5) my obedience, my (6)
" faithfulness, constancie, and voluntarie subjecti-
" oun, quhilk I tak for the plesandest gude that I
" micht ressaif, gif ze will accept it, and mak na
" ceremonie at it (7); for ze culd do me na greiter
" outrage, nor gif mair mortall greif (8)."

III.—

III.—" Je vous fupplie, que l'opinion d'une
" autre (1) n'efloingne voftre affection de ma con-
" ftance (2). Vous meffiez vous de moy (3), qui
" vous veux mettre hors de doute, et declarer mon
" innocence, o ma chere vie (4), ne le refufez pas,
" et ne fouffrez que je vous donne efpreuve de (5)
" mon obeiffance (6), fidelité, conftance, et volon-
" taire fubjection, que je prenda tres grand plaifir,
" autant que je le puis avoir, fi vous l'acceptez fans
" ceremonie (7), car vous ne me fcauriez faire
" plus grand outrage, ny offence plus mortelle (8)."

(1) Lady Bothwell's opinion of Mary's incon-
ftancy.

(2) " Be not hurtfull in zour mynde to my con-
" ftancie," Scotch; that is, do not injure the credit
of my conftancy in your good opinion. Yet the
French renders the claufe, " n'efloingne voftre af-
" fection de ma conftance," that is, do not *alienate*
your *affection from* my conftancy; a mode of expreffion, if any way proper in itfelf, certainly very
improper as a verfion of the Scotch.

(3) " Miftruft me; bot quhen," Scotch; " vous
" meffiez vous de moy, qui," French. The French,
fays Mifcellaneous Remarker*, " is as clear as
" words can be, when the thing alluded to is not
" certainly known;" and the Scotch, he adds, is
" words without energy, and indeed without mean-
" ing." The fenfe of the Scotch is this: miftruft
me if you will, but do not deny me the favour ot

* P. 27.

clearing

clearing myself, and removing all your doubts. I know not, what " energy" there is in this; but there is " a meaning" in it. Let us therefore now compare the French with the Scotch. You distrust me, it says, who would remove your doubts. Here the meaning is equally good, though somewhat different. But let us pursue the line of sense to the end. " Vous meffiez vous de moy, qui vous veux mettre " hors de doute, et declarer mon innocence, o ma " chere vie, ne le refusez pas." Here, for want of the words in the Scotch, " bot quhen," and so by turning " I" into " qui," the thread of connection is broken, and the sentence limps upon its legs. Yet the French, says the Remarker, " is as clear as " words can be," and the Scotch is " without mean- " ing."

(4) " My deir luse," Scotch; " ma chere vie," French. Here the Remarker might have seen *in his won way*, which was the original, and which was the translation. " Vie" could never be mistaken for " amie," but " luse" might easily be mistaken for " life." The Latin read the Scotch wrong, rendered it *vita*, and so gave " vie" to the French.

(5) " *Be* my obedience," Scotch; " *de* mon " obeiffance," French. But let us mark the train of ideas here. Mary befeeches him not to think ill of her *conſtancy*, " be not hurtfull in zour mynde to " my CONSTANCIE." He may mistrust her *con-ſtancy*, she says, but when she attempts to vindicate *it*; she begs he will hear her; and suffer her to shew her *conſtancy* in her conduct to him. " Suffer me

" to mak zow fum prufe," fhe fays, " be my obe-
" dience, my faithfulnefs, constancie, and volun-
" tarie fubjectioun." She thus requefts to give a
proof of her conftancy—by her conftancy.

(6) " My," Scotch, omitted in French.

(7) " Si vous l'acceptez fans ceremonie," fays
Remarker *, " is thus ungracefully rendered,
" gif ze will accept it, and mak na ceremonie at
" it.'" So trifling is this author, in his probable
proofs for the originality of the French! If any real
or fuppofed *ungracefulnefs* of language would prove
the point even probably, it could not have borne a
moment's argumentation. Could that balance remain long unfettled, which a mote would turn?
Yet even thefe motes are more in the mind's eye,
than in reality. The prefent particularly is. If the
Scotch had been, " gif ze will accept it *bot ony* ce-
" remonie," it would have been a little, and only a
little, more *compact*, but not more graceful, than it
is at prefent. And then the French would have
been literally conformable to it. Let me only add,
as punctuation is of fome confequence, that I have
taken the liberty of pointing the fentence as it now
ftands. Before, it ftood thus, " accept it; and mak
" na ceremonie at it, for."

(8) This is furely the very *bathos* of humiliation.
Mary is made to declare, that for Bothwell to *let*
her give *fome* proof of her love, by her *obedience*,
faithfulnefs, conftancy, and *voluntary fubjection*, fhe

* P. 27.

fhall

shall take for the greatest happiness that she can receive; and that if he makes *any* hesitation about accepting this proof, it will be to her the greatest of all possible outrages, and the sharpest of all possible sorrows. This is love " mounted to the lunar " sphere" at once. And it will appear peculiarly so, when we reflect, that this is said *during the life of her husband*, without any reserve concerning his death, and without one anticipation of approaching widowhood.

Let me add also, with regard to the main incident in the present letter, that this alone serves to prove the forgery. The marriage of Francis Sebastian is certainly the marriage alluded to. The coincidence of the first and fourth letter shews it. But then the first shews the fourth to be spurious. The fourth represents the marriage as only intended now for the first time, as intended now from a sudden and recent discovery, as hardly yet intended fully and absolutely, and as unknown, even in the very cause and principle of all, to Bothwell himself. Yet the first shews the marriage to be *then* intended, to be *then* known to be so, and to be known even to the King and to Bothwell. And the contradiction bewrays the imposture effectually.

§ IV.

§ IV.

I have thus gone over the letters from Glasgow. That they are fictitious, is too plain, I apprehend, to be doubted at present by any man of common sense. The evidence in this volume alone, is sufficient to convict them of imposture, in the eyes of all the world. The chronology, particularly, must stand as a deep and broad brand of knavery upon their front, to the end of time. But to make the brand still broader and deeper, let us attend to another chronology. This is contained in the *second* of the pretended confessions of Paris, which was peculiarly drawn up in order to strengthen the letters *, and ought therefore to be considered together with them †. Mr. Tytler had the honour of first opening this source of information against the letters; but afterwards closed it again, by withdrawing his remarks in a succeeding edition of his work ‡. I intend to break up the fountain a second time, and then trace the current to its termination. And, by doing this, I shall at once confirm the spuriousness of the letters, and prove that of the confession itself.

* Goodall, ii. 88. † See it in Goodall, ii. 76—79.
‡ See his Appendix, N° ii. superseded in 3d edition by other papers.

Nicholas Hubert, commonly called French Paris, or only Paris, entered first into credit with the Queen, as he tells us himself, " entra en credit avec " la Royne," when she was at Kalendar on her way to Glasgow, " comme la Royne fust a Kalendar al- " lant a Glasgow." This was by the rebel journal on Thursday January 23, 1566-7. She then gave him a purse with three or four hundred crowns in it, to be carried by him to Bothwell. This was done upon the road betwixt Kalendar and Glasgow, " sur le chemin entre Kalendar et Glasgow." But why was it given him *there*? To make haste after Bothwell, to be sure; to overtake him on his return to Edinborough; and so do, what the Queen ought to have done in the morning at Kalendar, before he left her. Yet this was *not* the design, it seems. The purse was given to Paris upon the road, not to post with it immediately after Bothwell; but—to carry it *whither the Queen herself was going*, to *Glasgow*; and merely to save *her* the trouble, of carrying thither so many hundred crowns in her own pocket. And this was done *openly*, and in the presence of all her retinue, " sur le chemin;" though she had gentlemen and ladies in her train, Joseph the brother of David Rizzio, Francis Sebastian, Joachim, and her maids of honour.

Paris thus attended her Majesty, as her privy purse, to Glasgow. " La Royne estant arrivée a " Glasgow," he staid there two days for a letter, which she said she would send by him to Bothwell. " Ayant demeuré là deux jours avec la dicte " dame, laquelle escript des lettres, et a luy les
" bailla,

" bailla, dyfant, Vous dires de bouche a Monf. de
" Boduel, que," &c. He ftaid therefore at Glafgow, *Friday* the 24th and *Saturday* the 25th of January, before he fet off with any letter to Bothwell.
This agrees exactly, as we have feen before, with
the internal chronology of the *firft* letter. And it
overthrows the date of the *fecond* decifively. Paris
fays himfelf, that he fet not off with the *firft* before
Sunday morning, THE DAY AFTER the date of the
fecond.

With this letter he fet out. He reached Edinborough. He does not fay *when*. But it could
not be till *Monday*. The diftance between Glafgow and Edinborough, by the route which was generally purfued then, and through Stirling *, is 66
miles, I believe. And it appears from the circumftances to have been, what from the feafon of the
year and ftate of the weather it might well be, the
former being " the deip of a fcharpe wynter," as
Buchanan has told us before, and the latter being
" the extremitie of this ftormy weather," as Lenox
has equally told us; the *evening* of Monday before
he arrived. For he delivers the letter; and the
next day, " le lendemain," comes three feveral
times, at eight, nine, and ten in the morning, for
the anfwer to it. Yet Mary is made in the *fecond*
letter, dated *Saturday morning*, to expect his arrival
then; though he was not then GONE, though he fet

---

* The Queen went this road. Lenox went it, when on his
way from Glafgow he ftopt fhort at Stirling, and requefted the
Queen to defer the trial of Bothwell (Anderfon, i. 54). And
Mary and Darnly went it before, with their army (Keith, 314).

not off till *Sunday* morning, though he was at Edinborough on *Tuesday*, and though he could not be back till *Wednesday*.

But Paris says, that, on his arrival at Edinborough, he found Bothwell in his lodgings at Holyrood-house; " arrivé a Lislebourg, trouvé le dict " de Boduel en son logis a l'abbay." He saw him, however, by the aid only of second sight. The Frenchman had been so far naturalized, as to be admitted to this the appropriated privilege of a Scot. By the aid of those magic spectacles, he saw Bothwell in his lodgings, he conversed with him that day, he again saw and again conversed with him the next. And yet, all the while, Bothwell was in a distant region, many, many miles from Edinborough, and upon the confines of England. On *Friday* the 24th in the evening, Bothwell set off from Edinborough for Lydisdale; and did not *set off* on his return from Lydisdale, till *Tuesday* January 28th.

On *Tuesday* however, at eight, nine, and ten in the morning successively, Paris went to his lodgings at Holyrood-house, where he thought he had seen and talked with him the night before. But he could not find him now. At last he found him in the High Town near Kirk-a-field, accompanied by a number of gentlemen, walking side by side with Sir James Balfour, and going to dine with Sir James. Paris addressed him, as actually Bothwell; and desired *before all the gentlemen* to be dispatched to the Queen. And the spectre answered, just as if it had been Bothwell. " Apres disner, dit il, je
" feray."

"feray." After dinner therefore Paris came again, "il retourna querir sa despeche apres disner." Bothwell wrote his letter; and Paris is sure that he wrote it with his own hand, "escrivit de sa propre "main." So much were his senses imposed upon! The deception indeed was very extraordinary. Bothwell appeared, spoke, and wrote. A real hand, and a real pen, seemed to be employed in the work. Real ink and real paper seemed to be used by him. And, when he had done, he seemed to say, "Voila "la response, retourne t'en a la Royne, et me re- "commandes bien humblement a sa bonne grace," &c. This was as courteous a ghost, as that of Sir Charles Grandison's to Mrs. Shirley. Yet it could not possibly be any thing but a ghost. The true, the genuine Bothwell, the ψυχη and the σωμα of Bothwell, were at this very time a number of miles off; while the shade, the ειδωλον, of Bothwell, was mimicking him at Edinborough, and calling up the apparitions of pen, ink, and paper, to assist in the mummery. And it is no wonder, that such a simpleton as Murray's Paris was imposed upon by the visionary forms; when the disquisitive Berkeley has *so fully convinced the world,* that papers, pens, ink, and men are all in their truest appearances a mere delusion, and merely spectres of the things which they represent.

Paris then went to Lethington, to whom was a letter inclosed in Bothwell's. Yet *our* letter to Bothwell *has strangely forgot to notice it.* She also sent (says Paris) a message by him to Lethington and Bothwell together, to know whether the King

X 3 should

should lodge at Kirk-a-field or at Cragmillar. Yet the same letter *has strangely forgot to notice this too.* It only refers to the bearer about the lodging at Edinborough. And it refers to Bothwell alone, not Lethington and him together, even upon this head. Paris however reports the message to Lethington. Lethington answers it, though Bothwell did not. " Le dict Liddington lui respondit, que le Kirk-de- " field seroit bon, et le dict Sieur de Boduel et lui " avoient advisé ensemble là-dessus." Lethington also writes a letter to the Queen, though *she* gives no hint of such a letter in *her own* from Glasgow. Bothwell also sends a diamond to her, with a gallant speech, that he would send her his heart if he had it in his own possession; and yet the *Queen* is even so uncourteous, as to take no more notice of *either* than of Lethington's letter. And Paris departs on his return for Glasgow, some time after dinner on *Tuesday* January 28.

The Queen, by the declaration of her own designs in letter the second, and by the journal which the rebels made of her actual movements, left Glasgow on *Monday* January 27. Yet she previously received a letter, which she answered in her third, and in which Bothwell had shewed " sa mony " contrary suspiciounis" of her, though he promised to meet her " the morne" or next day. But here Paris's confession and the rebel journal agree together, and pronounce the reception of *such* a letter to be IMPOSSIBLE. She must have received it before *Monday*; and Paris did not leave Edinborough

borough with a reply to her *firſt* letter, before *Tueſday* in the afternoon. Nor is this all. Mary received, not only this, but a ſecond letter, from Bothwell; one, in which he expreſſed his diſpleaſure at her, for the misfortune in one of her maids of honour. And the ſtrong bond of IMPOSSIBILITY is broken through, a ſecond time. She expects an anſwer to her firſt, ſhe receives one, and ſhe receives an anſwer to her ſecond; A WHOLE DAY before Paris, the bearer of the firſt, and the re-bearer of the reply to it, has even *arrived* at Edinborough with the *firſt*; A DAY AND A HALF, before he *ſets out* from Edinborough with the *reply*; and conſequently THREE DAYS, before he could reach her with it.

He ſet out on his return, " partit pour s'en aller " a Glaſcow vers la Royne." He arrived at Glaſgow. He waited upon the Queen. He reported the meſſage. He delivered the letters. And he afterwards returned from Glaſgow to Kalendar with the King and Queen, " retournoit de Glaſcow vers " Liſlebourg avec le Roy a Kallander." He reached Glaſgow, therefore, on WEDNESDAY NIGHT, January 29th. He could not reach it before. Yet he *found* the King and Queen *there*. And thus they, who certainly left Glaſgow on *Monday*, were there by Paris's forged depoſitions on the WEDNESDAY and THURSDAY following.

On the way betwixt Glaſgow and Kalendar, he ſays, he was addreſſed by a meſſenger of Bothwell's, who delivered *him* a letter to preſent to the Queen, inſtead of preſenting it to her himſelf. This was intended, no doubt, as an anfwer to her *second*, and to be the very letter to which fhe replies in her *fourth*. But it reached her, we fee, *not* at *Glafgow*, but *on the road* betwixt it and Kalendar. And it met her, when by the *third* letter Bothwell himfelf was to have met her. She anfwered it, fays Paris, upon the road betwixt Kalendar and Glafgow, " en al- " lant," and fent a *ring* with it. Yet NO·SUCH AN- SWER WAS EVER SENT. *The rebel journal rejects it.* Neither the *ten* nor the *eight*, neither the *Scotch* nor the *French* lift of letters, *will admit it for one of their number*. And it peculiarly cannot be that, which yet it peculiarly means to be, the fourth. When *this* was written, Bothwell was *very near to her*; becaufe he was to fend her word, as fhe fays, " this " nicht," concerning one of her maids of honour. But Bothwell was at *Edinborough*, when the letter with the ring was fent. Indeed he appears from Paris's confeffion and the rebel journal refpectively, to have come *no nearer than Edinborough* to her, all the while fhe was at Glafgow.

Paris fet out with the King and Queen from Glafgow for Kalendar, at fooneft by his own account, on THURSDAY January the 30th; when the King and Queen actually fet out on MONDAY January 27th. He accompanied them to Linlithgow, by his own chronology, on FRIDAY January 31ft, " apres la Royne et le Roy eftans a Lythgow;" when in fact they reached the town on TUESDAY January 28th. But there the Queen had a mind to fend Gilbert Curle to Edinborough, whom Paris afferts to have been a groom of her chamber, " va-
" let

"let de chambre;" though the firſt letter intimates, that both he and Paris were *private ſecretaries* to her *. So much do the letters and the confeſſion diſagree in the ſlighteſt points! He was to ſee, whether the houſe allotted for the King was prepared for his reception. But ſhe afterwards ſent John Hay in his ſtead to Bothwell. And *after* him, " en apres auſſi," ſhe diſpatched Paris with ſome bracelets to Bothwell; as if Paris, who carried the bracelets, could not alſo have carried the letter. *This* letter is evidently what is noticed in the rebel journal, when it ſays, that " ſhe remayned " all day in Linlythquow with the King, and *wraytt* " *from thence to Bothwell.*" But the *bracelets* are the ſame, that are mentioned in the *firſt* letter. Such a diſagreement is there again! Theſe Paris carried to Bothwell at Edinborough; " le " dict Paris, arrivant a Liſlebourg, lui baille les " braſſelets." He found him juſt going to mount his horſe, in order to meet the King and Queen. Paris accompanied him. And they conducted the King to his lodgings at Kirk-a-field.

This is the journal extracted from Paris's ſecond confeſſion. It goes directly againſt the rebel journal. Both go directly againſt the letters. And, in ſuch frail fabricks of chronology as theſe are, the beſt way of deſtroying them all is to daſh them one againſt the other. That the rebels, however, ſhould have formed no leſs than THREE ſyſtems of chronology, and all claſhing with each other; is an amaz-

* § 6.

ing incident in the annals of human folly. It shews the natural infatuation of impiety, in very strong colours. But it also shews something more. It lays open to the eye of FAITH, the providential spirit of GOD controuling the operations of villainy, by curbing its exertions of intellect; depressing the powers of the mind, to circumscribe the sphere of imposition; and even stimulating the soul to measures, that should finally blast its efforts. Had we not possessed this confession of Paris, we should have lost some good proofs against the authenticity of the letters. Had we not possessed the rebel journal, we should have been deprived of some of our best evidences against both. Yet these two papers were supplied by the rebels themselves. Murray sent up the confession. Murray presented the journal. Both were delivered in to the commissioners of England, and so were transmitted to the present times. They were delivered, in order to support the cause of the letters, to confirm their authenticity, and to sanction their veracity. And yet the seeds of detection were sowed deep in the ground of both, ready to come forth whenever they were invited by a spirit of fair enquiry, and sure to cover the letters which they were to befriend, with perpetual shame and infamy.

CHAPTER

CHAPTER THE FOURTH.

§ I.

LETTER THE FIFTH (1).

I.—" Allace! my lord, quhy is zour traift put in
" ane perfoun fa unworthie, to miftraift that quhilk
" is haillely zouris? I am wod (2). Ze had pro-
" miffit me, that ze wald refolve all (3), and that ze
" wald fend me word every day (4) quhat I
" fuld do. Ze haif done nathing yairof (5). I ad-
" vertifit (6) zow weill to tak heid of zour fals
" brother-in-law: he come to me, and without
" fchawing me ony thing from zow (7), tald me
" that ze had willit him to wryte to zow that "

I.—" Monfieur, helas! pourquoy eft voftre fi-
" ance mifé en perfonne fi indigne, pour foupcon-
" ner ce qui eft entierement voftre? J'enrage (2).
" Vous m'aviez promis, que vous vous refouldriez
" en toutes chofes (3), et que chacun jour (4)
" vous m'envoiriez dire ce que j'auroye a faire.
" Vous n'en avez rien fait (5). Je vous veux
                                            " bien

"bien advertir (6), que vous preniez bien garde a
"voftre defloyal beau-frere: il vint vers moy,
"fans me faire apparoiftre que c'eftoit de voftre
"part (7), et me dit que vous l'aviez"

(1) We are now come to the letters from Stirling. Of thefe the rebel journal fpeaks thus: "April 21 [1567], viz. Mounday, the Quene raid "to Stirling, and from thence wreyt the letteris "concerning—hir ravifhing—." And that here they begin, is plain from the tenor of the prefent letter. In the Englifh Detection of Buchanan, in which the letters were publifhed for the firft time all together, the fifth letter, as the firft from Stirling, bears this title, "ane uther letter fend fra Striviling to "Bothwell, concerning the practice for hir ravifche-"ment." Then comes the fixth with this title, "ane uther letter to Bothwell, for the practife and "devife to excufe the ravifhing." The feventh follows with this, "ane uther letter to Bothwell of "ye practice of hir ravifhment, and to advife him "to be ftrong to do it*." And the eighth, as I have noticed before, is ftrangely thrown in among the Glafgow letters, and made the third of them; when it is plainly one of the Stirling, and an anticipation of the approaching feizure and marriage.

(2) For remarks upon this, fee Section II.

(3) He had promifed her, it feems, to refolve all. But what needed to be refolved? NOTHING. The plan of feizure was already fettled, fay the re-

* Anderfon, ii. 151—155.

bels. And therefore nothing could remain to be settled at prefent. "The Quene raid to Stirling," fays the rebel journal, " *as it wes devyfit*, and from "thence wreyt the letteris concerning the *purpofe* "*devyfit of hir ravifhing*," meaning her feizure.— "That ze wald refolve all," Scotch; "que vous "vous refouldriez en toutes chofes," French. The Scotch fays, that Bothwell had promifed to refolve all difficulties for her, which fhould arife in their intended enterprize, and to fend her word from time to time how fhe fhould act in them; and that he had not done this. But the French afferts, that he had promifed to *refolve himfelf* in them all; which is very different in its import, and contrary to the two claufes immediately following. And yet the Mifcellaneous Remarker produces the variation, without adverting to the fenfe at all, as a probable proof that the French was the original *.

(4) This is another argument of the forgery. She fays, that Bothwell had promifed to fend her word " every day" what fhe fhould do. How many days then was fhe to ftay at Stirling, to admit of this addrefs from Bothwell to her " every day?" She was to ftay juft *one day* and *two nights*. She was to reach Stirling on Monday. She was to leave it on Wednefday. And thus the long train of days is fhrunk up into little more than four and twenty hours, like the Iliad compreffed into a nut-fhell.

* P. 27.

(5) Both-

(5) Bothwell has not executed his promise, it seems. He has not resolved all the difficulties for her, and sent her word "every day" what she should do. But how *could* he? She left him in the morning. She is writing to him in the evening. And what difficulties could he resolve for her in the interval? At this part of the letter, forgery faces us in every line, and almost in every word.

(6) "Advertisit," Scotch; "veux bien advertir," French. The Scotch speaks, says the Remarker, "as if the supposed writer of this letter referred to "what she had *formerly said*, instead of introduc- "ing," as the French does, "a subject *for the first* "*time* *." But the French is wrong, and the Scotch right. Mary is not introducing a subject for the first time. She refers to what she had formerly said. She is mentioning the neglects of Bothwell. He had promised to give her instructions from day to day; but he had not done it. She had warned him to beware of confiding in his brother-in-law; and yet he has confided in him. He has sent him to her too, without any token from himself. He has sent him to confer with her, on the business of their grand enterprize.

(7) This is another evidence of the forgery. The brother-in-law of Bothwell was Huntly, we know. He was at Edinborough on the Saturday night before. That day his forfeiture was taken off by the parliament †. That night also, say the

* P. 27.   † Goodall, ii. 141 and 249.

rebels

rebels themselves, "before the lords had such war-
"rant [from the Queen], there was none of them
"that did or wold set their hands [to the famous
"bond], saving onlie the Earl of Huntlie *." And
he actually appears as a subscriber to the bond †.
He was therefore in Edinborough on the 19th of
April, the day but one before the Queen set out for
Stirling. Yet he *came* to the Queen *at* Stirling,
says the letter. The rebel journal also speaks of
Stirling and of him, as the place " quhair Huntly
" *came to bir.*" Yet, as this is only Monday evening, how could he come to her? She had left
Edinborough only that morning. He must have
left it that morning too, as she complains that he
had brought her no tokens from Bothwell. How
then could he come to her? He actually AT-
TENDED HER THITHER. He actually STAID WITH
HER THERE. He actually ACCOMPANIED HER BACK
AGAIN. The proofs of these points will be dwelt
upon, as the proving passages occur in the letters.

" that I suld say (1), and quhair and quhen ze suld
" cum to me (2), and that that ze suild do tuiching
" him (3); and thairupon hes preichit (4) unto
' me yat it was ane fulische interpryse, and that
' with myne honour I culd never marry zow, seing
' that being maryit ze did cary me away (5); and

* Appendix, N° v.   † Keith, 382—383, and Ander-
on, i. 112.

" yat

" yat his folkis wald not fuffer it (6), and that the
" lordis wald unfay yamefelfis, and wald deny that
" thay had faid (7). To be fchort, he is all con-
" trarie. I tald him, that féing I was cum fa far,
" gif ze did not withdraw zourfelf of zourfelf, that
" na perfwafioun, nor deith itfelf, fuld mak me fail
" of my promeis."

" requis, qu'il vous efcrivit ce que je vous voudroye
" dire (1); et où et quand je pourroye aller a
" vous (2), et ce que vous deliberiez faire de luy
" (3); et fur cela il me remonftra (4), que c'eftoit
" une folle entreprife, et que pour mon honneur je
" ne vous pouvoye prendre a mary, puis que vous
" eftiez marié, ny aller avec vous (5), et que fes
" gens mefmes ne le fuffriroient pas (6), voir que
" les feigneurs contrediroyent a ce que en feroit
" propofé (7). Bref, il femble qu'il nous foit du
" tout contraire. Je luy refpondy, veu que j'en
" eftoye venuë fi avant, que fi vous ne vous re-
" tractiez, nulle perfuafion, non pas mefmes la
" mort, me feroit manquer a ma promeffe."

(1) The claufe means obvioufly all that Mary
fhould fay to Huntly. This is what Huntly was to
write to Bothwell. But the French alters it into
what Mary *wanted to fay* to *Bothwell*, " ce que je
" *vous voudroye* dire."

(2) Huntly was to fettle with Mary, " quhair
" and quhen" Bothwell was to meet her and feize
her. Yet this furely muft have been fettled before.
Common fenfe tells us it muft. And, as the journal

nal assures us it was, so *these letters never settle it.—*
" *Ze* fuld cum to *me*," Scotch; " *je* pourroye aller
" a *vous*," French. The latter has changed the
person; and made Mary to come, and (in the
Scotch sense of the words) *ravish* Bothwell.

(3) Huntly was to settle with the Queen, and
then to inform Bothwell, how Bothwell was to act
concerning Huntly, in this business of the seizure.
This is clearly the sense. Yet the Remarker, with
his usual indistinctness of ideas, says thus: " If this
" be joined with "' qu'il vous escrivit,'" it may
" seem impossible to explain, how the Earl of Both-
" well should have desired the Earl of Huntly to
" write to him, what use he, Bothwell, proposed, to
" make of him, Huntly. But "' me dit'" must be
" joined with "' ce que vous deliberiez faire de
"' luy;'" and the sense is, that Huntly told the
" Queen, or that the writer of the letter meant to
" have it supposed that Huntly told the Queen,
" what use Bothwell intended to make of him
" in the project of the *enlevement* *." He thus,
f I may be allowed to *compress his sense into percep-
'ibility*, makes Huntly to tell Mary from Bothwell,
what use Bothwell intended to make of Huntly in
he seizure. But Huntly was to settle with Mary,
nd then to inform Bothwell, *not* what use Bothwell
ntended to make of Huntly, *but* how Bothwell was
o act with regard to Huntly at the seizure.
Huntly was to be her *escort*. The difficulty was,
ow she was to be seized, and yet the seizure throw
o reflection upon her *escort*. This difficulty was to

* P. 28.

be removed by the conference between Mary and Huntly. And Bothwell was to act accordingly.

(4) "Preichit," Scotch; "remonstra," French. The latter loses the spirit of the former. To *preach* in conversation had *then* the same sense, as it has now. Thus in Paris's *first* confession, as it stands translated in Calderwood's MS history, Bothwell says to Paris on his objecting to the murder of the King, with all the pertness of a modern knave, "wouldst thou *preach* *?"

(5) "The Scottish copy," says Mr. Goodall, "makes the Queen use [report] these words to the "earl. This being a plain anticipation, in speak- "ing of the earl's rape [seizure] of the Queen as "past, which had not yet happened, the cautious "translators," the Latin and the French, "thought "fit to throw it out, and instead of the last five "words *ze did cary me away*, we find the words, *ny* "*aller avec vous*, in the French †." "This is in- "genious," the Remarker observes; but it "will "not," he thinks, "stand the test of sober criticism." His reasons for it are these. I must give them nearly in their full length, that he may be seen in his just proportions. "If it appear from any one "passage of the letter in question, that the French "is the original and the Scottish a translation, the "hypothesis of Mr. Goodall falls to the ground. "Besides, Lord Huntley is supposed in the Scottish "copy to remonstrate to the Queen against her "rash and ill-advised undertaking, une folle enter- "prise," as if *these words* and the *remonstrance* were

* Goodall, i. 139.   † Ibid. i. 98.

in the *Scottish* copy, " that is, her purpose of being
" carried off as by force, and then of marrying
" Bothwell; yet the very next words imply that
" Bothwell had already carried her off; and it is
" added, that even the vassals and dependants of
" Lord Huntley would not suffer it, that is, would
" not concur in the enterprize. All this is so mon-
" strously absurd, that we cannot suppose it to have
" been contained in a real letter, and still less, if
" possible, can we ascribe it to the invention of the
" enemies of Queen Mary, who, however wicked
" they might have been, were certainly intelligent
" and judicious. *It should seem*, that the Scottish
" translator either fell into an error, through his
" scanty knowledge of the French language, or
" that, from a less pardonable cause, he endea-
" voured to touch up and improve the origi-
" nal *." What then is the conclusion of all this?
Is Mr. Goodall's supposition to stand or to fall? It
is not to stand. Yet who has seen it fall? The
gentleman has so long habituated himself to the
contemplation of his own ideas, that he seems to
pay little respect to those of others. He is to *prove*
the Scotch a translation. Yet he always *supposes*
it, as he moves along. And he refers to this supposition at every turn, as the ground-work of all his
assertions, and as the pillar of all his conjectures.
Thus, when the French has varied so widely from
the Scotch, and for so important a reason as is suggested by Mr. Goodall, he, acting under the me-
chanical influence of his own prepossessions, steps

* P. 29.

forward

forward to *assume* what he is at that very moment labouring to prove, condemns the Scotch for deviating so much from the French, hints at the Scotch translator's ignorance of the French, and even throws out strong insinuations against his honesty. Just so may we conceive a child, after gazing fondly upon the scenery displayed in the reflection of a clear river,

> The pendent forests, and the downward skies,

and then drawing off his eye for a moment, to be surprized at the sight of woods shooting upward, and to stare at the absurdity of a sky over his head. And the whole difficulty of the passage lies in this. The seizure has not yet been made. Huntly even says, that his men will not suffer it to be made. And he declares, even if it had been made, Mary could not with honour marry Bothwell, because Bothwell was a married man at the seizure. This declaration, though it respects the future time, is yet, by an anticipation which is common to all languages, spoken of in terms of the past. Hence it is coupled with clauses all in the future. Such anticipations are never more than momentary. The mind immediately returns to its settled modes of speech. And a sentence becomes in that case just as our present one is, with one word of past time, and with other words of future on each side of it. He " preichit unto me," says Mary, " yat it *was* " ane fulische interpryse, and that with myne ho- " nour I *culd* never marry zow, seing that being " maryit ze *did* cary me away," catching the anticipation from the idea of the future marriage, to which the seizure must have been prior; " and yat
" his

" his folkis *wald* not fuffer it, and that the Lordis
" *wald* unfay yamefelfis, and *wald* deny that thay
" had faid." But the Latin, and the French after
it, not feeing this explanation of the difficulty, and
unwilling to adopt the feeming contradiction, left
out the exceptionable paffage, and boldly fubfti-
tuted another in its room. Mary, who before could
not with honour marry Bothwell after the feizure,
becaufe he would have then feized her while he yet
had a wife; now could not marry him becaufe he
has already a wife, and *could not go with him,* " ny
" aller avec vous."

(6) " His folkis," Scotch; " fes gens *mefmes*,"
French. This fhews Huntly to have had his retainers with him. " Wald not fuffer it." This
fhews Huntly and his retainers to be the Queen's
guard.

(7) This is thrown in, becaufe the lords *did* unfay themfelves, and *did* deny that which they had
faid. But the anticipation of the fact proves the
forgery. No friend of Mary's could *then* forefee,
that the majority of the lords would go fo directly
againft their folemn fubfcriptions, as they did afterwards. Huntly could laft of all have forefeen it
then, as (according to the rebel account) he was the
very firft man who figned [*]. We all bind ourfelves
they fay, that we " fall tak pairt—and fortifie the
" faid erle to the faid mariage, fo farr as it may
" pleife their foverane lady to allow; and thairin
" fall fpend and beftow our lives and guidis againis
" *all that leive or die may,* as *we fall anfer to*

[*] Appendix, N° v.

" God,

"God, and *upon our awin fidelities and confcience;* and in caife we doe in the contrare, *nevir to have reputatioun or credite in na tyme heirefter,* but to be *accounted unworthie and faithles traytors* *."
Yet Morton, Lindfay, Glencairn, the Bifhop of Orkney, and a variety of others, as foon as ever the marriage had been forced upon Mary by the enginry of this bond, directly broke through all their " fi- " delities and confcience," directly flew in the face of that GOD to whom they had bound themfelves to " anfer," directly condemned themfelves " ne- " vir to have reputatioun or credite in na tyme " heirefter," and directly branded themfelves in the fight of GOD and man for " unworthie and " faithles traytors." But this is fuch a pitch of wickednefs, as no *honeft* fagacity could have fore- feen. It was too monftrous to be expected, by any but *villains as great as themfelves*.

" The lordis wald unfay yamefelfis, and wald " deny that they had faid," Scotch; " voire que les " feigneurs contrediroyent a ce que en feroit pro- " pofé," French. " Here the tranflator," fays the Remarker concerning the Scotch original, " feems " to have gueffed, that the expreffion alluded to " *Ainflie's fupper*, and to the famous bond of the " nobility, and, on that miftaken guefs, to have " formed his tranflation †." Into what a labyrinth has the author led himfelf, by his boldnefs in *arro- gating* the very point which he pretends to prove! He feems to have ftudied the ingenious Mr. Hil- drop's new fyftem of logick, in which the PETITIO

* Anderfon, i. 110—111. † P. 30.

PRINCIPII,

principii, that proscribed fallacy of the schools, is converted into a true principle of reasoning—for a deist, and honoured with a very particular distinction. The French translation is thus mounted into an original. The Scotch original is thus depressed into a version. The latter alludes to the bond of association. This he saw. Yet he would not see it. The French had not seen it. This was enough for him. He therefore rambles with the French, to make the lords contradict what *shall be proposed* concerning the seizure: as if the seizure was *now* to be proposed to the lords. And, sense or nonsense, he swallows it all, if it is but administered in a vehicle of French.

II.—" As tuiching the place, ze are tó negligent,
" pardoun me, to remit zourself thairof unto me.
" Cheis it zourself, and send me word of it (1), and
" in the meane tyme I am seik, I will differ, as, tuich-
" ing the matter, it is tó lait (2). It was not lang
" of me zat ze have not thocht thairupon in time
" (3). And gif ze had not mair changeit zour
" mynd sen myne absence, then I have (4), ze suld
" not be now to ask sic resolving. Weill (5), thair
" wantis nathing of my part,"

II.—": Touchant la place, pardonnez moy, si je
" vous dy que vous estes trop negligent de vous, re-
" mettre a moy. Choississez-la donc vous-mesmes,

"et m'en advertiffez (1); cependant je ne fuis a
"mon aife, car il eft ja trop tard (2), et n'a pas
"tenu a moy, que vous n'y ayez penfé de bonne
"heure (3). Et fi vous n'euffiez changé d'opi-
"nion depuis mon abfence, non plus que moy (4),
"vous ne demanderiez maintenant d'en eftre refolu
"(5). Tant y a qu'il n'y a point defaute de ma
"part; et"

(1) From this paffage, we muft fuppofe Mary and Bothwell not to have yet fettled the *place* of the feizure. Huntly was accordingly to afcertain the "quhair" with her. Yet he does *not* afcertain it. Bothwell refers it to Mary. And Mary refers it back to Bothwell. All this is a pofitive proof of the forgery. The time of Mary's ftay at Stirling did not admit of either of thefe references. The *place* was alfo as much afcertained, as the feizure. For this we have the authority of Buchanan himfelf. And Mary, he tells us exprefsly, had fettled with Bothwell *before fhe left Edinborough*, that he fhould feize her *at Almond Bridge*, and thence carry her off: "antequam Edimburgo difceffiffet, cum eo
"tranfegerat, ut ipfe revertentem ad Almonis Pon-
"tem eam raperet, ac fecum quó vellet, velut per
"vim, abduceret *."

(2) "In the meane tyme I am feik, I will differ, as,
"tuiching the matter, it is tó lait." This concurs with the journal and with truth in intimating, that if the place of feizure was not yet fettled, it was too late to fettle it now. Her vifit at Stirling would

* Hift. xviii. 356.

not allow of it. And it is equally furprizing and agreeable, to fee the truth thus ftart out from the covert of fiction. But this paffage in the Scotch, fays our Remarker*, " exhibits an affemblage of " words without connexion or meaning." Yet both are clear. " In the meane tyme," fays the Queen, that is, till you can choofe the place and *fend* me word of it; " I am feik," not I will be fick, as if fhe was to feign herfelf fo, but " I am" fo, as fhe afterwards appears to reprefent herfelf: " I will differ," I will put off my return: " as, " tuiching the matter, it is tó lait," becaufe, with regard to *the* bufinefs, it is too late to execute it now, if I fhould return as I originally projected to have done. Such is the " meaning," and fuch the " connexion," of the words in Scotch. Let us now turn to the French. " Cependant je ne fuis a mon " aife, car il eft ja trop tard." Here half is left out, " I will differ" and " tuiching the matter." Both are effential to the meaning. The ficknefs of the Scotch, alfo, is converted into uneafinefs in the French. And Mary is made, not to defer her return, becaufe it is too late to execute the bufinefs; but to be uneafy, becaufe it is too late. Yet the Remarker cries out thus †: " can partiality for an " hypothefis induce any perfon, although but mo-" derately fkilled in the French language, to affert, " that the Scottifh copy is at this place the original, " and the French a tranflation?" The Scotch, it feems, would have retained all its rights of originality, if it had only run thus like the French, " in the

* P. 30. † Ibid.

" meane

" meane tyme I am not at myne eis, for it is tó lait."
But presuming to have more and better things in it
than the French, to raise the uneasiness into sickness,
to say she will put off her return, and to add that it
is too late to do the business now; it reduces itself
to the rank of a translation from the French. And
we are thus provided with a new and happy cri‑
terion, to distinguish copies from originals.

Let me also mark another proof of forgery
here. The sickness, here and hereafter alluded to,
seems to have been real. But then it was equally
sudden and temporary. And it did *not* happen at
Stirling. " In itinere," says Buchanan, speaking of
Mary's *return,*—" *repentino* dolore cruciata, in *do-*
" *munculam pauperculam* concessit, ad quatuor ferme
" millia passuum a Sterlino: *remittente se deinde do-*
" *lore,* ad iter reversa, *Limnuchum* eâ nocte venit*."
This was such an illness, as was impossible to be
mentioned like the present illness, in a letter during
its continuance. It was too sharp, to admit of her
prosecution of the journey. It was too transitory,
to stop her long upon the road. And it came on
four miles on this side Stirling, and at her return
from it; when that befell her before she set out to
return, even while she was in Stirling, and even the
first evening of her arrival at Stirling. So plainly
is Lethington's first letter from Stirling, quite con‑
trary even to Buchanan's narrative of Mary's jour‑
ney to it!

(3) This again informs us, that the plan of seiz‑
ing Mary could not be put in execution, unless her

* Hist. xviii. p. 356.

stay at Stirling was prolonged. Accordingly, we have seen already that it is to be prolonged. We owe the sight indeed to the *Scottish translation*, as the Remarker so illogically persists in calling it. The *French original* did not know the fact. And the stream has risen higher than the fountain.

(4) Bothwell, it seems, has changed his mind since his absence. But how long was this absence, to work such an effect upon him? It was no less than—from morning till evening. Such is the absence that can change the minds of lovers! It was the whole life of an *ephemera*; a compleat generation, as calculated on *its* cycle of time. The sun had risen, the sun had even reached its noon, the sun had even come to its fall, since this pair of lovers had been torn from each other's arms. And what cannot be effected by such a *Julian period* in love?

(5) " *Weill*, thair wantis nathing of my part." I look upon this little word *weill*, as a full proof of itself that the Scotch was the original. I have already demonstrated the point, I trust, by that strongest of all evidence, the facts of history. But I apprehend that this alone would prove it. It is a word peculiar to the common language of England and Scotland. It is also used in a very peculiar manner by it. It may come into original writings of the familiar kind, because it frequently occurs in the familiarities of conversation. But it never occurs in more formal writings. Nor, even in familiar compositions, did it ever appear, I believe,

lieve, upon the face of a tranflation; becaufe it has no correfpondent term in any other language. And it appears here, not anfwered in the French by any word or words like it in meaning; " tant y a " que," the French for it, being very different from it, and fignifying *however*.

" and feing that zour negligence dois put us baith
" in the danger of one fals brother, gif it fuccedet
" not weill, I will never ryfe agane (1).

III.—" I fend this beirar unto zow, for I dar not
" traift zour brother with thir [thefe] letteris, nor
" with the diligence (2). He fhall tell zow in
" quhait ftait I am, and judge ze quhat amendment
" yir [thefe] new ceremonies have brocht unto me
" (3). I wald I wer deid, for I fé all gais ill (4).
" Ze promyfit uther maner of mater of zour foirfe-
" ing (5), bot"

" en cas que voftre negligence ne nous mette tous
" deux au danger d'un defloyal beau-frere, fi les
" chofes ne fuccedent, jamais ne puiffe-je bouger de
" cefte place (1).

III.—" Je vous envoye ce porteur, d'autant que
" je n'ofe commettre ces lettres a voftre beau-frere,
" qui n'ufera auffi de diligence (2). Il vous dira
" de mon eftat. Jugez quel amendement m'ont
" apporté

"apporté ces nouvelles ceremonies (3). Je vou-
"droye eftre morte, car je voy que tout va mal (4).
"Vous me promiftes bien autre chofe par vos pre-
"mieres promeffes (5); mais l'abfence a pou-
"voir"

(1) "Brother," Scotch; "beau-frere," French:
"never ryfe agane," Scotch; "ne puiffe-je bou-
"ger de cefte place," French. To "ryfe agane" alludes to her prefent illnefs. She has faid before, "I am feik." She fays afterwards, that the bearer fhall tell Bothwell "in quhat ftait I am," meaning as to her health; and that he himfelf may judge, "quhat amendment" of health fhe has got from his conduct. And the King fays fimilarly in the firft letter, "I fall never ryfe out of yis bed." The French has accordingly preferved the meaning, in fome meafure; only changing the intimation of not recovering from her ficknefs, into another intimation of not being able to remove from that place. This however fhews the ficknefs before not to be intended for a feigned one in Mary, as an excufe for deferring her return; but to be reprefented as a real one, heightened indeed by Bothwell's neglects, but ftill real, and the reafon for deferring her return. It therefore furnifhes another proof of the forgery. Mary had no illnefs *at* Stirling. Mary did not defer her return *from* Stirling. She could not intend to ftay lefs than one day there. And fhe ftayed not more.—"Séing," Scotch; "en cas," French; the latter fuppofing that it *may be*, when

the

the former concurs with the whole tenor of the letter, to say that it *is*.

(2) Huntly then was to return to Edinborough, and the messenger was to carry the letter thither, and both to return to Stirling; before she could set off. This marks the forgery again. The present letter could not be written, before the night of Monday April 21st. It, the bearer, and Huntly could not set off till the next morning, Tuesday April 22d. The journey was six-and-thirty miles thither. Bothwell was then to consider the " quhair" and the " quhen" for seizing her, to settle too with Huntly how the seizure was to be made with a salvo to his honour, and then to write back to her concerning both. The messenger therefore could not reach Stirling, till Wednesday evening. And yet Mary actually left it on Wednesday morning, and came that evening to Linlithgow, according to the rebels themselves. " April 23d," says the journal, " she came to Linlythquow." " Limnuchum," says Buchanan before, " *eâ nocte* " *venit.*"—" Nor with the diligence," Scotch, meaning the speed requisite to be made; as Bishop Lesley in his Negotiations says, that " the ambassa- " dor did his *diligence* so well," &c.; as Mary's commissioners say, that the rebels " left the doing " of all *diligence*;" and as the proctor in Lady Bothwell's suit is said to have taken " the next day, " —to do farther *diligence* *."

* Anderson, iii. 149; Goodall, ii. 165; and Robertson, ii. 449.

(3) All

(3) All this is totally inconsistent with the time, that the very rebels themselves have allowed for Mary's stay at Stirling. It implies her to have been come from Edinborough some days. She has been seized with sickness. Her sickness has been aggravated by the indecisive and formal manner of Bothwell's acting, concerning the seizure of her person. And yet, all the while, she must have come from Edinborough the very morning of her writing.

(4) Bothwell had promised to send her word " every day," what she should do. He has not done this. He has at last sent his brother-in-law Huntly to her, against her warnings, and without any written commission from himself, to settle some points with her concerning the seizure. She refuses to treat with him. She sends off an express to Bothwell, requiring him to settle the place of seizure. But she declares herself to be sick. His indecisive mode of acting has increased her sickness. And she wishes she was dead, as she sees every thing go cross to her desires. All this implies such a length of time, as shews the forgery at once; when we measure it upon the scale of the journal.

(5) " Foirseing," Scotch; " premieres pro-" messes," French. The meaning is, that Bothwell promised a different kind of conduct in foreseeing, in forethought, in looking forward to all the parts of the intended business. It is to the same effect as before, when she says: " ze had pro-" mysit me, that ze wald resolve all, and yat ze " wald send me word every day quhat I suld do."

But

But the French has altered the meaning greatly. It reads "foirſéing" through the ſpectacles of the Latin, as *fore-ſaying*. It then turns the *fore-ſaying* into *promiſes*, even into the *firſt* promiſes, as if there were any others; and ſo leaves out all hints of the forethought. And the Miſcellaneous Remarker has been prudent enough, to paſs over this variation in ſilence; though it had previouſly been noticed by Mr. Goodall *.

" abſence hes power over zow (1), qua haif twa
" ſtringis to zour bow. Diſpatch the anſwer that I
" faill not, and put na traiſt in zour brother for this
" interpryſe (2); for he has tald it, and is alſo all
" aganis it (3). God give zow gude nicht (4)."

" ſur vous (1), qui avez deux cordes en voſtre
" arc. Depechez vous de me faire reponſe, afin
" que je ne faille, ne me voulant fier en voſtre
" frere (2), car il en a babillé, et y eſt du tout con-
" trair (3). Dieu vous donne la bonne nuict (4)."

(1) It well might, conſidering how long it had been; no leſs than—ten or twelve hours.

(2) The Scotch reminds *Bothwell* to put no truſt in Huntly, as Mary had advertiſed him before to take heed of Huntly. But the French tells him, that *ſhe* would put no truſt in Huntly,

* i. 91.

Yet

Yet the Remarker observes*, that the Scot has "mis-understood" the Frenchman. He *will* have the French to be the original, though the French author declares expressly to the contrary. He *will* believe and assert his favourite Dulcinea del Toboso, to be a lady of high rank and birth; even though her own mother deposes, that she is only a clown's daughter. And he takes no notice of the omission in the French, the clause "for this "interpryse" having no words to answer it there; though it is so important, that he is obliged himself to interpolate some words to the same effect, in his version of the French into English. The French, he observes, is to this effect in English: "make haste to return me an answer, that I "may not fail (miscarry *in my part of the enter-* "*prize*) for I do not chuse to rely on Lord "Huntley; he has been blabbing *it*, and is wholly "against *it*."

(3) "He is all aganis it," Scotch; "y est du "tout contraire," French. Before, the expression was this, "he is all contrarie," Scotch; "il semble "qu'il nous soit du tout contraire," French. *Then* the Remarker observed †, as an additional evidence "of the French being the original, and the "Scottish a translation," that an "emphatical "word" was "omitted in the Scottish copy." It is, he said, in French, "il *semble* que," or "he "*kytheth* to be." But he says nothing to the *present* passage, where the emphatical word, as he calls it,

* P. 31.   † Ibid.

it, is " omitted" in both the copies. The word indeed is so little emphatical, that it is quite the reverse. It does not augment the force and power of the meaning. It actually diminishes it. And the import of the passage, which is, that Huntly was *actually* all against the enterprize, is diluted by this " emphatical" word into an assertion, that he *seems to be*, or rather that *it seems he is*, all against it.

(4). This shews the letter to be written late at night. There are only two nights, to which we can attribute it, that of Monday April 21st, and that of Tuesday April 22d. And, as it is the first letter, I assign the first night to it. If we refer it to Tuesday night, the difficulties urged before will be all enhanced greatly.

§ II.

§ II.

Mary is made in the foregoing letter, to speak of some mistrusts in Bothwell concerning her. I wish to consider these at a greater length, than I could allow myself to do in the transient course of the notes. And I doubt not but I shall add one more to the many proofs of forgery, which I have laid already before my reader.

Mary left Edinborough on Monday April 21st. She left Bothwell there. "In the mene tyme," says the rebel journal, "Bothwell remainit at Edin-"brough." She left him therefore at Edinborough that morning. And when was this letter written to him? She staid at Stirling only Monday night and all Tuesday. On Wednesday she returned to Linlithgow. "April 23d," says the journal, "she "came to Linlythquow." We have only one day and one night, therefore, for these letters. And the first must of course be written on Monday night, as at night it expressly declares itself to have been written. Mary, then, came away from Edinborough and Bothwell on Monday morning, and writes to him from Stirling on Monday night. Yet she is made to complain of his distrusts. "Alace, "my lord," she cries out, "quhy is zour traift put "in ane persoun sa unworthie, to mistraist that "quhilk is haillely zouris? I am wed." But how *could* Bothwell have shewn any mistrust in this period? He could certainly have shewn none, *since she came away.* She only came away that morning. He must consequently have shewn it *before.* Yet he was *then* shewing just the reverse. This we know from a particular fact. On Saturday before, the parliament was dissolved. That evening Bothwell invited the members of it to a grand supper at a tavern, which has been made memorable since by the transactions at it, and from the keeper of the tavern is known by the name of AINSLIE's SUPPER. The design of it was to draw the members into a bond of association, urging Bothwell upon Mary for a husband, and engaging to stand by her and him for ever. This bond was accordingly produced. And the rebel journal informs us, that " April 19, " quhilk wes Setterday,—the same nycht the lordis " *past* the band—to the Erle Bothwell."

A dispute has arisen indeed, concerning the *day* on which the bond was signed. An un-authenticated copy of it in the Cotton library, is dated the 19th. But another copy, which is at Paris and authenticated by Sir James Balfour, is dated the 20th. This therefore is alledged by the friends of Mary [*], as an argument against the date of the other, and as an evidence against the alledged use of force in the subscriptions. The " parliament," said the rebels at York, " was the occasion that so many lords were " there assembled, which, being all invited to a sup-

---

[*] Keith, 382; Tytler, 217; Guthry's Scotch Hist. vii. 21 —22; and Stuart, i. 212—213.

" per

"per by Bothwell, were induced—more for fear "than otherwayes, to subcribe to the said bond; "two hundred harkebusiers being in the court, and "about the chamber-door wheare they supped, "which weare all at Bothwell's devotion *." Yet I still think, that the bond was signed at the supper. The next day was Sunday. It is by no means probable, that such a meeting would be convened upon such a day. Nor could the meeting and supper on Saturday have served any purpose, if the bond had not been then produced and signed. That it *was* then produced, the rebels say at York †, the copy in the Cotton library asserts, the rebel journal avers, and every circumstance confirms. And these are sufficient, to weigh down the solitary authority of the Paris copy.

But how comes *this* to be so dated? From a very natural circumstance, no doubt. The meeting and the supper were purely for the sake of the bond. It was not produced however, till the supper was over. So the rebels say at York, that the lords " were induced *after supper* to subscribe to the "said bond." So the rebel journal affirms, that "the lordis past the band *efter supper* to the Erle "Bothwell." This would make the business late in a large assembly. But the national habit of hard drinking would make it much later. And as Buchanan adds, and as we may be very sure the fact was, the bond was not produced and signed before the spirits of the company were properly prepared

* Appendix, N° v. † Ibid.

for the bufinefs, by a free circulation of the bottle; "folutis ad hilaritatem animis omnium *." From all, the meeting had plainly advanced far into Sunday morning, before it broke up. We are told by the rebels at York, that "the *next* morning, by *four* "*of the clocke*, few or none of them weare left in the "towne, but departed *without taking their leave* †." And it is utterly incredible, that the BISHOPS would be prefent at fuch a meeting. Yet eight of them are fubfcribers to the bond. They are fo in the Paris copy, dated the 20th. But they are not fo in the Cotton copy, dated the 19th ‡. This ferves to fhew us, that *fome* fubfcriptions were *added on the Sunday*, though the main part of them was put down on the Saturday; that, particularly, a fpace was left for the fpiritual peers, at the head of the fubfcribers; that this fpace was afterwards filled up by them; and that *then* the 20th day of the month was written over the 19th. The general fact, too, is furprizingly confirmed by the authority of Buchanan, who informs us in his hiftory, that, the day after the fupper, fuch bifhops as were then in town were called upon to fubfcribe the bond; "poftridie, quod in urbe fuit epifcoporum, convo- "catur—ut et ipfi fubfcriberent §." And, in this authenticated view of the whole, no violence is offered to either of the copies; the rebel dates at York, and the rebel journal at Weftminfter, are adhered to; and all the parts of the hiftory are made to unite together.

* Hift. xviii. 355.   † Appendix, N° v.   ‡ Keith, 382—383; and Anderfon, i. 112.   § Hift. xviii. 355.

But

But let me observe something farther, concerning this memorable bond. That, which is called the Cotton-copy, *is one of Cecil's papers* in the Cotton library. And from this circumstance, and from the manner in which Cecil says it came into his hands, it must have been furnished by the rebels at the conference in England*. They do not appear indeed upon the journal of the commissioners, exhibiting any copy of the bond at Westminster. But they do at York. An account of the fact is thus given us by the commissioners there. They " shewed unto us," they say, " a copie of a bond, bearing date the 19th " of April, 1567, *to the which* the most part of the " lords and counsaillors of Scotland HAVE *put to* " *their hands*†." This therefore was a copy with the subscriptions to it. But that in Cecil's papers is not. It is however the very same, except only in this single circumstance. It was presented to Cecil by John Read, Buchanan's own amanuensis ‡. This Cecil himself avows. " Of whom," he says concerning John Read, " I had *this copy*, being in " *his own hand* §." And this points out to us the very channel, through which Cecil received the papers, that were not publicly exhibited by the rebels, and yet were furnished by their authority. Buchanan appears to have had the keeping of all their papers. They were lodged in his hands, that he might draw up his Detection from them. He had therefore an amanuensis. This man from his

---

* Anderson, i. 112.   † Appendix, N° v.   ‡ Keith, 382.   § Anderson, i. 112.

office became secretary to the commissioners. As amanuensis, he copied the papers that were to be presented to Cecil. Hence this paper, hence the rebel journal*, and hence all the other papers probably, are in his hand-writing. And, as secretary, he carried this paper particularly to Cecil himself. But whence did he derive it? From that very copy undoubtedly, which the rebels had already exhibited at York, and which was in his own custody at present. We can even *demonstrate* that he did. " There was also in the copie of the bande," say the commissioners at York, " A COPIE OF A WAR-" RANT,—which bears date *the 14th of Maye* †." And to Cecil's copy of the bond is actually subjoined A COPY OF A WARRANT, with these words preceding it; " to this the Queene gave her con-" sent the night befoir the marriage, quhilk was the " 14 day of May, the zeir of God forsaid, in this " forme ‡."

* Carte, iii. 818. † Appendix, N° v. ‡ Anderson, i. 111.—This John Read is said in the first volume of Calderwood's MS History, at Glasgow, to have been " servitur " and writer to Master George Buchanan." But a MS translation of Buchanan's History into English, which is equally at Glasgow, asserts itself to have been made " by John Read, " esquyar, brother to James Read, parson of Banchor Ternam " whyle he lived: they both ly interr'd in the parish-church " of that town, seated not far from the bank of the river " Dee" (Nicholson's Hist. Lib. iv. 122, edit. 1702). He was " servitur and writer" to Buchanan. But then he is called by his entitler here " esquyar," with that petty affectation of consequence, which is so ridiculous a feature of the times at present.

Yet

Yet why did the rebel secretary, when he copied the bond exhibited at York, leave out the subscriptions that were to it? Because he was so ordered by his masters. Since the conference at York, they had altered their plan of proceedings in this, as well as in other respects. They had a reason for not suffering him to copy the subscriptions now, though they had exhibited them before. There was *one* name in them, which they *now* thought it most prudent to conceal for the future. And they concealed this by withholding all. But Cecil was too cunning for them. He must have remembered the copy at York, in the letters of the commissioners, to have been exhibited *with* the signatures to it. He must have seen at once the unnatural appearance of it, *without* them, now. He marked the artifice. He resolved to counteract it. Yet to call for the subscriptions would not answer the end. They, who had suppressed, might vary them. He must act to the present moment. He therefore detained the secretary. He questioned him about the subscriptions. He made his memory in some measure supply, what his pen had studiously omitted. And in a paper, which he afterwards annexed to the bond, he wrote down with his own hand " the " names of such of the nobility as subscribed the " band, so far as John Read might remember *."

Whence then did Read derive the names of the subscribers? From that very copy of the bond, which was now in his own custody, to which were annexed the subscriptions, and of which he had been

* Anderson, i. 112.

taking

taking a transcript just before. He therefore could not be mistaken in the names, which he mentioned as there. He could least of all be mistaken in the leading name. He might omit names that were actually there. But he could not mention any as there, which were not so. And he could not possibly mention a name, as the very first of all there, which was not there at all. Yet the VERY FIRST name in this rebel secretary's list, is MURRAY's. This is very astonishing. This is little known. But it is very certain, and ought to be known to all. And it lays open a large scene of villainy in that singular man, who affected in general a character just the very reverse of what he merited; who particularly assumed a bluntness of spirit *, to conceal an hypocrisy of heart; so became a greater hypocrite from the assumption; and was in this and in all his conduct, I suppose, the most finished hypocrite, that human viciousness, working upon human wisdom, has ever engendered.

He had gone off the stage just as the curtain drew up, at the seizure of Mary, and at the murder of Darnly. The one retirement reflects a strong light upon the other. He went away only *one* day before the murder. He went away *several* before the seizure. He *then* retired on the 9th of April †. But he signed the bond which produced the seizure, *before* his departure. He was *therefore* the FIRST who signed it. So eager was he to push on a business, of which he reaped all the advantage after-

* Keith, 196. † Appendix, N° x.

wards!

wards! And so long had the plan been in agitation, among his party!

We have thus seen Cecil's copy of the bond. Let us now turn to Balfour's. This is in the Scotch college at Paris. It is also attested to be a genuine copy, by the formal subscription of Sir James Balfour. He was clerk of register, and clerk of the privy council, at the time of signing the bond. But that was not the reason, for lodging the original in his hands. It was not lodged there at first. Bothwell retained it for some time in his own possession. He had it in his possession, when he seized Mary on April the 24th afterwards. He actually shewed it to Mary, while he kept her a prisoner in Dunbar castle*. He therefore took it with him, when he removed her on May the 3d to the castle of Edinborough, of which Balfour, his friend, was then governor. He kept it in his own apartment, during his residence there. In that apartment he had " a green velvet desk," in which he reposited some of his most valuable papers. He reposited in it " the principal band of the conspira-" tors in that murder" of Darnly. He therefore reposited in it, we may be sure, the bond which had been signed at the supper, and which he had just before shewn to Mary at Dunbar. He left both there, on his passing with the Queen upon the 12th of May, from the castle to the court of session, and from the court of session to the palace †. Both remained there in quiet, till the associates of his vil-

---

* Anderson, i. 97.   † Appendix, N° x.

lanies

lanies turned most perfidiously upon him, exclaimed against the guilt in which they had assisted him, and on June 15th ruined all his fortunes at a blow. Then Balfour, with the general meanness of mankind on such a revolution, broke open the velvet desk, and made himself master of the papers. "He found,—and saw, and had in his hands, the principal band of the conspirators in the murder." He also found, read, and took into his own custody, the bond of association. In 1580 he was called upon to produce the former, as evidence against the Earl of Morton. And on January 30, 1581, he inclosed an attested copy of the latter, in a letter to Mary herself[*].

All this gives as great an appearance of accuracy to the copy, as could be wished for. Yet the reality is not answerable. On the whole, Balfour's copy is less accurate than Cecil's. Had Murray indeed delivered a formal and attested copy to the commissioners of England, it would undoubtedly have been as inaccurate as Balfour's. It would have been garbled for the same reason. It would most probably have been more garbled than his. But the design of Murray to conceal his own signature by suppressing all, and the desire of Cecil to extort the names of the subscribers from the memory of the secretary, accidentally coming in collision together, produced a copy superior in exactness to Balfour's. Sir James suppressed the name of MURRAY, for the same reason which made

[*] Robertson, ii. 463; and Keith, 382.

Murray

Murray willing to suppress all. On the same principle he suppressed HIS OWN too, Lord LINDSAY's, and the Earl of GLENCAIRN's. He suppressed their names and his own, because he was sending the list to MARY; and because he and they had been most hypocritically active, in turning the very marriage, which they had pushed on themselves, into a strong evidence of criminality in her. That he suppressed his own name and Lord Lindsay's; is plain from this authentic paper. "The maist part of the nobilitie," say the lords of Mary's side, "and principallie of the usurparis, sic as the Erle Morton, Lord Sempil, LORD LYNDSAY, and MR. JAMES BALFOUR, gave thair consent to the Erle Bothwel" marrying Mary*. Sir James and Lord Lindsay, therefore, were subscribers to the bond. Yet they do not appear in Sir James's copy of it. This omission is a very gross one. It speaks to very mind. Nor can it be palliated by the excuse, which has been unwittingly made for it by the *friends* of Mary, as if Sir James took down " only the names of the *great men*," and for that reason omitted these †. On *this* ground of acting, Sir James *would* have inserted his own. And he *could* n't have omitted Lord Lindsay's. The omission of his own name is the leading clue to the rest. The omission of his own and Lord Lindsay's shews clearly, why he omitted Murray's and Glencairn's, when both appear in Cecil's copy. And all throw

* Goodall, ii. 361.   † Ibid. i. 364.

such

such a discredit over Balfour's boasted copy of the bond, as sets it much below Cecil's.

Nor let it be surmised, that if Murray had been a subscriber, and the very first subscriber, to the bond; his name would have been particularly mentioned by the peers of Mary's party, as one "principallie "of the usurparis" who signed it, and even in preference to "the Erle Morton, Lord Sempil, Lord "Lyndsay, and Mr. James Balfour." That Murray actually signed the bond, and was the very first who signed it; stands upon such a broad basis of evidence, as is not to be shaken by mere omissions. Negative evidence can never supersede positive. Nor is it wonderful, that the peers omitted Murray's name. They were not speaking from any copy of the bond. Even the Queen, even her embassador in France, had none till many years afterwards; and then had it only from the keeper of the original, who transmitted it to her embassador in a letter to Mary, and so left it to be found among the embassador's papers a few years ago*. They were speaking only from memory. This might well deceive them. Murray was not present at the supper Murray was actually absent from the kingdom a the time. Their recollection of both would unit to mislead them. And even if they had some indistinct remembrance, of seeing his name upon th paper that evening or the next day; yet they woul be afraid to rely upon this, in contradiction to bot and still more afraid to assert the fact upon th

* Keith, 382.

authori

authority of this, in a formal address. We see them even omitting the name of a person, who was actually in the kingdom, actually at the supper, and more important than either Lord Semple, Lord Lindsay, or Sir James Balfour. This is the Earl of Glencairn, the most ferocious leader of the most ferocious sectaries, and in himself and in his followers so much, what Mr. Pope *once* characterized the English sectaries of the *last* century to be, a

——sacrilegious brood,
Sworn to rebellion, principled in blood *.

Yet this very man is omitted by the peers; though we know him to have been equally a subscriber with the others, and though he was so much more formidable in his power, his spirit, and his zeal, than any of them. And if their memory failed them concerning such a hero in rebellious violence, " the " fellest of the fell;" it might well be unable to give them all the certainty that they could act upon, concerning Murray. Yet the lords of Mary's party did afterwards get such good intelligence, of Murray's having signed the bond; that Bishop

---

* This man, on June the 17th 1567, the day after the Queen's imprisonment, " accompanied only by his domesticks, " entered the Queen's chapel of Holyrood-house, and," with all the religious barbarism of our own sectaries in 1641, " not " only *demolished the altar*, but *broke* the *pictures*, and *all* the " *other ornaments*, without regard to *price* or *workmanship* " (Crawford 42). " The preachers," says Spotswood, 208, " did commend it as a work of great piety and zeal." And see Keith, 88, 401, 403, and 406—407, for Glencairn, as a very *Hot-spur* in rebellion and blood.

Lesley,

Lesley, in his Defence of Mary's honour, openly addresses him thus. Having first asked, " Cal you " this—a voluntary assignation of the regiment to " YOU, Earle Murray?" he proceeds in this manner: " I aske then, as before, of YOU, why, " through the special sute and procurement of *your* " *faction*," meaning, as he says in another place, " Earle Morton, the Lord Simple, the Lord Lind- " zay, with their adherents and affinitie," " he," Bothwell, " was acquited, and set on cleare bord ? " Why did YOU, with a great number of the no- " bilitie, MOVE FURTHER, AND WORKE THE SAID " MARIAGE " of the Queen with Bothwell, " as " most meete and necessary for your Quene ? Why " did YOU, AS BY YOUR HAND-WRITING IT WIL " APPEARE, proffer and promisse to HIM your faith- " ful service, and to HER your loyal obeisance ? " Why did none of *al your faction*," &c*. And the exactness of the writer, in distinguishing what he attributes to the whole party in general, and what to Murray in particular, serves to prove the accuracy of his observations, and to give a greater certainty to all.

Nor let it even be supposed, upon this hypothesis of a wilful suppression of names by Balfour, that he should equally have suppressed others; and that, as he screened Murray and Glencairn, he must also have screened Morton, Glammis, Ruthven, and Semple. The fact is plain, that he did conceal the names of Murray and Glencairn. The fact is also

---

* Defence, 38, 42, and 26.

plain,

plain, that he equally concealed Lindsay's and his own. And problematical reasonings can never be adduced, in opposition to plain facts. Besides the public cause, he had reasons of private enmity and of private love, no doubt, to actuate him in this bold falsification of the bond. These would mingle with the public principles, pervert their direction, and destroy their uniformity. He therefore mentioned some, while he past by others. He put down Morton, and left out Murray. He passed over Glencairn, Lindsay, and himself, and he lighted upon Glammis, Ruthven, and Semple. And he noticed not Seton, Sinclair, Oliphant, Rosse-Hacat, Carleile, Hume, and Innermeith, some of whom we know to have been rebels*, and all of whom except Seton, who was probably omitted by a mere casualty, we therefore presume to have been such. But every one of these names, almost, is preserved very faithfully in Cecil's copy. The hasty call upon Read's memory, allowed no time for party-selection there. He gave in the names of rebels or of royalists, as they arose to his memory. And his copy accordingly answers to that description, which is given of the signatures by the peers of Mary; while Balfour's differs widely from it.

They say, that the *major* number of the subscribers was of *the rebels themselves*. This is a fact, which is of great consequence in the history of the bond. Yet it has never been observed. It appears however in a passage, that I have cited already:

* Goodall, ii. 65—66, and Anderson, ii. 228—229, and 233, compared with Goodall, ii. 354.

"The

" the maist part of the nobilitie, and PRINCIPALLIE
" of the USURPARIS,—gave thair confent to the
" Erle Bothwel." It is also confirmed by the authority of Bothwell himself, in his referring the bond, particularly, to *the great leaders of the Proteſtant party in Scotland*. In Mary's inſtructions to her embaſſador in France, for informing the King and Queen of France concerning her late marriage with Bothwell, ſhe apologizes for her marrying him in the PROTESTANT form, becauſe Bothwell inſiſted upon it; he, ſhe ſays, " having mair reſpect
" to content YAME, by QUHAIS CONSENT GRANTIT
" TO HIM BEFOIRHAND he thinkis he hes obtenit
" his purpois,—than regarding our contentatioun*."
In Cecil's copy, this is actually the caſe. It enumerates the Earls Murray, Argyle, Huntly, and Caſſils, Morton, Sutherland, Rothes, Glencairn, and Cathneſs; and the Barons Boyd, *Seton, Sinclair*, Semple, and *Oliphant*, Ogilby, *Roſſe-Hacat, Carleile*, Herris, Hume, and *Innermeith* †. Of theſe, I ſhall not conſider either Argyle or Boyd to be rebels. They were indeed in the original conſpiracy with the rebels. But they broke not out into rebellion with them ‡. They therefore cannot, in any propriety of ſpeech, come under the denomination of " uſurparis." And I'ſhall rank them both under the royal banner. But of others we muſt determine differently. Some engaged in the uſurpation at firſt, and vigorouſly returned to their duty

---

* Anderſon, i. 99. † Anderſon, i. 112. I have *italiciſed* ſuch names as are omitted in either liſt, that the eye may catch them the ſooner. ‡ Crawford, 23, and 26.

afterwards.

afterwards. These must still be reputed as rebel subscribers to the bond. And we must repute all for rebels, whom we know to have been connected in rebellious designs with them at the time, if we do not know them to have deserted at the breaking out of the rebellion; and also all, that we find to have embarked with them in the usurpation, however they might revolt from them afterwards. But the Cotton copy has Murray, Morton, and Glencairn, Semple, Hume, and Innermeith, the *certain* followers of rebellion*; and Argyle, Huntly, Boyd, Seton, and Herris, the *undoubted* champions for royalty. Cathness must also be numbered with the former, though in July 1568 he took part with the latter; because we know him to have been actually combined with the rebels, in the month immediately preceding the execution of the bond, and ready to enter immediately upon rebellious courses with them; and because we know him not to have left them, till fifteen months afterward †. But Cassils,

---

* Innermeith appears a rebel July 24, 1567, Keith, 427; and December 4, 1567, Goodall, ii. 66. † Goodall, i. 353 for his union with the rebels, and Anderson, iv. part i. 124, for his association with the royalists.—The list of peers in Spotswood, 208, and Keith, 408, represented in Stuart, i. 247, as a list of royalists, is only an enumeration of such nobles, as in June and July 1567 "did *either assist the adverse party*" to the rebels, "or then *behaved themselves as neuters*" (Spotswood, 208; see also Keith, 577). Nor are the names, I believe, much to be depended on. Ochiltree is one of them in Spotswood and in Knox (Keith, 408), though we know him to have been really acting with the rebels at the time (Keith, 406, 424).

Caſſils, Sutherland, Rothes, and Sinclair, Oliphant, Ogilby, Roſſe-Hacat, and Carleile, ſeem to take a middle place between both. They were indeed all royaliſts afterward. Yet the higheſt that we can aſcend in the courſe of their loyalty, is September the 12th and May the 8th 1568 *. And then we find Errol, a plain and evident rebel †, in company with them. We have SIX certain rebels, therefore, againſt FIVE certain royaliſts. But if we add Cathneſs to the former liſt, as we ought to do, we have SEVEN againſt FIVE. This is the amount of both, even if we leave out the doubtful ſigners. We might perhaps with propriety attach Sinclair, Oliphant, Roſſe-Hacat, and Carleile, to the cauſe of uſurpation. We are wholly ignorant of their conduct, prior to September and May 1568. And Balfour's omiſſion of their names, with thoſe of Murray and Glencairn, Hume and Innermeith,

---

424, &c.). The name is accordingly Ogilvie in a MS. of Spotſwood's (Keith, 408). But this does not clear away the error in Knox. And ſo groſs a miſtake in one name renders all ſuſpectable. See alſo Keith, 583, for Innermeith, July 20, 1567, ſubſcribing with the rebel chiefs, though mentioned in the liſt as either loyal or neuter; and July 24 acting boldly with the rebels (Keith, 427).

* Keith, 476, for Caſſils, Sutherland, Rothes, Sinclair, Oliphant, Ogilby, Roſſe-Hacat, and Carleile, May 8, 1568; and Goodall, ii. 353—354, for them, September 12, 1568. Carleile is in Keith *Carlieure*. But this is only a miſ-print (Douglas's Peerage, 121). And Roſſe-Hacat is only *Roſſe of Halk-head* (Peerage, 582), I ſuppoſe, abbreviated in pronunciation. He is therefore called ſimply Roſſe, in Keith and Goodall, ibid.   † Keith, 476, and Goodall, ii. 65.

throws

throws a deep shade of suspectability over them. Yet let us leave them to remain with their companions, in their original state of dubiousness. Let us add only what we are sure ought to be added, those two names of Balfour and Lindsay, which, in a singular coincidence of action, have been omitted by both the copies. And then we shall see the balance still more in favour of the rebels, and Cecil's copy coming still closer to the standard set up by the peers of Mary. But in Balfour's this is just the reverse. His copy exhibits for its subscribers, the Bishops of St. Andrews, Aberdeen, Whitern, Dumblain, Brechin, Ross, the Isles, and Orkney; the Earls Huntly, Argyle, Morton, and Cassils, Sutherland, *Errol, Crawford*, Cathness, and Rothes; and the Barons Boyd, *Glammis, Ruthven*, Semple, Herris, Ogilby, and *Fleming*. But, of the eight bishops, only one took part against Mary; the infamous Bishop of Orkney. Of the nine earls, Morton and Errol certainly, and Cathness probably, stand opposed to Huntly and Argyle; while Crawford, whose loyalty first appears on May the 8th 1568 *, files off upon one side with Cassils, Sutherland, and Rothes. Of the seven barons, we have Ogilby equally filing off; and Glammis, Ruthven, and Semple †, facing Boyd, Fleming, and Herris. And thus, instead of FIVE royalists against NINE rebels, as in Cecil's copy, we find in Balfour's TWELVE royalists against SEVEN rebels; and when

* Keith, 476, and Goodall, ii. 65.   † Goodall, ii. 65.

we add Balfour and Lindsay to the number, TWELVE against NINE.

So clearly is Cecil's copy a more authentic one than Balfour's! Nor does any *number* of *inferior* lords, as has been surmised, appear to have been omitted by either. Cecil's indeed reckons only nine earls and eleven barons. Even Balfour's enumerates only nine earls, seven barons, and eight bishops. And " the *maist* part of the nobilitie," say Mary's friends upon one side; and " the *most* " part of the lords and counsaillors of Scotland," say her rebels on the other; subscribed to it. But then both these copies actually contain " the most " part" of the lords, that appeared in parliament at the time. This is evident from the rolls of parliament. Neither copy includes any of the abbots. These were secular gentlemen, who had taken possession of the abbies a few years before, and had then arrogated to themselves the nobility of the abbots. They sat as nobles, for the first time, in the rebel parliament of 1560. But they sat not in council after the return of Mary, before May 15, 1565. And they sat *regularly* in parliament for the first time, I believe, at this period*. They were yet, therefore, a kind of candidates only for a legal nobility. They were for that reason not invited, with the other nobles, to the supper. And for the same reason they were not solicited, like their half-brothers the bishops, for their subscriptions to the bond the day afterwards. But of the nine

* Anderson's General Preface, xxxi, Keith, 277, and Anderson, i. 113.

bishops, of the eight earls besides Bothwell himself, and of the sixteen barons, that are upon the rolls, only seven barons, one earl, and one bishop did *not* sign *. Nor is this all. We know the parliamentary rolls to be considerably defective in this respect. We know Huntly, particularly, to have been at the supper; though he is not in the rolls. We know also Glencairn, Sinclair, Oliphant, Carleile, Hume, and Innermeith, to have subscribed the bond on the dissolution of parliament; though not one of them is noticed by the rolls of it. And these, added to the list of signing nobles, give a decided majority to the latter. Even if we take in the abbots to our account, we can enumerate only eighteen lords (besides Bothwell), who were non-subscribers; when there are (besides him) twenty-six upon the rolls, and there were at least seven more, who were actual subscribers †.

In this view of the signers and of the parliament, the rebel secretary had no great exertion of memory to make. The whole list of them, as made up in Cecil's and Balfour's copies together, is only twenty-five, besides the bishops; eleven earls, and fourteen barons. He may have forgot Errol, Crawford, and Glammis, Ruthven, Fleming, Balfour, and Lindsay. But most probably he did not. Some or all of these may equally have subscribed on the next day, the 20th. They would then be never inserted in his copy of the subscriptions, and his memory could never recur to them. His copy

* Anderson, i. 113—114.   † Ibid.

was taken that very night. This is evident from the date, and from the total omission of the eight bishops by him. His memory could never have leaped over them all; ranged too as they all stood at the head of the whole. He could only have omitted them, because his copy did not contain them. And there is a slight intimation at the close of his list, that at once shews the general accuracy, with which his memory recollected the names in his copy, and proves both his copy and his memory to have been confined, entirely, to the subscriptions of the 19th. " Eglinton," says Cecil from him, " subscribed not, but slipped away *." He not only recollected those who were specified in his copy. He also remembered one who was *not*. And he mentioned the reason, which had always been suggested for his non-appearance there; that though he was actually present at the supper, and actually stayed till the production of the bond, yet, when he found what sort of business was going forward, he very wisely stole out of the company, and departed without subscribing.

This plan of a supper and a bond, in order to recommend himself to Mary for a husband, was certainly an amazing stroke of villainy in Bothwell. It was a stroke of refined villainy, beyond the reach of his poor understanding. It was suggested, no doubt, by the rebels themselves. The bond accordingly appears to have been signed by Murray himself, no less than TEN days beforehand. It was

* Anderson, i. 112.

peculiarly

peculiarly calculated, though none of our hiſtorians have noted the connection, to produce the ſeizure of Mary's perſon, to lead on to the brutal act of raviſhment, and to terminate at laſt in her neceſſary marriage with the raviſher. And it actually ended in a long train of miſeries, to Mary and to all the kingdom.

But ſtill did Bothwell uſe any armed force to produce the ſignatures? It is not credible that he did. It is indeed ridiculous to ſuppoſe he could. Yet let me additionally obſerve, that this circumſtance of terror is plainly of a later date than the bond or the ſupper, and was even fabricated poſteriorly to the formation of the rebel journal; being totally omitted there, and omitted even when an apology is attempted to be made for ſigning the bond. " The " ſame nycht," it ſays, " the lordis paſt the band " efter ſupper to the Erle Bothwell, *being drawin* " *ſecretlie be him to the ſupper**." And, what is ſtill more deciſive, the rebels themſelves even *diſproved* the circumſtance effectually, *in the very moments* in which they *firſt* aſſerted it. " In proufe " that they did it not willinglie," ſay the commiſſioners of Elizabeth, " they procured a warrant, " which was now ſhewed unto us, bearing date the " 19th of Aprill, ſigned with the Quene's hand, " whereby *ſhe gave them licence to agree to the ſame*; " affirming that, before they had ſuch warrant, " there *was none of them that did or wold ſet to* " *their bands*, ſaving onlie the Earl of Huntley †."

* Appendix, N° x.   † Ibid. N° v.

Where

Where then are the "two hundred harkebusiers," that compelled them to subscribe for fear? Nowhere, plainly. There was no compulsion, they allow themselves. There was only a licence. Till this was produced, they would not subscribe. And, when it was produced, they subscribed, not for fear of Bothwell's "harkebusiers," but from reverence to the Queen's licence. So clear is it even from the rebels themselves, that Bothwell made use of no force in procuring the subscriptions! The warrant produced at York was ashamed to shew itself at Westminster*, and was therefore confessed to be spurious. It was too compleatly ridiculous in its nature indeed, to be obtruded upon the faith of any, that had spirit to examine and sagacity to discern a gross incredibility. Mary is represented by it, as wanting her nobles to recommend Bothwell, and therefore licensing them under her sign manual to recommend: when she might have taken him without any recommendation at all; and when she might as well have taken him without one, as have openly and formally licensed them to give one. But it serves very strongly to prove the falsity of the force asserted. In concurrence with the rebel journal also, it shews the rebels to have first formed the story of the harquebusiers at the York conference, and not to have properly incorporated it yet with their other falshoods. And, as I cannot but observe at the close of all, Murray must have been one of the most impudent of *human* be-

* Goodall, ii. 235—236, 256—258, and 87.

ings,

ings, to pretend, as he thus did by his deputies at York, that the Queen granted a warrant, " bearing " date the 19th of Aprill," and licenfing the perfons to fign; that all the peers, except Huntly, refufed to fign before the warrant was produced; and that at laft they figned, becaufe they were compelled by Bothwell's harquebufiers: when, at that very inftant, *his own name*, and not Huntly's, appeared in *his own copy of the bond* as exhibited at York and reported at Weftminfter, *the very firft* upon the file of fubfcriptions; when he was well known to have left Scotland fome days before the fupper, and had actually left it no lefs than ten before*; and when therefore he muft have fubfcribed at a time, at which there was no warrant exifting, and in which there could be no compulfion ufed.

I have entered into this long examination of the whole fact, partly becaufe I thought I could throw a new light upon it; partly becaufe it fhews the villainy of the rebels in a new point of view; and principally becaufe it proves Bothwell, at this period, not to have been in any poffible humour of miftrufting the Queen. He had formed his plan for marrying her. He had been fecuring himfelf on Saturday and Sunday from any interruption in the act, by procuring fubfcriptions to his bond of affociation. He had nothing now to do, but execute the deed that he had projected. He ftood on the very tiptoe of ambitious expectation, no doubt. His vanity flattered him with the hope, of gaining the Queen's heart. His pride was continually holding

* Appendix, N° x.

up

up to his mind, the present proof, as he thought it, of his vast popularity among the nobles. And all must have been hope and joy within him. Yet these moments above all others has the letter-writer selected, for Mary to complain of his distrusts. He has been busy in procuring the bond, with a view to marry her; yet he is mistrustful of her. He has been singularly active, in shewing his regard and affection for her; yet, all the while, he is making her mad with his expressed distrusts. And in the gayest and happiest minutes of his whole life, when

> Hope elevates, and Joy
> Brightens his crest;

even then, he is represented as peculiarly suspicious and rude.

§ III.

§ III.

LETTER THE SIXTH (1).

I.—" Of the place and the tyme, I remit myſelf
" to zour brother and to zow (2). I will follow
" him, and will faill in nathing of my part (3). He
" findis mony difficulteis (4); I think he dois ad-
" vertiſe zow thairof, and quhat he defyris for the
" handling of himſelf (5). As for the handling of
" myſelf, I hard it anis weill devyſit (6)."

I.—" Du lieu et de l'heure, je m'en rapporte a
" voſtre frere et a vous (2). Je le ſuivray, et ne
" faudray en rien de ma part (3). Il trouve beau-
" coup de difficultez (4): je penſe qu'il vous en a
" adverty, et de ce qu'il deſiroit pour bien jouer ſon
" perſonnage (5). Quant a jouer le mien, je ſcay
" comme je m'y dois gouverner, me ſouvenant de
" la façon que les choſes ont eſté deliberées (6)."

(1) When was this letter written? There is no note of time in it. But from the whole turn and tenor it appears, not to have been written till two days at leaſt after the former. This carries us at once beyond the line of time, which Mary ſtaid

at

at Stirling. And it concurs with all before, to prove the forgery plain.

(2) Behold the backward and forward operations of this and the preceding letter. Bothwell was to settle the time and place, and send Mary word. He does not do this. He sends Huntly after her to do this, and to settle another point concerning Huntly himself. Mary refuses to settle with Huntly. She sends off an express to Bothwell. She insists upon his chusing the place. Of the time she says nothing. But she now refers the time as well as the place, not merely to Bothwell, but to him and to Huntly; to the very man in conjunction with Bothwell, with whom she had refused to settle it before, when Bothwell sent him to her. All this reciprocation of reference is done, we must remember, at the distance of six-and-thirty miles, and within the compass of one whole day and one evening. And, what aggravates the whole, it is plain from her manner, that she has heard from Bothwell in answer to her first letter; and that she is now writing a reply to his answer.— " Time," Scotch ; " homme," French, as misprinted in Goodall, for " heure," as in Buchanan.

(3) How different is this from the preceding letter ! " I advertisit zow weill," she *then* said, " to " tak heid of zour fals brother-in-law ;" and yet Bothwell, she complains, had sent him to settle all the circumstances of the seizure with her. " Zour " negligence," she adds, " dois put us baith in the " danger of ane fals brother." And " put na
" traist

" traift in zour brother," fhe concludes, " for this " interpryfe; for he hes tald it, and is alfo all " aganis it." But *now* fhe remits the place and the time to this very man and Bothwell together, and declares boldly that fhe " will follow him." Her ficknefs too is all gone off. She no longer wifhes fhe " wer deid, for I fe all gais ill." She " will fol- " low Huntly," and, " will faill in nathing of her " part."

(4) Juft now, fhe was leaving the time and the place to Huntly and Bothwell, and declaring fhe would follow Huntly without fail. But here we find Huntly, whom fhe was to *follow*, is not fo forward as herfelf. He fhrinks behind her. And " he findis mony difficulties" in a plan, of which, the very moment before, the time and the place were to be fettled by him and Bothwell. All this is amazingly contradictory. But the contradictorinefs is heightened by a fact. In the laft letter, Huntly was fetting off for Edinborough. " I dar " not traift zour brother," fhe there fays, " with thir " letteris nor with the diligence." Yet he is now with her. She has alfo received a letter from Bothwell, which has altered her opinion of Huntly, and makes her remit the time and the place to him and Bothwell, and to declare that fhe will follow Huntly. And Huntly has gone to Edinborough fince the laft letter, has fettled the time and place with Bothwell, and has returned with an account of both to Mary;—all within the compafs of four-and-twenty hours. He moved upon a witch's broom.

He

He beftrode the wooden horfe of the Perfian Tales. Or he failed in an air-balloon.

(5) This augments all the difficulties of the chronology. But indeed, when once the laws of nature are broken through, a great deviation may as well be allowed as a little one. And a palace may rife " like an exhalation" in five hours, as well as in fifty. Huntly, returned a fecond time from Edinborough, ftill finds many difficulties in the bufinefs, and ftill is referring (as Mary thinks) to Bothwell at Edinborough, for the folution of them. This is furely one of the bufieft days in all the hiftory of the human race. It is full of uncommon activity. Huntly has been at Edinborough, has confulted, has returned, is now fending back to Edinborough, and is to have an anfwer again before the morning. And, what perhaps marks it ftill more, all this activity hitherto has been buftle without efficiency. The time and place indeed are fettled, we muft fuppofe. But how the honour of Huntly is to be falved, is not fettled. He has been fo eager about Mary's and Bothwell's parts in the play, that he has totally overlooked his own. Yet he was, when we laft faw him, fo much averfe to the whole, fo " all aganis it;" that he had even betrayed the fcheme, " he hes tald it." He was then alfo folicitous to know, what Bothwell " fuld do tuiching " him." Mary very naturally forgot this in her late letter. She might well forget *his* concerns, when fhe forgot a material one of her own, the *time* of the feizure. And, though he remembered the

time

time for her as well as the place, he wholly forgot his own honour.

(6) "As for the handling of myself, I hard it "anis weill devyfit," Scotch. I once thought "hard" to be a mis-print for "hald," and the sense to be, I hold it to have been well devised once. But "hard" is as good or better, and signifies, that it was once well devised in her hearing. Either way, the clause shews the plan of the seizure to have been settled, before Mary left Edinborough. Common sense shews that it must have been. But then common sense shews equally, that not merely the general plan would be settled, that the circumstances must have been settled with it. They were the necessary parts of the plan. They were necessary to be settled before she went away. Her stay was so peculiarly short at Stirling, that, if they were not settled before she went, the plan itself could not be executed as she returned. This passage even says that they were, by declaring that the very line of behaviour, which the Queen was to pursue, had been settled to her satisfaction. "As for the handling of "myself, I hard *it* anis weill devyfit." And this cuts up these four letters by the roots, at once.

The French version here is very strange. "Pour "bien jouer son personnage" in the preceding sentence, and "a jouer le mien" in this, seem to *me* very absurd substitutes for "pour bien se conduire" and "a me conduire." But the translation of "I "hard it anis weill devyfit," into "je scay comme "je m'y dois gouverner, me souvenant de la façon

" que les choses esté deliberées," is most ridiculously loose and wild. Yet the Remarker, in his usual strain of *sombrous* confusedness, observes *; that in the Scotch " a material part of the French is " omitted, and the reason supposed to have been " given by the Queen is lost in the translation," meaning the original. And thus that Ovidian addition of Dryden's to Virgil,

And her last sighs came bubbling up in air,

proves Dryden's to be the original, and Virgil's only a translation; because " a material part" of the English is " omitted" in the Latin, and the effect of Juturna's sorrowful retreat under the waters " is " lost in the translation."—The expression " hand-" ling of himself" and " handling of myself," is not so *antique*, but some traces of it have come down to modern times. Keith, speaking of Mary's ministers at one time, calls them " those who had pre-" sently the chief *handling* about the Queen." And the language carries no particular dissonance with it, even to our English ears at present.

II.—" Methinkis that zour services, and the " lang amitie (1); having ye gude will of ye lordis " (2); do weill deserve ane pardoun, gif abone the " dewtie of ane subject yow advance yourself (3),

* P. 31—32.

" not

" not to conftrane me (4), bot to affure yourfelf of
" fic place neir unto me (5), that uther admoni-
" tiounis or forane perfwafiounis may not let me
" from confenting to that, that ye hope your fervice
" fall mak yow ane day to attene: and, to be
" fchort,"

II.—" Il me femble que voftre long fervice, et
" la grande amitie (1) et faveur que vous portent
" les feigneurs (2), meritent bien que vous obte-
" niez pardon, encor qu'en cecy vous vous avan-
" ciez aucunement par deffus le devoir d'un fubjet
" (3). Or eft-il que vous entreprenez de le faire,
" non pas afin de me forcer et tenir captive (4),
" ains pour vous rendre affeuré pres de moy (5),
" et que les remonftrances et perfuafions des autres
" ne m'empefchent de confentir a ce que vous ef-
" perez que voftre fervice vous fera un jour obtenir.
" Bref, c'eft pour vous"

(1) " Zour fervices and the lang amitie,"
Scotch; "*long* fervice, et la *grande* amitie,"
French.

(2) This alludes to the bond of affociation.
But the French has taken the " amitie," which
fhould go with the " fervices," and fo exprefs in
conjunction the fidelity fhewn by Bothwell to the
crown, and the friendfhip fhewn by the crown to
him; and united it to the " gude will of ye
" lordis."

(3) The enormity of feizing the Queen's perfon, and carrying her captive to the caftle of Dunbar,

bar, wanted some covering from the hand of forgery, to make us believe it was done by Mary's consent. This covering is here attempted to be spread over it. But the leaf-gold is stretched out so thin, that we see the rottenness of the wood below it.—" Gif," Scotch; " encor que," absurdly, French: " en cecy," French, as absurdly added: and " aucunement," French, interpolated in direct opposition to the sense.

(4) The French, beginning a new sentence, prefixes this clause, " or est-il que vous entreprenez " de le faire," and then renders " constrane me" by " de me forcer et tenir captive." The Remarker, with a *prudence that is the better half of his valour*, passing over the former variation unnoticed, settles upon the latter. And " this is imper-" fect" in the Scotch, he says, " and does not express " half of the meaning of the French."

(5) " Sic place neir unto me," Scotch; " pres " de moy," French; the words " sic place" being omitted, though important in themselves, and though leading to the next clause.

" to mak yourself sure of the lordis, and fré to
" mary (1); and that ye ar constranit for your
" suretie, and to be abill to serve me faithfully (2),
" to use ane humble requeist, joynit to ane impor-
" tune actioun (3)."

III.—

III.—" And, to be schort (4), excuse yourself,
"and perswade thame the maist ye can (5), yat ye
"ar constranit to mak persute aganis zour enemies
"(6). Ze sall say aneuch, gif the mater or ground
"do lyke zow; and mony fair wordis to Lething-
"toun (7). Gif ye lyke not the deid, send me
"word (8), and leif not the blame of all unto
"me (9)."

" asseurer des seigneurs, et vous mettre en liberté
" de vous marier (1); comme y estant contraint
" pour vostre seureté, a ce que puis apres me ser-
" vant loyaument (2), vous me puissiez presenter
" une humble requeste, conjointe toutesfois avec
" importunité (3).

III.—" (4) Excusez vous donc, et les persuadez
" le plus que pourrez (5), que vous estes forcé par
" necessité de faire ainsi vostre poursuite a l'encontre
" de vos ennemis (6). Vous aurez dequoy dire
" assez, si l'argument et le subjet vous plaist; et
" donnez beaucoup de belles paroles a Ledington
" (7). Que si cela ne vous semble bon, adver-
" tissez m'en (8), et n'en mettez pas du toute la
" faute sur moi (9)."

(1) How would the seizing of the Queen make him " sure of the lordis, and fré to mary?" It would make him sure of them, I suppose, by the future marriage of her. But how then would it make him free to marry? By the subsequent divorce from his own wife, no doubt. He seized

Mary

Mary on April 24, and the firſt proceſs of divorce was iſſued the 26th *. Yet all this leads to a detection of the forgery. The obtaining of a divorce is here made to reſult from the ſeizure. But it was intended long before. The preparatory ſteps had alſo been taken long before. Even in the ſecond of Murray's own contracts it is expreſsly declared, that ſo early as the 5th of April Bothwell's wife " hes " thairunto conſentit †." Even the " procuratory," by which ſhe authorized her proctor to appear for her before the commiſſaries of Edinborough, and to inſtitute a ſuit for divorce, was ſigned by her on or before that day. " April 5th," ſays the rebel journal itſelf, " the ſecund contract of marriage, per verba " de præſenti, was maid and wryttin be my Lord of " Huntly, quha for his reſtoring agane the forfal- " tour," to have his forfeiture taken off, " *had* pur- " chaſit ane *procuratory ſubſcryvit with his ſiſter's* " *band*, then wyif to Bothwell ‡." The divorce therefore did not depend upon the *ſeizure*, though it undoubtedly was occaſioned by the hope of a marriage with the Queen. And the letter, which makes it to depend upon that, cannot be genuine.

(2) How would the ſeizure enſure Bothwell's ſafety, and enable him to ſerve her faithfully? Exaltation, not ſafety, was his object. Nor could he ſerve her more faithfully as a huſband, than as a common ſubject. Nor could Mary, in any view, think theſe were his motives. If he and ſhe were

* Appendix, N° x.   † Ibid, N° xiv.   ‡ Ibid, N° x.

linked

linked in adultery together, her's would be to secure her lover entirely to herself, and his to obtain all the honour and elevation that he could reach. And suggestions, so contrary to all this, could never come from the pen of Mary. They came indeed from Bothwell originally. They are the very arguments used by Bothwell to Mary, when he had seized her person, and secured her in Dunbar-castle *. They were very natural to Bothwell, who wanted to colour over his profligate ambition with some less offensive pretences. But they are very unnatural in Mary, who could have had no profligacy of ambition to cover. And the forgery is betrayed at once; by the act of borrowing suggestions from a paper, posterior in date to the present letter; and by the absurdity of transferring the suggestions, from the real and natural user, to one who could not use them at all.

(3) "Ane humble requeist joynit with ane "importune actioun," Scotch; "une humble re- "queste, conjointe toutesfois avec importunité," French. "The Scottish translator," says the Remarker †, still keeping his old *mumpsimus* in spite of the new *sumpsimus*, "does but guess at the im- "port of this passage, and he guesses ill." The French means, he adds, " a humble but earnest pe- " tition in the way of marriage." But *should* not it mean more? Is this *all* that has been so long alluded to in the letter? Is it indeed any part of that?

* Anderson, i. 96.   † P. 32.

Is not the whole aim and substance of the letter, concerning an "actioun," and a very "impor-"tune" one indeed? The fact is, that the Scotch keeps steadily to the prevailing idea of the letter, and the French deserts it at a leap; that the Scotch pursues the subject of the seizure, only adding its necessary adjunct, a petition for marriage, to it; and that the French sinks the seizure from the sight, and makes the petition to stand for both. And thus the cypher, which in union with its proper figure was of real consequence, is compelled to appear by itself, when it could be of no consequence at all; and yet is supposed by our arithmetician, to carry even more than the consequence of both with it. " To be abill to serve me faith-" fully," Scotch; " a ce que puis apres me servant " loyaument, vous puissiez," French. The French says, as the Remarker himself observes, " untill, in " consequence of your loyal services, you might " present a petition." But the meaning is, as the Scotch says, that, to be able to serve me faithfully, you are constrained to use a request and a seizure. *That* makes Bothwell to seize Mary, till, in consequence of his loyal services done after the seizure, he could request her to marry him; which is infinitely absurd. And *this* makes him to seize her and request her marriage, that he might be able to serve her the more faithfully afterwards. Yet the Remarker adduces this whole passage as a proof, that the French is the original and the Scotch a translation.

(4) " T

(4) "To be fchort," omitted in the French.

(5) Bothwell is directed to excufe himfelf to the lords, and to " perfwade thame the maift he can," that his intended feizure of the Queen was neceffary in itfelf. This implies a confiderable time yet to pafs, before the Queen was to be feized. So far it concurs with the reft of this letter, and all the former letters. And fo far alfo it concurs with the whole of both, to prove the forgery. But it likewife affords a diftinct evidence of the forgery itfelf. There were few or no lords in Edinborough at this very time, to whom he could make ufe of his excufes and perfuafions. Mary muft alfo have known of this, before fhe fet out. The parliament, which had brought the lords to Edinborough, being diffolved upon Saturday; they would naturally be gone from it. Accordingly, the rebels themfelves fhall fhew us that they were. They exhibited unto the commiffioners at York " a copie of
" a bond bearing date the 19th of Aprill 1567, to
" the which *the moft part of the lords and coun-*
" *faillors of Scotland* have put to their hands—: it
" appeared alfo, that the felf-fame daye of the date
" of this bond—the Earl of Huntley was reftored by
" parliament; which parliament was *the occafion* that
" *fo many lords were there affembled*; which being all
" invited to a fupper by Bothwell, were—induced
" —to fubfcribe to the faid bond—;" and, " the
" next morning by four of the clocke, *fewe or none*
" *of them* were left in the towne, but departed
" without taking their leave *." And there muft

* Appendix, N° v.

therefore

therefore, on the Monday and Tuesday afterwards, have been "none of them" at all "left in the towne," for Bothwell to try his excuses or persuasions upon.

(6) What enemies had Bothwell *at this time?* He had none, except those who were leading him to the seizure of the Queen, in order to ruin both him and her. Yet these the *adulterous* Bothwell and the *adulterous* Mary could not have considered as enemies. And all the lords assembled in parliament, being "the most part of the lords and " counsaillors of Scotland," had just before shewn a remarkable instance of their seeming attachment to him.—" Yat ye are constranit to mak persute " aganis zour enemies," Scotch; " que vous estes " forcée par necessité de faire ainsi vostre poursuite " a l'encontre de vos enaemis," French. Knowing, as we do know, the Scotch to be the original and the French a translation; it is an object of literary curiosity, to see with what earnestness and eagerness, with what wrigglings and writhings, the Remarker endeavours to prove true by verbal criticisms, what we are certain to be false from fact. But it is peculiarly curious to observe, what little points he fastens upon at times, in order to prove it. And we have a lively instance before us here. " The translator," he says, and means the Scotchman, " not understanding the sense of *poursuite*, has " made Bothwell *pursue* his enemies, not solicite " the Queen's hand ;" as if, even on this interpretation, the Scotch " persute" was not just the same in meaning with the French " poursuite ;" and as if

the

the real interpretation was not, that Bothwell was obliged to seize her person, and then solicit her marriage, in order to make pursuit against his enemies.

(7) This is another of the false mint-master's marks. Bothwell before was to make excuses and to try persuasions, upon lords that were *not* at Edinborough. He is now to speak " mony fair wordis " to Lethington," *who was actually with the Queen at the time*. This is an amazing stroke of imposture. Yet it is a plain one. " April 24," says the rebel journal itself concerning the seizure, Bothwell " met hir upon the way, seemit to ravish " hir, and tuik Huntly and the SECRETARIE pri- " soneris, &c. *" That this was secretary Maitland of Lethington, cannot be doubted. So Mary says †, that on her surrendering herself to the rebels at Carberry Hill on June 15, 1567, and their rude behaviour to her in Edinborough, she sent " her " secretare Lethingtown" to them. So Lesley makes Huntly and Argyle speak of " secretaire " Lethingtoun" twice, in their account of the conference at Craigmillar, during the month of November or December 1566 ‡. A MS. also cited by Bishop Keith and Dr. Robertson, which is only Crawford's Memoirs as they stood in the original, and not as they now stand in the printed copy §, informs us expressly; that, when she was seized, she was " accompanied with the noble Earl of Huntly,

---

* Appendix, N° x. † Goodall, ii. 165. ‡ Ibid. ii, 317, and 318. § Keith, 330; and Appendix, N° xiii.

" and

" and secretary Maitland of Lethington*." And another cotemporary writer, even Melvill, says that Bothwell " took the Earl of Huntly, *the se-* " *cretary Lidingtoun,*" &c. † Here then is a *demonstration* of the forgery; and one that conspires with a variety of others to shew, that the letters have never been attentively examined before.

" Ze fall fay aneuch," Scotch; " vous aurez de- " quoy dire affez," French. This is another of the Remarker's proofs. And to shew us where the force of it lies, he italicizes *fall* in the Scotch, and translates the French " you will." He did not know what these very letters shew in every page, that *shall* was generally used for *will* at this period.

(8) This concurs to shew, that some time was yet to intervene between the present letter and the seizure, and so unites to prove the forgery.

(9) Before I close the Section, let me make two or three observation upon what has recently occurred in it.

The circumstance concerning Lethington is the more amazing, as we have hitherto supposed Lethington himself to be the very fabricator of the letters. Yet it is incredible, that in *this* work he could so far forget his own ideas and his own life, as to fix himself at Edinborough, when he was actually at Stirling, and to overlook his own presence at the very memorable seizure of the Queen

---

* Keith, 383; and Robertson, Diff. 19.   † P. 80.

by Bothwell. And this incredibility seems to bear forcibly against the supposition. But it cannot bear it down. The latter is too strongly grounded, to be overset even by an incredibility. This indeed is opposed by another. For, even if he was *not* the personal fabricator of the letters, yet as he was certainly a peruser of them, and a careful peruser too, since he united with others to produce them at York, and offered with others to swear them to be Mary's writing; it is equally incredible, that in *this* work he should so far forget his own ideas and his own life, as to fix himself at Edinborough when he was actually at Stirling, and to overlook his own presence at the very memorable seizure of the Queen by Bothwell. The opposed incredibilities thus counteract each other, like contrary impulses of air; and enable us to stand unmoved upon our own ground, between them. And all serves to shew in a most convincing manner, the astonishing hurry and negligence which attended the creation or revisal of these famous letters, in the very producers of them.

Having obviated this argument against the presumed fabrication of the letters by Lethington, let me obviate another that has arisen at times to my own mind, and will probably arise to the mind of my reader. There is such a strain of low breeding in the language, in the address, and in the deportment, of the Queen and her courtiers; as could never (we are apt to surmise) be thrown in by a Lethington, a man conversant for years with the court, and a man for years attendant upon the Queen.

Queen. Yet this cannot in reality affect the pretenſions of Lethington, to the honour of this capital forgery. He did not ignorantly or inadvertently fall into theſe abſurdities. He fell into them wilfully. He was obliged to do ſo. He could not write of the Queen and her court, as he knew them to be. It would not comport with his flagitious deſigns, to delineate them in their native colours to the public. He muſt repreſent her in maſquerade. And he muſt repreſent them as equally maſquerading with her. He accordingly holds her out to the eye of the world, and them as catching their manners by reflexion from her, the very reverſe of what they were. He has dreſt up the accompliſhed and dignified Queen, all whoſe deportment was a frank but poliſhed courteſy, and all whoſe language was propriety and delicacy itſelf, in the looſe garb of the loweſt adulteresſ. He has ſhewn her unaccompliſhed, undignified, unpoliſhed, and very groſs. He has given her all the bold familiarities of a common hoyden. He has ſuperadded all the vulgarities of a common whore. And he has thus written a ſet of letters for her, which in every feature of their complexion, and in the ſtronger features peculiarly, deny all reſemblance to hiſtory, and diſclaim all affinity to Mary.

Yet ſtill how ſhall we account for his ſtrange inſertion of his own name in the letters? He *muſt know* in the moments of compoſition, that he was actually with the Queen at the ſeizure. No hurry could efface this from his memory. No negligence could keep him from attending to it there. How came

came he then to write, in so direct a contradiction to fact, and in such an impudent violation of his own memory? This can only be accounted for, I believe, from a very signal sort of mystery in the frame and texture of his mind. He was, say Crawford's Memoirs, " a man of great parts, well versed
" in all the intreagues of the court, and the incli-
" nations of the common people; singularly *cun-*
" *ning, bold,* and eloquent, but *prone to changes*; and
" so fond of being great, or of appearing consider-
" able, in a party or cabal, that no tyes of honour
" or friendship could bind him to the interest of
" his sovereign or his country *." No ties of friendship or of honour could even bind him to his own party. The same principle went on regularly in its operations. And Lethington was uniformly a traitor to all his connections. Buchanan accordingly wrote a libel against him in 1570, under the title of CHAMELEON. In that he recites some curious facts, which lay this retired and unobserved part of Lethington's character very open before us.
" The first experience the said Quene" regent " had
" of him," he says, " was in sending him to France
" for certane bisines occurrent for the tyme, quhair
" he did his commissioun *sa weill to his awin inten-*
" *tion,* and *sa far from the Quenis mynd,* that *he*
" *dissavit the Cardinal of Lorayne,* quha untill that
" day thocht himself, not only auld practicien, bot
" also maister, zea Doctor Subtilis, in sic matters
" of negociatioun." After Mary's arrival in Scotland, when he was acting in union with Murray,

* P. 5—6.

" sche,"

"fche," Mary, "then being deliberat to diftroy
"him," Murray, "be the Erll of Huntlie, went to
"the North, and he," Murray, "in her company;
"and howbeit the treffoun wes oppynnit planelie,
"and Johne, Gordoun lying not far of the
"town," *Aberdeen* *, "with an greit powar, and the
"Erll of Murray exprefslie ludgeit in ane hous fe-
"parate frae all uther habitatioun, and his deid
"[death] be diverfe wayis focht; this Chamæleon,
"quether of fempilnes, or for layk of foirficht, or
"for bauldnes of courage, I refer to every manis
"confcience that doith knaw him, *he alone could fe
"no treffoun, could feare no dangeur, and wald nevir
"beleif that the Erll of Huntlie wald tak in hand fic
"ane interpryis.*" On the intended marriage of the
Queen with Darnly, when fome objected to it on
account of religion, "the Chamæleon *in fecreit*
"flatterit the Quene, and *openlie* tuke the colour of
"religioun." Afterwards "being fent divers
"tymes to commune with the Lord Flemyng," he
"*evir* did the *contrair of the propofe that he wes fend
"for.*" And when Murray was fetting out for the
conference at York, being doubtful "quhethir he
"fould tak him with himfelf, or leif him beheind,
"for, taking him, he *doubtit not bot he wald hinder
"the actioun in al manner poffibill,* and, leaving him
"behind, that following his natural complexioun
"*he wald trubill the cuntre,* in fick manner that it
"fould not be eafelie in lang tyme brocht to reft
"agane; at lang having deliberat to take him

* Crawford's Lives of Officers of State, 87.

"with

"with him, and *perſwadit him bayth be giftis of* "*landis and money,* he fand to be trew in deid all "that he fuſpectit afore; for *everie nycht* in a man- "ner *he communicat all that wes amangis us with* "*ſum of our adverſaris,* and *armit thame ſa far* "*as he culd agains the ſaid Regent* *." Such a very extraordinary man does Lethington appear, under the pourtraying pencil of Buchanan! Nor can we make many deductions from this imputed extravagance of perfidiouſneſs in him, becauſe of the ſlanderous tendency of Buchanan's temper. Some of theſe facts we know to be true. All of them ſerve only to give us back the image, a little enlarged and a little disfigured perhaps, which the mirror of hiſtory has held up to us before. Lethington felt a perpetual verſatility in his ſpirit, a perpetual unfaithfulneſs in his principles, and a perpetual fund of reſources, at the call of both, in the dexterities of his own management. He was happy to render himſelf an important aſſociate to his party, by the exertions of his natural cunning. But he was alſo happy, in a ſtrange ſuperfœtation of cunning, to be plotting againſt the very party which he was actually ſerving at the time. To undermine his enemies, and to countermine his friends, appears to have been the great ambition of his refining genius. And thus, in the very moments when he was fabricating this grand ſyſtem of impoſition againſt Mary, he would plume himſelf

* P. 14, 15, and 16, Ruddiman's Buchanan.

at once on forming it, and on giving it during the formation such private marks, such secret signatures, by little errors in time, and by petty variations from fact; as would escape the notice of every other eye, and yet should enable him, whenever he pleased, to expose the whole villainy to the world compleatly.

§ IV.

§ IV.

Here let us examine an argument, which has been strongly urged in favour of a French original to the letters. Mr. Hume, I think, was the first who insisted upon the Gallicisms in the Scotch copy, and alledged them as a proof of its being a translation from the French *. Mr. Tytler replied to him. And the Miscellaneous Remarker has rejoined to Mr. Tytler. It is pleasing enough to a philosophical surveyor of the human mind, to see it contending with such weak weapons on either side, when history would have furnished it with weapons of force and power. Such have been actually produced, I trust, in the course of the present work. Nor can any Gallicisms in the Scotch have the weight of a feather at present, against the full measure of historical evidence before. Yet it may be useful to notice the argument, in order to answer it as an objection; as one that is really light in itself, but has been made respectable by the contest about it.

* v. 147.

The objection, as advanced by Mr. Hume, consisted of various IDIOMS, and of one WORD, that were Gallic. To the idioms we need not say much. They are such unsubstantial evidences, that there is hardly any grasping of them. They run thus: " make fault, faire des fautes;" " make it seem that I believe, faire semblant de le croire," which is literally, to make a semblance of believing it, and therefore different from the Scotch; " make brek, faire breche;" " have you not desire to laugh, n' avez vous pas envie de rire," which is plainly no idiom, and has no similarity at all; " the place will hald unto the death, la place tiendray jusqu'a la mort," where the point of similarity lies only in *the* and *la*, the former of which was then used in this connection, though it seldom is now, and the latter is sometimes not used at present; " he may not come forth of the house this long time, il ne peut pas sortir du logis de long temps," which is no idiom, and has no more similarity than what a translation necessarily gives; " to make me advertisement, faire m'avertir," which is different from the Scotch, and signifies only, to *make advertise me*; " put order to it, mettre ordre a cela," which is different again, and as different as to *put* and to *send*; " discharge your heart, decharger votre cœur," and " mak gud watch, faites bon gard," in both which the similarity is in one word, and the dissimilarity in two and three. And at the close we may ask, If such arguments as these can prove any thing, what will be too difficult to be proved? Yet the Miscellaneous

neous Remarker * has even heightened the folly, by adducing thefe additional Gallicifms out of one of the letters, though thefe are as much Anglicifms as almoft any modes of fpeech in our language; " the difdane that I can not be in outward effect " yours," " my only wealth," " fall not part furth " of my bofom," " to the quhilk I pretend," and " for evil nor gude fall nevir mak me go from it." And I cannot but obferve upon both, that, if we were to liften to fuch empirics in language as thefe, we fhould be like the honeft Alderman with his *profe*, and ftare to find we had been talking FRENCH all our lives.

The languages of France and England were originally the fame. They were fo in the days of our Britifh anceftors. They were fo ftill, in the time of our Saxon fathers. And *Frenchmen were brought hither by Auguftine and his fellow-miffionaries, to be their interpreters to the Englifh.* The fact is little known. But it ought to be called out into general notice. It is recorded by Bede himfelf † : " acceperunt autem, præcipiente beato Papâ "Gregorio, DE GENTE FRANCORUM INTERPRETES." This being the cafe, the two languages may well retain a variety of fimilar idioms to the prefent day. They muft ftill be *fubftantially* the fame. They apparently are fo. The fame words, the fame combinations of words, are perpetually recurring in both. And we may as well argue in general from any coincidences of this nature, *that the French are*

* P. 33.   † Hift. i. 25.

derived

derived from the English, as that the English are borrowed from the French. Yet, from the natural variations of time in two separate kingdoms, there are many idioms and words peculiar to each at present. Some of the French were common once to our own language, though they are retained only in the other now; and some are still common. Thus, " to *discharge* your heart" was used at the period of the letters, and is still used among us, as it is among the French; though it is almost superseded in familiar life among us, by the expression " to *open* your heart." Thus also, " to *make* good " watch," was used then for " to *keep* good watch;" though the French still adhere to their old expression, "*faire* de bon gard." The French and we also once said, "*faire* un faut," or " to *make* a " fault," as the Scotch letters say; but we now say, " to *do* a fault," while the French preserve their ancient term. And " to make a breach" is as good English, as "pour faire breche" is French.

Having thus dispatched the idioms, I turn to the words. Mr. Hume mentions only one; " this " is my first JOURNEY, c'est ma premiere JOUR- " NE'E." He thought *journey* in this sense to be purely French. Though a Scotchman; though so thoroughly a Scotchman, that even to the last he could not clear his tongue, from his native provinciality of pronunciation; yet he had never heard the word, it seems, among his cotemporaries of the town or country about him. In itself, and in its derivatives, it forms a very important set of words in the English language. In all the English

extremities

extremities of the island, it signifies just as it does in the letters, a day's work. And, as Mr. Tytler has justly observed *, *journey-man* and *journey-work* are common to all parts of it.

This single instance furnishes us with a striking proof, of the hasty superficialness and the wanton decisiveness, with which Mr. Hume pretended to disprove the originality of the Scotch letters. In the violence of his assault upon it, he forgot his native tongue. His zeal operated with all the force of a fever upon his brain. He did, as Rousseau said he did afterwards in his hearing. *He talked nothing but French in his sleep.* The whole English language was lost to him, during the continuance of the paroxysm. And the loudest conversation of the street or the farm, could not awaken him from his delirium.

But the English language, *at the period of the letters*, appears to have been particularly furnished with words, that either in their nature or in their orthography were purely French. Indeed, the foppery of adopting such terms seems to have been fully as prevalent among the grave statesmen then, as it is among our writing and conversing coxcombs at present. And some of these actually make their appearance in the letters.

Secretary Cecil, says Mr. Tytler †, mentions a thing " to be BRUITED." Throgmorton also, says Miscellaneous Remarker ‡, uses BRUIT for rumour.

* P. 87. † P. 86. ‡ P. 18.

And half a hundred writers ufed thefe words at the time, and have ufed them fince. But this argument, adds the Remarker, "feems not to the "purpofe, for Cecil was an Englifhman, and *bruited* "is not a French word." Are not the Scotch and the Englifh languages, then, the fame? Are not the Scotch letters, particularly, written in Englifh? They certainly are. And, though *bruited* be not ufed by the French, the radical *bruit* is, which is fufficient. We took this word from the French, and then founded our own *bruited* upon it.

Sir James Melvill, fays Mr. Tytler*, ufes the word FINEST for "the moft fubtile, cunning, or "penetrating genius, from the French words *fin* and "*finet*, a cunning or fubtile man; a word not "known or ufed, either in writing or in common "fpeech, at this day." This is furely a good inftance of the humour then current among writers, of adopting French words into the language; and fo helps to account for the appearance of fuch words, in the Scotch letters. Yet the Remarker does not like it. "Neither is it of moment," he fays†, "that "Melvill, who had paffed much of his time in "France, ufed *fineft* ;—thus forming, by analogy, "a fuperlative from the French *fin*." What makes Mr. Tytler's obfervation of no moment in the opinion of his critic is, that Melvill "had paffed "much of his time in France." But had not Mary, who muft have written the letters, if they

* P. 86. † P. 18.

are genuine, and in whose name they must have been written, if they are forgeries? Yet the Remarker adds: "as to what the author says of *fin* "and *finet*—having the same sense, he might as "well have said, that a *smatterer* in the French "language and an *adept* are synonimous." How trifling an advantage will kindle the natural pride of our spirits, into an instant blaze! " I once "knew," said that good and ingenious man, the late Mr. Hooke the historian, " a fellow vain of "tying a string adroitly to a rat's tail." But *there* was some ground for the vanity. The fellow was adroit. And the Remarker is not so. *Fin* signifies cunning or subtle, and *finet* signifies subtle or cunning.

In the protestation drawn up for the earls of Huntly and Argyle, as Mr. Tytler remarks [*], " Lethington says, "'Tak you na care, we sal find "' an *moyen* to mak her quit of him.'" But this, replies the Remarker [†], " is merely the word *mean* "spelt in a different way." It is spelt however in the *French* way. It therefore shews the tendency of the times to the *French* language, in a very strong manner. Even when the word was English as well as French, even when it was used in an English as well as a French meaning, the tongue or the pen imperceptibly formed it in the French fashion. And, so formed, the word occurs continually in the Scotch papers of those times; in the intimations given by the nobles of Mary's party to

[*] P. 86. [†] P. 20.

her

her commissioners*; in Mary's register of the proceedings at Hampton Court, on Feb. 2d, 1568 †; in Murray's letter to Cecil, Jan. 31, 1569‡; in a letter of Mary's to her friends in Scotland ‖; in a letter of Murray's to Mary herself §; and in bishop Lesley's Negotiations ¶.

So also the English commissioners at York, use an English word formed exactly in the same mold of France; and speak of DEPECHING, instead of dispatching, an answer to a letter ⊥. Murray does the same, in a letter from England to the Lord of Craigmillar; dating it thus, "at Kingstoun, the "xi of Januar, 1568;" and then adding this posterior note to it, " *depefchit* the xiii day **. Mary does the same too, in her account of Rizzio's murder to her embassador in France; writing to him in these words, " we received your *depefche*, sent by " captain Mure ††." And her and Elizabeth's commissioners are said to be waiting, till the former should hear " from the Quene their mistress, by " their next *depeche* ‡‡."

Yet it was not merely in Frenchifying the form or the meaning of English words, that this pedantry of politeness shewed itself in that age. It took a bolder step. It introduced words that are supposed to be purely French, and in what is believed to be

* Goodall, ii. 355. † ii. 335. ‡ ii. 332.
‖ ii. 325—326. § Anderson, iv. part i. 117. ¶ P. 76. Anderson, iii. ⊥ Goodall, ii. 127. ** ii. 306. †† Keith, 330.
‡‡ Goodall, ii. 156.

a purely

a purely French meaning. "Queen Mary, in anſwer to Murray's and Morton's accuſation againſt her, ſays they have MESCHANTLIE ſclanderit her." "Lethington, confeſſedly the beſt Scotch writer of that time," and, as I muſt beg leave to add, the very fabricator of the letters, " in his own letter to Cecil—uſeth the word APPUY for ſupport*." Randolph alſo, the Engliſh embaſſador in Scotland, ſpeaks of the INGROSSMENT or pregnancy of the Dutcheſs of Savoy†. Quintin Kennedy too, Abbot of Croſraguel, in a treatiſe which he publiſhed 1558, ſays thus of the clergy; " this wer the way to cum in att the dure,—quhare now,—as it wer thevis or BIGANTIS, we creip in at wyndois or bak-durris ‡." Nor is the word *brigants*, in its derivatives at leaſt, peculiar to the preſent writer. It was even uſed in the judicial forms of the nation, at this period. In 1581 a Scotch peer being tried for the murder of Darnly, he is charged in his indictment to have murdered him, " be way of hameſukin, BRIGANCIE, and foirthowght fellonie §." And what intimates even ſome of theſe very words to have been originally in the Scotch language, though they are only preſerved in the French at preſent; the ſame Abbot, in a letter of April the 7th, 1559, ſays to the Archbiſhop of Glaſgow, " zit I may write un MOT to your lordſhip:" thus uſing a word, that is well known to be French; uſing it too, with a numerical term that has particu-

* Tytler, 86.   † Keith, 209.   ‡ Keith, App. 203.
§ Arnot's Crim. Trials, 390.

larly

larly a French appearance; and yet using a word, that is exceedingly familiar to *all* the inhabitants of *Lancashire* at this day *.

To any of these instances, either of casual French or of French affectation, among the Scotch or the English of those days, the Remarker cannot object. He does not. Yet he wants some " better " evidence," to " account for the numerous Gal- " licisms that occur in the Scottish copy." Those instances are not very numerous. We have just seen a long string of his own, not *one of which* was a Gallicism. And Mr. Hume's too have been all accounted for. The Remarker, however, now adds five, taken out of the first letter. But two of them have been noticed in my remarks upon that letter before, and shewn to be the creation of his own errors †. A third is only one of Mr. Hume's repeated, " mak fault, faire faute." Of the other two, one is " maid my *estat*," which is plainly French in its application, though our English word *state*, as implying circumstances of stateliness, approaches very near to it; and comes under the same class with *depeche, moyen, finest,* and *bruit,* before. The other is this, " he belevit to die for " gladness;" which *may* be a French mode of expression, like " mak fault," before, but is ap-

---

* Keith, App. 194. The Lancashire word is pronounced with that *y* final, which is still retained in so many words among the Cornish; and is formed into MOTT-Y. " Why do you " put in your *mott-y?*" is a very common question to any person interposing a word in conversation.

† Lett. i. § xiv. and xvii.

parently

parently so nearly a Scotch one too, as not to be worth our notice. And those purely French words, and that purely French meaning of an English word, which are actually used in the letters, and two of them used repeatedly, are totally overlooked by all parties. Thus, says the author, " I held " PURPOIS to na body*," " the *purpois* of Schir " James Hamilton †," and " the *purpois* that he " and I had togidder ‡." So Murray, in his answer to the protestation from Argyle and Huntly, speaks of " ony *purposis* haldin at Craigmillar in " my audience;" and mentions " the effect of " the haill *purposis*, spokin in my audience at the " famin tyme §." And so Randolph says of Mary, that after she had spoken to him for some time, " after these *purposes*," he offered to address her as she was leaving the council-room; and that then, " in long *purpose* of this matter, and other like, " she saith," &c ||. The writer of the letters, also, speaks of his " MALHEUR ¶." " I am FASCHIT," he adds, " that it stoppis me to write newis of my- " self ⊥;" and " I am now passand to my *fascheous* " purpois **." " I am thinkand," he says in a third place, " upon nathing bot *fascherie* ††." And, as he *once* said in his second letter, " I am soe " *faschit* with it ‡‡." Just so Mary, in her instructions to her embassador sent into England upon her

* L. i. § i.   † L. i. § xxi.   ‡ Ibid.   § Goodall, ii. 321.
|| Keith, 195.   ¶ L. iii. § ii.   ⊥ L. i. § x.
** L. i. § xxiv.   †† L. i. § xxxii.   ‡‡ Appendix, N° vii.

marriage

marriage to Bothwell, characterizes her subjects very justly, for " a peopill als factious amangis " yameselfis, and als *fassious* for the governour, as " any other nation in Europe *." Nor was this French word un-familiar to the English *south* of the Tweed. The Duke of Norfolk, writing to Cecil at the time of the York conference, says, that " their action ys like to *fawche* them †." And, as this English use of the word shews how it came to be introduced among the Scotch; so the appearance of it among both nations, proves the common propensity of both at this period, to adopt the terms of the French, when their own were as elegant and as forcible as they. We see and feel too much of this ridiculous fashion at present, not to catch the reflection of it in the manners of Mary's age. We are fully convinced by our own experience, that we have no need to recur to the wild hypothesis of a translation from a French original, in order to account for the existence of French words, either in Norfolk's or in Lethington's letters. And we actually see an author quoted above, Quintin Kennedy, Abbot of Crosraguel, in his popular address to the Scotch against the Reformation in 1558, calling upon the Romish clergy to do " their dett and DEVORE to the simpyll " peple committit to their cure;" and exclaiming against the princes suffering spiritual preferments to be extorted from them, by solicitations for un-

* Anderson, i. 103. † Goodall, ii. 133.

worthy perfons, as " the MALHEURIUS prince fall
" warry [curfe] the tyme, that evir he wes fua
" MISCHEANTLIE fubject to the unreffonable defyre
" of his fubjectis *."

The *Scotch* indeed appear to have been peculiarly free, in naturalizing French words among
them, and allowing them all the privileges of na-
tives. This may be accounted for hiftorically,
" from the long and continued intercourfe and
" connection between the Scotch and French na-
" tions †." They had a Queen of France for their
Queen, in Mary. They had had a French lady for
their Queen and their Regent, in her mother. And
their nobles were continually moving to and from
thefe allied kingdoms. Hence we have fo many
more inftances before, of fafhionable impertinence
in the ufe of French among the Scotch, than among
the Englifh. And hence we have fome remains
of French among the vulgar Scots of the prefent
day, that are utterly unknown to England.

" Every Scotchman," fays Mr. Tytler, " knows
" well what the vulgar mean by giving a BONNE-
" ALLÉE, or parting-cup ‡." This is certainly a
very fingular proof, of the prevalence of French in

* Keith, App. 203. So Bothwell is faid in the famous bond
to have " offerit to do his *devoire* be the law of armes," Anderfon, i. 109. So Mary in a charter fpeaks of " fies and
' *devories*," fees and duties, " pertening to the keiping of the
" faid caftell," Ibid, 118. So likewife, in Sir Ralph Sadler's
letters, we have " *demeure*" for refidence, in 214, 253, and
61; " *retour*" for return, in 326; and " *manjouring* " for
half-inclination, in 338.

† Tytler, 85.   ‡ Ibid, 109, edit. 3d.

Scotland.

Scotland. It is curious to the antiquary of manners. It is curious to the critic in language. Yet the Remarker objects to it. He objects, but he cannot anſwer. "*Bonne-allée,*" he ſays*, " if it " be a French phraſe at all, means a garden-walk, " convenient and well-kept." He choſe not to ſee. I *muſt* pay *this* compliment to his *underſtanding*. *Bonne-allée* could never have ſignified a fine garden-walk, if it had not previouſly ſignified ſomething elſe. The word properly and primarily ſignifies a *good going*. It thence branched out into two meanings, *a good journey*, or *a good road to journey on*. The latter of theſe eaſily reſolved itſelf into a *good walk*, in a garden or any where elſe. And the hoſpitable ſpirit of the Scotch retained the expreſſion, for what uſed to be called in England a *ſtirrup-cup*; when the French had loſt the object and the name together.

The Scotch alſo retain, as appears from Mr. Tytler †, another expreſſion of the ſame import, and equally French, for the ſame object. Nothing but a continued ſpirit of hoſpitality could have continued ſuch terms, even amongſt the loweſt orders of the ſtate. They are, therefore, as much monuments of their hoſpitality, as of their intercourſe with France. But the latter expreſſion is " giving one's FOY." This is plainly French in its ſubſtantial word; and is equivalent, in its *general* acceptation, to our Engliſh " pledging " of a friend in drinking. But the word *foy* has a

* P. 19.   † P. 85, edit. 1ſt.

peculiar

peculiar meaning in Scotland, and signifies that " pledging" which a friend gives a friend in a parting-cup. And what can the Remarker say to this? He *says* nothing, though he *speaks* much. " Does *foy*," he asks, " mean a parting-cup in " French, or *donner sa foy* to give a parting-cup?" Nobody pretended that it did. Mr. Tytler only argued, that *foy* was a French word, and yet that it was used in the Scotch language to this day; in a particular signification indeed, but still used. It may be lost in the present French. The signification may have perished with the thing. But the word is plainly French. And the thing and the signification are plainly preserved in the Scotch. No! says the Remarker. " The Dutch phrase, *de foy* " *geven*, means according to Skinner, who writes an " English Etymological Dictionary, *cænam profec-* " *titiam dare*, i. e. *fidem amicitiæ, etiam per absentiam* " *duraturæ*, dare." Yet this is plainly the same with the Scotch *foy*. This also explains the meaning of it more fully, and makes it to be *fidem amicitiæ etiam per absentiam duraturæ*. This also explains our English " pledging," to mean *originally* a cup given as a *pledge* of friendship, *etiam per absentiam duraturæ*. And all serves to shew the custom, which in Holland is, and perhaps in France was, a parting-supper; but which in England and in Scotland, from the superior love of drinking here, was a parting-cup; to have been retained in France, in Holland, and in Scotland, under the one appellation of a *foy*, and in England under that of

VOL. II.   D d   a *pledge*:

a *pledge:* and, in all, to have been confidered as a *fides* or *pledge* of friendſhip, that was to continue even during the abfence of the parties.

But I will give one more inftance of thefe notable relicks of French, in the prefent body of colloquial Scotch. "A JARDELOU, or *gare de l'eau*," fays Mr. Tytler, "I believe, is pretty well under-"ftood in Edinburgh, even at this very day *." This is a word, adds the Remarker †, "of which "Scotfmen, unlefs fuperior to national reproaches, "are not wont to treat. It means foul water or "other noifome things thrown from a window. "The vulgar amongft us have turned a French "phrafe, *gare l'eau*, into a fingle word, and have "perverted both its found and its fignification." The word appears to be, as Mr. Tytler ftates it, *gare de l'eau*, beware of the water. Water, it feems, was the only thing at *firſt*, that was permitted to be difcharged from the windows into the ftreets at night. Other things were permitted afterwards. Yet ftill the monitory notice from the windows was, *gare de l'eau*, and that from the ftreets, *hold your hand*. And this fhews us, very ftrikingly, the predominance of the French language among the Scots; when one half of thefe *cries of Edinborough* was in French. But the Remarker is out of humour with it. Not able to difprove the fact or the inference, he takes pet at both. "This example "is produced," he fays, "for proving, that in the

---

* P. 110, edit. 3d. † P. 19—20.

"days

"days of Queen Mary the Scottish language abounded in French words, and even in Gallicisms." Mr. Tytler had said with more propriety, that it "abounded with Gallicisms, and even with French words;" though the Remarker presumes *formally* to correct the arrangement of his language. An idiom is a much weaker proof than a word. But Mr. Tytler does not produce *this* example *alone*, to prove his point. He produces it in concurrence with others. Each proves a single word of French to have been incorporated into the Scotch. Some prove more. *Foy* proves one. *Bonne-allée* proves two. *Gare de l'eau* proves four, all formed into one; as RENDEZVOUS amongst ourselves is two French words compacted together, and used, like *jardelou*, for a substantive. All demonstrate a variety of French words, to have once been engrafted on the stock of the Scotch; since the remains of them are so striking, even at this day. And the writings of Queen Mary's days reflect a light back upon these again, shew the fact which these image out to us, and so unite with them to exhibit it in its full proportions.

All serves to prove in the clearest manner, that if the French idioms or the French words in the Scotch copy of the letters, had been ten times more than they are, they might easily be accounted for, from the predominating affection of the times for French; that this spirit reigned in England, but carried a much greater sway in Scotland; and that the best writings of Scotland then, and the language of the vulgar now, concur together in a very extraordinary manner, to prove the adoption of French words, and even of French combinations of words, for some of the commonest ideas, and some of the pettiest operations, in life.

§ V.

§ V.

LETTER THE SEVENTH (1).

I.—" My lord, fen my letter writtin, zour bro-
" ther-in-law yat was (2), come to me verray fad,
" and hes afkit me my counfel, quhat he fuld do
" efter to morne (3), becaus their be mony folkis
" heir, and amang utheris the Erle of Sudderland,
" quha wald rather die, confiddering the gude they
" have fa laitlie reffavit of me (4), than fuffer me
" to be caryit away, thay conducting me (5); and
" that he feirit their fuld fum troubil happin of"

. I.—" Monfieur, depuis ma lettre efcrite, voftre
" beau-frere qui fuft (2), eft venu a moy fort trifte,
" et m'a demandé mon confeil de ce qu'il feroit apres
" demain (3), pour ce qu'il y a beaucoup de gens
" icy, et entre autres le Conte de Southerland, qui
" aymeroient mieux mourir, veu le bien que je
" leurs a fait depuis n'a gueres (4), que de fouffrir
" que je fuffe emmenée, eux me conduifans (5);
" et d'autre part qu'il craint"

(1) When

(1) When this letter pretends to be written, will appear from some circumstances in it hereafter.

(2) I have already, in the preceding parts of the work, shewn what a striking mark of forgery this is.

But let me make another remark upon it. The *cause* of this strange anacronism, was the *posterior* formation of this and the next letter. And, what is very remarkable, the same cause produced the same effect in the preceding series of letters. In those from Glasgow, as well as in these from Stirling, two were additional letters; the third and the fourth, as well as the seventh and eighth, of the whole. This is peculiarly manifest concerning the third and seventh. The error about the divorce here, and the blunder about the lodgings there, shew it very evidently. And both were letters added to the original number, added when the original ideas were considerably effaced by time, and added when there was no attention paid to an accurate renovation of them. The third particularly appears to have been added, *before* the journal had been presented at London, *before* the letters had been exhibited at York, but *after* the letters had been produced to the parliament of Scotland. It was added undoubtedly, on Elizabeth urging the rebels to come to her conference in England, and on their preparing to attend her there. Then resolving to augment the number, in a fond conceit of enlarging the power, of their fictitious proofs

against

against Mary; they extended the original two from Glasgow into three, as they afterwards extended these, and the original two from Stirling, equally and respectively into four. Lethington thus sitting down to continue what he had composed at first, sitting down to do it at the distance of eight and twelve months from the first composure, acting under the immediate spur of the moment at both periods, and yet too confident in his practices to suspect his inaccuracy in the work; he naturally found himself confused in his chronological ideas for it. He therefore began to write his third letter, as from Kirk-a-field; when he finally meant it all for Glasgow. He first noticed the King's apartments, as " thair-up" or " là-haut ;" but afterwards referred to them, as " the place here besyde," or " de lieu qui est prochain d'icy *." And this is exactly in the same strain of self-deception, from which he afterwards spoke at the head of his seventh letter, concerning Bothwell's divorce from his wife as already passed; when the letter itself is apparently calculated for a period, that was antecedent to the divorce by several days.

(3) " Efter to morne," after to-morrow. This letter therefore pretends to be written on Tuesday April 22d, as the seizure was on Thursday April 24th †. The fifth letter therefore, the first of the four from Stirling, demonstrably claims to be

* § i. and ii. † Appendix, N° x.

written

written on Monday night; as I have already stated it to be. And the sixth, the second of the four, must be attributed to Tuesday morning. Having thus settled the claimed chronology of the letters decisively, let us now compare the train of incidents in them with their own standard of time. Huntly, according to them, has come from Edinborough since Mary, since Monday morning, and, as appears from Bothwell's sending him to consult with Mary, some time since both. Yet he arrives at Stirling time enough, for Mary to write an account of his conversation in a letter that night. Indeed he well might, as many days had passed in that one. For she complains in that very letter, of Bothwell having promised to write to her " every " day," and of his having not done it; of his having changed his mind since her absence; and of his absence having power over him, because he has two strings to his bow, his own wife and Mary. And this alone will serve to shew, how contrary the letters are even to their own assumed chronology, as well as to that of the rebel journal.

(4) The favour which they had so lately received of Mary, was this. On April 19th the forfeiture, which had lain for some time upon the Earl of Huntly's estate, was taken off by the Queen in parliament. " Aprill 19, quhilk wes Setterday, the " decreyt of reduction wes gevin for the Erle of " Huntly, and all his friendis *." And one of

* Goodall, ii. 249.

these

these was the Earl of Sutherland *; who had been attainted, and was now restored, with him.

(5) This shews clearly, that Huntly and his friends, even the Earl of Sutherland and others, who had had their forfeitures repealed the Saturday before, had "conducted" Mary from Edinborough to Stirling on Monday April 21st, according to the present letter, and were to conduct her back again "efter to morne." Huntly and Sutherland were both in Edinborough at the repeal; and both at Bothwell's supper afterwards. Sutherland also subscribed the bond, as well as Huntly †. And, according to this plain passage, he had come with Huntly on Monday. This therefore proves a gross contradiction in the letters. Huntly, who came with the Queen, is represented as coming some time, even some days, after her; as coming commissioned from Bothwell, to settle with her the circumstances; as distrusted before by Mary, as distrusted by her then, as treated with contempt by her, and as returning to Edinborough. This is said, we see, directly in the teeth of the present passage. And the violent opposition is a full evidence of a forgery.

But let us dwell upon another circumstance here. Huntly undoubtedly attended the Queen in this journey. But did Sutherland also? I believe not. We have three accounts of the persons then in her train, all from cotemporary writers, and one of them from a person actually of the number. And in

* Keith, 380. † Anderson, i. 117; and Keith, 383.

none of these is the Earl of Sutherland mentioned. She was, say Crawford's Memoirs, "accompanied with the noble Earl of Huntly and secretary Maitland of Lethington *." Bothwell, says the rebel journal, seized Mary, "tuik Huntley and the secretarie prisoneris, and led them all to Dumbar †." Bothwell's men, says Melvill, "took the Earl of Huntly, the secretary Lidington, and *me*, and carried us captives to Dumbar; all the rest were permitted to go free ‡." Melvill therefore was one of the persons seized. Lethington was another. And Huntly was another. The Earl of Sutherland was not with them. Had he been, his rank must necessarily have caused him to be mentioned. Crawford's Memoirs and the journal, both which notice Lethington, would certainly have noticed Sutherland. Melvill, who even specifies himself, could not have refrained from specifying Sutherland too. And, had there been one gentleman of consequence in the Queen's train more than these, had Sutherland particularly been that gentleman, Bothwell must have carried him equally with them to Dunbar. Here then we have another proof of the forgery. The letter was written long after the incident on which it rests, and when the original knowledge of persons and circumstances was grown confused in the memory. Huntly was made to be no longer the brother-in-law of Bothwell, though he was so in reality for se-

---

* Keith, 383, p. 80.   † Goodall, ii. 250.   ‡ Melvill.

veral

veral days afterward. And Sutherland was supposed to be there, becaufe Huntly was; and therefore was put down in the room of Melvill.

———————

" it: of the uther fyde, that it fuld be faid that he
" wer unthankfull to have betrayit me (1). I tald
" him, that he fuld have refolvit with zow upon all
" that, and that he fuld avoyde, gif he culd, thay
" that wer maift miftraiftit (2).

II.—" He hes refolvit to wryte thairof to zow be
" my opiniqun (3); for (4) he hes abafchit me to
" fé him fa unrefolvit at the neid. I affure myfelf
" he will play the part of an honeft man: bot I
" have thocht gude to advertife yow (5) of the feir
" he hes, yat he fuld be chargeit and accufit of tref-
" foun, to ye end yar,"

" que s'il en furvenoit quelque trouble, on ne
" l'eftimaft ingrat, comme s'il m'avoit trahié (1).
" Je luy dy, qu'il devoit eftre refolu de cela avec
" vous, et mettre hors de fa maifon ceux defquels
" on fe meffioit le plus (2).

II.—" Suivant ce mien advis, il s'eft refolu de
" vous en efcrire (3); et (4) me fuis eftonnée de
" le voir fi peu refolu en temps de neceffité. Je
" m'affeure bien qu'il fera tour d'honnefte homme:
" mais je vous ay bien voulu advertir (5) de la
" crainte

"crainte qu'il a, d'eſtre chargé et accuſé de tra-
"hiſon,"

(1) "And that he feirit thair ſuld ſum troubil
"happin of it: of the uther ſyde, that it ſuld be
"ſaid that he wer unthankfull to have betrayit me,"
Scotch. "It is not in the power of man," ſays the
Remarker*, "to diſcover the tendency of theſe
"words, unleſs he conſult the French." The words
are pretty plain, I think. But let us conſult the
French: "*et d'autre part* qu'il craint, que s'il en
"ſurvenoit quelque trouble, on ne l'eſtimaſt ingrat,
"comme s'il m'avoit trahié." And we now ſee,
that the French is ſo far from explaining the
Scotch, as, like ſome of the Remarker's own expla-
nations, it perverts the ſenſe of it. The Scotch
ſays, that Sutherland and others would rather die,
than ſuffer Mary, while under their guard, to be
carried off by Bothwell; that Huntly was therefore
apprehenſive there would be a *conflict* about it, for
ſuch is the old meaning of *trouble* †; and that *on the
other hand*, if no conflict took place, he ſhould be
charged with ingratitude, as having *betrayed* her to
Bothwell. But the French ſays, that Sutherland
and others would act as above; and that *on the other
hand* Huntly was afraid, *if any conflict ſhould take
place*, he ſhould be charged with *ingratitude*. And
who does not ſee, that there is a regular conſecu-
tion of ſentiments in the one, and that there is a
compleat confuſion of them in the other?

* P. 33.   † See Robertſon, ii. 373, "*trouble* among
"his own countrymen."

All

All this however, both in the Scotch and in the French, shews Huntly to be the commander of the Queen's escort upon this occasion, and the others to be only his friends and adherents.

(2) This means, that he should keep Sutherland and others, who would rather die than suffer Bothwell to carry her off, from attending as guards upon Mary. But what does the French make of it? " Mettre hors de sa maison." So " all that" is rendered only " cela," and " gif he culd" is wholly left out.

(3) Huntly is writing by Mary's advice, late on Tuesday, to Bothwell at Edinborough. No hint is given, that the answer will find either him or her at any place but Stirling. And there is no urgency, for Bothwell to return the answer with expedition. The strain of the letter implies, that there was time enough for him to write, for Bothwell to answer, and for the answer to find him at Stirling. Yet Mary set out the very next day, Wednesday, for Linlithgow; and the day afterwards, Thursday, was carried off by Bothwell. What however was Huntly to ask, and Bothwell to answer? He was afraid, that the gratitude and bravery of his own followers would produce a battle, at the attempted seizure. What could Bothwell say to this fear? He was apprehensive, if no battle ensued, that he should be considered as having ungratefully betrayed her. What could Bothwell reply to this apprehension? He certainly could not lessen either. And neither Huntly nor Mary could suppose, that he could. All this application

plication and re-application from Bothwell to Mary, from Mary to Bothwell, and from Huntly to both, so far as concerns Huntly's share in the business, is all impertinence and absurdity.

(4) "For," Scotch, very properly; "et," French, very improperly.

(5) Not only Huntly, but Mary also, is writing to Bothwell very calmly, as if time was not pressing, and as if Bothwell's answer to *her* would equally find her at Stirling; without any urgency for dispatch.

" without mistraisting him, ze may be the mair cir-
" cumspect, and that ze may have the mair power
" (1). For we had zisterday mair then iii. c. hors of
" his and of Levingstoun's (2). For the honour of
" God (3), be accompanyit rather with mair then
" les (4); for that is the principal of my cair.

III.—" I go to wryte my dispatche (5), and
" pray God to send us ane happy enterview schortly.
" I wryte in haist, to ye end ye may be advysit in
" tyme (6)."

" a ce que, sans vous meffier de luy, vous y regar-
" diez de plus pres, et que vous vous rendiez d'au-
" tant plus fort (1). Car nous avions hier plus de
" trois cens chevaux des siens et de Leviston (2).
" Pour

" Pour l'amour de Dieu (3), foyez pluſtoſt accom-
" pagné de trop, que de trop peu (4): car c'eſt le
" principal de mon foucy.

III.—" Je m'en vay achever ma depeſche (5),
" et prie Dieu, que nous nous puiſſions entrevoir
" bientoſt en joye. Je vous eſcry en diligence,
" afin que foyez adverty a temps (6)."

(1) Mary then thought, that there was ſo much time yet to the execution of the plan, as would allow Bothwell, not merely to anſwer Huntly in time and at Stirling, but even to raiſe a larger number of forces. Yet the bearer of this letter could not reach Edinborough, before Wedneſday noon. And the plan was executed on Thurſday.

(2) I have ſhewn already the only gentlemen of the Queen's train, to be Huntly, Lethington, and Melvill. She muſt have travelled to and from Stirling, therefore, with only a ſlight number of attendants. She *could* not have had 300 horſe of Huntly's and Livingſton's with her. She particularly had not, as I have already ſhewn, the Earl of Sutherland in her retinue. And ſhe explicitly tells us herſelf, and Crawford's Memoirs expreſsly confirm her report, that ſhe travelled not with any parade of retainers about her. " Bothwell," ſhe ſays in a letter of inſtructions to her embaſſador in France ſoon afterwards, " finding opor-
" tunitie, *be reſſoun* we wer paſt SECREITLIE to-
" wartis Stirling, to viſite ye prince oure deireſt
" ſone;

"fone; in our returning he awayted us be the way, "accompaneit with a greit force, and led us, with "all diligence, to Dunbar *." "She was com-"ing," fay the confirming Memoirs, "but "SLIGHTLY guarded, from Stirling to Edin-"burgh †." Here then is another fact that detects the forgery. And the 300 horfe are like Bayes's invifible army at Knightfbridge.

There is alfo another proof of forgery in this paffage. I have already fhewn the only attendants of confequence in the prefent expedition, to have been Huntly, Lethington, and Melvill. Livingfton therefore was no more there, than Sutherland. He was only fuppofed to be there, at a time when memory was confounded by the interval fince the event, becaufe Mary called probably at his houfe on her way to Stirling. And thefe letters plainly appear fpurious again! Nor can it be furmifed, in removal of this evidence of forgery, that Livingfton probably was *not* with Mary *at the feizure*, and yet was with her at Stirling; that he attended her, only from his houfe to Stirling; and that he re-attended her, only from Stirling to his houfe again. This paffage actually precludes the furmife. It intimates him to have accompanied her to the very feizure; becaufe it enumerates his men and Huntly's together, and advifes Bothwell to bring "rather *mair* then les" againft them. And the appearance of Livingfton here, concurs with the appearance of Sutherland before, to form a *double* demonftration of the forgery.

* Anderfon, i. 95. † P. 19.

But

But all shews the Queen decisively to have come to Stirling, according to the present letter, escorted by Huntly and his retainers. It therefore proves the falsity of the fifth letter, which represents Huntly to have come to Stirling after her, and to have brought her a message from Bothwell. And the mention of " zisterday," as the day of her coming, concurs with the antecedent notice concerning " efter to morne," to refer this letter to Tuesday, the day after her arrival; to refer the sixth letter to an earlier part of the same day; and to refer the fifth to Monday night; the night of her arrival. It thus disproves all the intimations in letters fifth, sixth, and seventh, of any large interval of time coming in betwixt her arrival and her return. It turns them all into proofs of forgery. And it gives us a very remarkable fact, in the closer adherence of one of the posterior letters to the dates of the journal, as to Mary's present visit, than of either of the prior; though it made such an egregious deviation from it at the outset, as to the time of Bothwell's divorce from Huntly's sister.

(3) " Honour," Scotch; " amour," French.

(4) Bothwell's force was about eight hundred horse[*]. Yet the letter desires him to have rather over than under—three hundred. This therefore I consider as an evidence of the forgery. Mary's

---

[*] Crawford, 19, says 800; Buchanan, Hist. xviii. 356, says 600; and yet a thousand is the number in Goodall, i. 367, Robertson, i. 417, Guthry's Scotch Hist. vii. 32, and Stuart, i. 216.

fears would have operated stronger than Bothwell's. If his made him raise eight hundred, hers would have suggested to him fifteen hundred or two thousand. And she was present with the three hundred, while he was at a distance from them, and yet knew their number as exactly as she.

(5) "I go to wryte my dispatche," Scotch; "je m'en vay achever ma depefche," French. "*To wryte*," says Remarker *, " as if it had not been written already." He therefore prefers the French "achever," to finish my dispatch; as if she was *going* from her present letter — in order to finish her present letter. The fact is, that " my dispatche" does not mean the present letter at all. This is demonstrably certain. What it does mean, I cannot say. And therefore I must consider it as an absurdity of forgery, the prints of sand in this Birmingham coinage, which betray the place and the mode of its manufactory.

(6) This also shews, that Mary thought her letter would apprize Bothwell in time, to collect a larger number of horse for the enterprize of Thursday.

* P. 33.

VI.

§ VI.

LETTER THE EIGHTH (1).

I.—" My lord, gif the difplefure of zour ab-
" fence, of zour forzetfulnes (2), the feir of dan-
" ger fa promifit be everie ane to zour fa luifit per-
" fone (3),"

I.—" Monfieur, fi l'ennuy de voftre abfence,
" celuy de voftre oubly (2), la crainte du danger
" tant prouvé d'un chacun a voftre tant aymée per-
" fonne (3),"

" may gif me confolatioun ; I leif it to zow to juge :
" feing the unhap, that my cruell lot and con-
" tinuall mifadventure hes hitherto promyfit me;
" following ye misfortunes and feiris, as weill of
" lait, as of ane lang tyme bypaft, the quhilk ze
" do knaw (4).

II.—" Bot for all that I will in na wife accufe
" zow, nouther of zour lytill remembrance (5),

" nouther

" nouther of zour lytill cair, and leift of all of
" zour promeis brokin, or of ye cauldnes of zour
" wryting (6), fen I am ellis 'fa far maid zouris,
" yat yat quhilk pleifis zow is acceptabill to me;
" and my thochtis ar fa willingly"

(1) This letter pretends alfo to be written from Stirling. *When* it pretends to be written, muft be determined from fome circumftances in it.

(2) Bothwell was ftill abfent and ftill *forgetful*, it feems. Mary thus returns to the complaint of her firft letter from Stirling. But fhe has heard from him fince that. This forgetfulnefs, therefore, muft be of a later date. And it muft of courfe be fince fhe wrote her laft letter. But what forgetfulnefs could he poffibly fhew fince this? It was written late on Tuefday. It could not reach Edinborough before Wednefday. And on Wednefday fhe left Stirling. This therefore is another proof of the forgery.

(3) *Every one* then knew of the intended feizure. She faid before, that Huntly had " tald it." And now we find, that " everie ane" at Stirling was apprized of it, and talked of the danger which Bothwell would incur in the act. But let us attend the Remarker in his *laft dying fpeech*. " Of letter " VIII," he fays, " there are only a few words re-" maining in the French; but, few as they are, " they have been mifunderftood by the Scottifh " *tranflator* *." The prefent paffage is accordingly

* P. 33.

produced

produced to prove the affertion. But the whole centers in one word, " promyfit," a *tranflation* for " prouvé." Yet " prouvé" is obvioufly wrong, and " promyfit" is obvioufly right. Mary is not fpeaking of danger *realized*, but *threatened*. Every one at Stirling tells her of this threatened danger. And this fhe calls a *promifed* danger, agreeably to the old ufe of the word, not, as now, confined to a good fenfe only, but then free to admit either a good or a bad one; and agreeably alfo to her own ufe of it immediately afterwards, when fhe fpeaks of " the unhap that her cruell lot has hitherto *promyfit* " her."

(4) The French ended with my laft note. The Remarker therefore has nothing more to do. Yet he ftill finds a little bufinefs for himfelf. He can fee the French original ftill, by the dim reflection of the Scotch tranflation. When the fun is fet, " the " moon takes up the wonderous tale." In " one " paffage at leaft of the Scottifh copy, the French " word," when there is no French left, " feems to " have been mifunderftood, '" following ye mif- "' fortunes,'" inftead of *according* to or *after the* " *form of*, fuivant les malheurs." This is a very extraordinary mode of coming at the French original, by *diving after it* in the Scotch. But alas! he may

———dive into the bottom of the deep,
Where fathom-line could never touch the ground;

and yet will not be able to " pluck up this " drowned" original " by the locks." He has only

miftaken

mistaken the sense here. The passage means merely, that Mary's cruel lot threatens her with unhappiness, *following* her former misfortunes, that is, *in addition to them.*

I thus take my final leave of the Miscellaneous Remarker. Who he is, I have not pretended to guess. The report of London, I understand, makes him to be Lord Hailes. But I know by experience the fallaciousness of such reports. This, I see, is peculiarly false. The Remarker* speaks of his lordship in the following terms. " My " Lord Hales quotes a writing in his possession, " which proves," &c. " See his *Remarks on the* " *History of Scotland*, p. 167, a book little known, " in which the author IS ALTERNATELY A SCEPTIC " AND A DOGMATIST." This is not the language of a man concerning himself. And I have been since instructed to believe, that the author is the gentleman of Gray's Inn, who is well known for some controversial writings; who particularly wielded his *leaded bludgeon* so remarkably against the Historian of English Poetry, and made it to fall with such a *heavy*, and such a *decisive*, weight upon his head; who merits every commendation, for the extent of his researches and the depth of his knowledge, contrasted with the avocations of his profession and the disadvantages of his education; who has all the vigour of a man, that feels he can confide in himself; and who wants only the cool correctness, that only a regular education can furnish.

* P. 4.

furnish. But I believe this information to be equally a mistake, with that concerning Lord Hailes. Mr. R. I understand, is no Scotchman. He has certainly not been resident of late in Scotland. Yet the author of the pamphlet is avowedly a Scotchman. And, as in one place he mentions what was " the old-fashioned word within his me-" mory" for a watch in Scotland *; so in another he refers to " Records, B. 29, N° 285, and B. 30, " N° 572," though he " will not answer," he says, " for the accuracy of these references †;" and in a third place ‡ refers to the " Detection, i. 2 (or " p. 65)—a copy marked by Mr. Goodall as the " first edition" *in English*, and now, no doubt, in the advocates library at Edinborough. Nor is the work worthy of Mr. R. We have no appearance of Mr. Warton's antagonist in it. And I attribute it still to some young Scotchman, who has been a pupil of Dr. Robertson's, and who has stepped forward to teach before he has been properly taught himself.

(5) This is another touch concerning Bothwell's forgetfulness of Mary. And it serves with the others, to shew the violation of the chronology. Indeed this pair of lovers does in fact, what Lee's pair only wishes the Gods to do; and

> Annihilates both time and space,
> To make two lovers happy.

(6) She has therefore heard from him since her

* P. 19. † P. 3. ‡ P. 2.

last.

laſt. This laſt being written on Tueſday, the anſwer could not arrive before *Thurſday*. Yet ſhe left Stirling on Wedneſday. And, beſides this, there muſt be an interval of two or three days at leaſt, to allow for the forgetfulneſs. This will carry us to Saturday or Sunday, for the date of this letter. And yet ſhe was ſeized by Bothwell upon Thurſday.

"ſubdewit unto zouris, that I ſuppois yat all that
"cummis of zow proceidis not be ony of the
"cauſis foirſaid, bot rather for ſic as be juſt and
"reſſonabill, and ſic as I defyre myſelf. Quhilk is
"the fynal order (1), that ze promyſſit to tak for
"the furetie and honorabil ſervice of ye only up-
"hald of my lyfe. For quhilk alone I will pre-
"ſerve the ſame, and without the quhilk I defyre
"not bot ſuddane deith.

III.—" And to teſtifie unto zow how lawly I
"ſubmit me under zour commandementis, I have
"ſend zow, in ſigne of homage, be Paris, the orna-
"ment of the heid (2), quhilk is the chief gude of
"the uther memberis; inferring thairby that, be
"ye feiſing of zow in the poſſeſſioun of the ſpoile
"of that quhilk is principall, the remnant cannot
"be bot ſubject unto zow, and with conſenting of
"the hart. In place quhairof, ſin I have ellis left
"it unto zow (3), I ſend unto zow ane ſepulture
                                          "of

" of hard ſtane, collourit with blak, ſawin with
" teiris and bones (4). The ſtane I compair to
" my hart, that as it is carvit in ane ſure ſepulture
" or harbor of zour commandementis, and, abone
" all, of zour name and memorie that ar thairin in-
" cloſit, as is"

(1) Here then let us look back to all the proceedings in this buſy period. Mary had been at Stirling *ſome days* before ſhe wrote the fifth letter, becauſe ſhe ſays Bothwell promiſed to ſend her word *every day*, and had not done ſo. This, as we know ſhe reached Stirling on Monday night, will carry us to Thurſday or Friday at leaſt. She *then* ſends off a letter to him. An anſwer could not come under a day and a half. Yet ſhe appears in the ſixth letter to have received one. And this ſixth, therefore, muſt be written on Saturday or Sunday. The next letter was written ſoon afterwards, on the ſame day probably. But the anſwer to either could not have reached her before Monday or Tueſday, in the week following. Yet ſhe has received an anſwer, when ſhe writes her eighth letter. She complains however of his " lytill re-
" membrance," and of his " forzetfulnes." And, from both, the eighth letter cannot be written before Wedneſday or Thurſday. This however is her laſt. It was to produce Bothwell's " fynal
" order." But that order could not reach her before Friday or Saturday. And thus long, by the letters, muſt ſhe be ſuppoſed to have ſtaid at Stirling.

ling. Yet she reached Stirling on Monday, and left it on Wednesday; riding thither on Monday from Edinborough, and riding back on Wednesday to Linlithgow. She staid only one whole day at Stirling. And this day the letters have cut and minced into ELEVEN at least.

(2) What is this, that Mary sends him? It is " the ornament of the heid." Of whose head? Of her own. She sends it " in signe of homage;" " and that, by seising of him in the possessioun of " the spoile of that quhilk is principall, the rem-" nant cannot be bot subject unto him." It was one of *Mary's own head-dresses*, one of her own SCOTCH MOBS. This was surely a very strange present for a man. And the letter-writer must have been compleatly infatuated, to think of such a present for him.

(3) By her Will, I presume she means.

(4) This appears to be a ring, the stone of which was black in the ground, and represented a sepulchre strewed with bones and tears. But, to shew the eternal clashing of falshoods, the letters send the ring from Stirling in April, while Paris's second confession sends it from the road betwixt Glasgow and Kalendar, in the January preceding. " Elle rescript une lettre, et y mist dedans un an-" neau *."

* Goodall, ii. 78.

" my

"my hear [hair] in this ring, never to cum furth,
"quhill deith grant unto zow tó ane trophee of
"victorie of my banes; as the ring is fullit, in
"figne that yow haif maid one full conqueis of
"me, of myne hart, and unto yat my banes be left
"unto yow in remembrance of your victorie, and
"my acceptabill lufe and willing, for to be better
"beftowit then I merite (1). The ameling that
"is about is blak, quhilk fignifyis the fteidfaftnes
"of hir that fendis the fame. The teiris ar without
"number, fa ar the dreddouris to difpleis yow, the
"teiris of your abfence, the difdane that I cannot
"be in outwart effect zouris, as I am without fen-
"zeitnes of hart and fpreit; and of gude reffoun,
"thocht [though] my meritis wer mekle greiter
"then of the maift profite that ever was, and fic as
"I defyre to be, and fall tak pane in conditiounis
"to imitate, for to be beftowit worthylie under your
"regiment.

IV.—" My only wealth, reffaif thairfoir in als
"gude part ye fame, as I have reffavit your mar-
"riage (2) with extreme joy, the quhilk fall not
"part furth of my bofum, quhill yat mariage of
"our bodyis be maid in publict, as figne of all that
"I outher hope or defyris of blis in yis warld."

(1) What all this means, it is not eafy to divine.
" To" I fuppofe to be *too*. I have therefore
printed

printed it " tó." The mention of " deith" shews " banes" to mean *bones*. And then the sense, such as it is, seems to be this: that she sends the stone as an emblem of her heart; that the stone, being carved into the form of a sepulchre, represents her heart sepulchred in his love; that his name and memory are inclosed in her heart as firmly, as her hair is in the ring; that they shall never part from her heart till she dies; and that the ring is " fullit," either filled with the hair, or (as I rather think, and as we call the moon a *full* one, when it is quite round) is compleatly circular, in token of his full conquest of her till death.

All this is, as Dr. Robertson observes very justly*, " much refined mysticism about devices, a folly " of that age; of which Mary," he adds, " was " very fond, as appears from several other circum- " stances, particularly from a letter concerning " *impresas*, by Drummond of Hawthornden. If " Mary's adversaries forged her letters," the Doctor proceeds to say, " they were certainly employed " very idly when they produced this." They certainly were. Mary, however fond of devices, could never have written such nonsense as this about them. To be fond of devices, and to write with the folly of a driveler concerning them, are very distinct things; however the Doctor may choose to confound them. Homer sometimes nods; but then his dreams are superior, even to the waking thoughts of a Zoilus. And, when Mary conde-

* Diss. 34.

scends

scends to write upon " impresas," she will be found, I doubt not, to write like Mary. Some sparks of elegant vivacity must be struck off from her pen. But here the whole is unmeaning dulness. Nor is this all. There is a much greater absurdity than this behind. Mary is made to indulge herself in these weak and silly speculations, at a time when her head and heart must have been full of the great enterprize before her. The pretended seizure of her was to be attempted. She had some persons in her retinue, who would rather die than suffer it. The commandant of her retinue was afraid of their resolution, and trembled for the consequences. It was her decisive stroke for appropriating Bothwell to herself. On this critical incident hung the balance of her happiness. And her heart must have been torn with hopes and fears. Yet this very period of her life, and the very last minute of this period, have the forgers chosen; to make her sit down to her table in one stupid apathy of unconcern, to be unthinking of the moment of decision that was pressing upon her, and to be wholly taken up in hunting some fantastical devices, in pursuing some imaginary resemblances, in marking the course of a butterfly, or in gazing at the combinations of the clouds. And thus the woman, " all " whose sensations were exquisite, and all her emo- " tions strong*," becomes blunt in her sensations

---

* Robertson, i. 386.—This touch of Mary's character, like a variety of other particulars, is all borrowed from Buchanan, 39, Anderson, ii. and 251, Jebb, i.

and

and weak in her emotions, at the very instant when they would naturally have been most exquisite and most strong.

(2) This means the marriage-contract, as it is not to " part furth of her bosum." It must also mean the second or large one; as the first was only signed by Mary, and would certainly be kept by Bothwell. Yet the second was rather too large to be kept in a Queen's bosom. It would be too ample, even for a modern *bouquet*. And why should Mary have it rather than Bothwell? It was signed by both. Indeed this and the other contract were actually kept by Bothwell, " as Jesuits say, who " never lie." Murray, that *general of the order*, says so. Morton also, that *prime-assistant* to him, says the same. In their respective receipts for *their own* originals, they mention " ane silver box, overgilt " with gold, with the missive letteris, *contractis or* " *obligatiounis for marriage,*" &c.; " quhilk box, " and haill pecis within the samin, wer takin and " fund with umquhill George Dalgleische, servand " to the Erle Bothville*." Bothwell therefore kept the two contracts. And the letter, which intimates Mary to have kept one of them, is as contrary to fact according to the rebels, as it is repugnant to reason in the opinion of others, and is proved by both to be a forgery.

* Appendix, Nº iv.

V.—

V.—" Zit my hart feiring to difpleis you as
" mekle in the reiding heirof, as I delite me in ye
" writing, I will mak end; efter t'iat I have kiffit
" zour handis with als greit affectioun, as I pray
" God (o ye only uphald of my lyfe) to gif yow
" lang and bliffit lyfe, and to me zour gude favour,
" as the only gude yat I defyre, and to ye quhilk I
" pretend.

VI.—" I have fchawin unto this oeirer that
" quhilk I have leirnit, to quhome I remit me,
" knawand the credite that ze gaif him; as fcho
" dois, that will be for ever unto zow humbill and
" obedient lauchfull wyfe, that for ever dedicates
" unto zow hir hart, hir body, without ony change,
" as unto him that I have maid poffeffour of hart;
" of quhilk ze may hald zow affurit, yat unto ye
" deith fall na wayis be changeit, for evill nor gude
" fall never mak me go from it."

END OF THE SECOND VOLUME.

www.ingramcontent.com/pod-product-compliance
Lightning Source LLC
Chambersburg PA
CBHW051727300426
44115CB00007B/501